# Wisdom of Our Elders

# Wisdom of Our Elders

*Living in Spirit, Wisdom, Deep Mercy, and Truth*

EDITED BY
Karen E. Simms Tolson

WIPF & STOCK · Eugene, Oregon

WISDOM OF OUR ELDERS
Living in Spirit, Wisdom, Deep Mercy, and Truth

Copyright © 2024 Wipf and Stock Publishers. All rights reserved. Except for brief quotations in critical publications or reviews, no part of this book may be reproduced in any manner without prior written permission from the publisher. Write: Permissions, Wipf and Stock Publishers, 199 W. 8th Ave., Suite 3, Eugene, OR 97401.

Wipf & Stock
An Imprint of Wipf and Stock Publishers
199 W. 8th Ave., Suite 3
Eugene, OR 97401

www.wipfandstock.com

PAPERBACK ISBN: 979-8-3852-0560-8
HARDCOVER ISBN: 979-8-3852-0561-5
EBOOK ISBN: 979-8-3852-0562-2

VERSION NUMBER 05/20/24

All Scripture quotations, unless otherwise indicated, are taken from the Holy Bible, New International Version®, NIV®. Copyright ©1973, 1978, 1984, 2011 by Biblica, Inc.™ Used by permission of Zondervan. All rights reserved worldwide. www.zondervan.com. The "NIV" and "New International Version" are trademarks registered in the United States Patent and Trademark Office by Biblica, Inc.™

Scripture quotations marked (NRSV) are from the New Revised Standard Version Bible, copyright © 1989 by the Division of Christian Education of the National Council of Churches of Christ in the USA. Used by permission. All rights reserved.

# Contents

*Acknowledgments* | ix
*About the Conception of This Book* | ix

. . . And So, We Begin | 1

Part 1  **Introduction: Clarity of Purpose, Resilience, Courage, and Forgiveness** | 23

Chapter 1  Unshouted Courage: Testifying in the Public Square | 25
—A. Vanessa Hawkins

Chapter 2  For the Love of Black Women-Folx | 37
—Lisa Anderson

Chapter 3  Resilience, Strength, and Inner Power as Spiritual Practice | 50
—Argrow "Kit" Evans-Ford

Chapter 4  The Grace in Forgiveness | 57
—Karen Simms Tolson

Part 2  **Introduction: Identity and Spiritual Callings** | 71

Chapter 5  Black Cool, Wisdom Deep | 75
—Eric Wilson

Chapter 6  My Jesus of Color | 83
—Jason Villegas

| | |
|---|---|
| Chapter 7 | The Authentic Self and Desire: Listening to the Voice of the Heart \| 93 |
| | —Deborah A. Wade |
| Chapter 8 | Journeying to Our True Nature \| 98 |
| | —Grace J. Song |
| Part 3 | **Introduction: Change Is an Inevitable Certainty \| 109** |
| Chapter 9 | Blessed Troubles: Reading the Bible as Multivalent Voices \| 115 |
| | —Sophia Park |
| Chapter 10 | Cleaning Out the Attic \| 125 |
| | —Claire Cox-Woodlief |
| Chapter 11 | Out of Resistance Comes Revelation and Change \| 132 |
| | —Wilfredo Benitez |
| Part 4 | **Introduction: New Beginnings: A Clarion Call \| 147** |
| Chapter 12 | Living the Questions \| 149 |
| | —Lib Campbell |
| Chapter 13 | *Pirkei Avot*: Chapters of Wisdom \| 159 |
| | —Sheila Peltz Weinberg |
| Chapter 14 | Expanding on Spiritual Eldering: A Quaker-Hindu Dialogue \| 171 |
| | —Preeta M. Banerjee |
| Chapter 15 | Take Me into a Suffering World \| 182 |
| | —Mary Glazer |
| Part 5 | **Introduction: Reaching for Higher Ground: Humans, Earth, and Spiritual Connections \| 187** |
| Chapter 16 | Bless to Me, O God, the Earth Beneath My Feet \| 189 |
| | —Mary C. Earle |
| Chapter 17 | We Cannot Create What We Cannot Imagine: Creation and Imagination \| 200 |
| | —Donna Coletrane Battle |

Chapter 18   God's Wisdom Implanted in All Things | 212
          —Jessica Felix Romero

  Part 6   **Introduction: Love, Hope, and Beauty in All Things** | 229

Chapter 19   I Am a Dreamer | 233
          —Marsha Holmes

Chapter 20   Liturgy of the Hours: A Need for Daily Practice | 242
          —Robert Benson

Chapter 21   Spiritual Guidance in the Qur'an | 247
          —Jamal Rahman

Chapter 22   The Bursting of Bubbles | 259
          —Leslye Colvin

# Acknowledgments

From birth to the end of our lives, we are always in companionship, first with God and our parents; for this, I am grateful. I honor and thank my ancestors, both named and unnamed, who I could feel urging me to use my voice and to keep going. I honor my life-long mentor, Dr. Hazel Harvey, who knew about this project and is now among the ancestors. I am thankful to each contributor to this anthology for your time, attention, words of wisdom, and willingness to share your truth. To my Simms family and the family to come, remember *there is only one thing that cannot be taken from you*: keep this legacy alive. To my circle of trust—Diane Butler, Sharon Curry, Susan Hunt, Gloria Murray, Gloria Wangia LaSalle, Natalie Boeyink, and Erica Scott Lawrence—you are always there with love, sisterly conviction, and support. I will never forget each of you, as you have played a vital role in my efforts to become me. To Vanessa Hawkins, Leslye Colvin, and Jessica Felix Romero, thank you for stepping in to support the development of this book at a very precarious time, putting aside your tasks and asking, *"What can I do to help?"* and not letting this project miss a beat; you supported me in ways you cannot imagine. To Wilfredo Benitez, thank you for using your beautiful gift with a camera. Dwight Dozier, thank you for your patience and insight in creating the website. Thank you to Dr. Teresa Reed and Dr. Kimberly Hundley for your encouraging words and support. To my editor and the staff at Wipf and Stock, Matthew, George, Elisabeth, and many others, thank you for gracefully holding my words and concepts with care. Most of all, to my husband Jerry Tolson, who listened, loved, and stood by me without fail, it is indeed forever.

# About the Conception of This Book

I HAVE ALWAYS KEPT a journal. My first journal was given to me by my Grand Aunt Alice and Grand Uncle William Farrison while I was in elementary school. It was an old-fashioned "diary" with a lock and key that I proudly kept around my neck. As a child, I diligently recorded my thoughts and daily activities. As I matured, I began to explore topics and my ideas about the issues within the pages of my diary. Since then, the diary has become a journal where I present my spiritual concerns and cares. Writing has been a lifelong passion that led to my first career as an English teacher.

This book began to take shape during the last four years as I journaled about discernment and topics related to growing in wisdom and how truths and knowledge align with social concerns. Being somewhat isolated for an extended time when COVID-19 was rampant encouraged me to formalize my ideas, and I felt the urge to begin a book from this grain of insight. I started to select contributors for this anthology, and, unfortunately, not everyone selected made it through the final editing process. I connected with Claire Cox Woodlief and the North Carolina Institute for Spiritual Direction and Formation. Claire was quite helpful in identifying six of the contributors to this book as well as contributing a chapter. For that, I extend my appreciation.

While writing this book, I had the opportunity to journey to places foundational to the Civil Rights Movement—Montgomery, Birmingham, and Charleston. The experience served as a spiritual reminder of the importance of truth and wisdom as vital constructs to societal change. It was also a reminder of the importance of speaking with clarity as I proceeded with this project and of holding the development of this book as a sacred trust.

Finally, to the reader. No matter who you are or where you are in life, you were conceived, and you stand on the shoulders of:

2—parents

4—grandparents

8—great grandparents

16—second great-grandparent

32—third great-grandparents

64—fourth great-grandparents

128—fifth great-grandparents

256—sixth great-grandparents

512—seventh great-grandparents

1,024—eighth great-grandparents

2,048—ninth great-grandparents

You needed at least 4,094 ancestors over 400 years to be born. May we walk together through the door that our ancestors opened.

For more information about this anthology or any of the contributors, please contact info@awisdomofoureldersbook.com or visit https://awisdomofoureldersbookcom.wordpress.com/.

# ... And So, We Begin

Growing up in the South, I became familiar with the sacred verse *"Then you will know the truth, and the truth will set you free"* (John 8:32). Having lived in a segregated environment and attended segregated elementary and middle schools during the 1960s, I was intimately familiar with this scripture. I kept it near my heart because it reminded me that truth will always win, regardless of the circumstances. During this time, I remember this verse was often used in various ways: as a mantra, a personal reminder to do your best, and, most frequently, a rallying cry during social protests and injustices. At first glance, *truth* and its use in this context seem readily apparent. It was an outward expression of internal pain. However, as I moved through life, I began to view *truth* as necessary components that are companions to concepts such as *justice, righteousness, freedom,* and *equity*. Truth became foundational cornerstones connecting spiritual concepts such as *wisdom* and the *spiritual self*, creating a more profound, richer, and deeper perspective.

As I "matured" in my faith, I took a keen interest in the expansive way my interior life evolved. I began seeking studies on spirituality, including the works of mystics and contemplative figures. Contemplatives and mystics such as Saint Augustine, Sojourner Truth, Jarena Lee, Julian of Norwich, and Teresa of Avila became familiar names to me. The modern-day writings of Howard Thurman, Joy Bostic, Otis Moss, III, Thomas Merton, Barbara Holmes, Michael Curry, Don Miguel Ruiz, Chanequa Walker-Barnes, Joseph Campbell, Zenju Earthlyn Manuel, and Natalie Gutierrez have greatly influenced me. Such writers have also played a role in my examination of culture and the development of personal convictions and beliefs as a construct for spiritual and community change. I was guided into professional studies in historical, philosophical, and comparative education, which aligned with my spiritual interest. I grew in understanding contemplative reflections, ideas, and the expansive nature of spiritual practices. I embraced wide-ranging aspects of contemplative thought and reexamined my belief about contemplation and how contemplation could only be achieved through silence when guided by meditation. I adopted the belief that the purpose of contemplation is an alignment of my spirit, awareness, and purpose with God's desires and love for me and my love for God. I also found that it is through reflective interaction, with God at the center, that I draw closer to a new consciousness and awareness of who I am. There was a new awakening within me that understood the need to explore and wrestle with sometimes uncomfortable and difficult questions, which is at the center of my faith.

I began to explore the need for the link between truth and spirituality. My perception of personal truth is mostly derived from experiential learning, witnessing, listening as well as seeking sage wisdom and advice of wise ones. My personal truth takes on forms that embrace culture, situation, background, and context. I became more aware that divine truths, or God-centered truths, are essential tenets that bind the world together through sacred texts and are carried out through canons and teachings within denominations, religions, and various faith traditions. In contrast, eternal truths and personal truths are developed by human experience and bear the imprint of time as a witness to change and consistency. Such truths are often most clearly recognized through "lived experiences" and can be presented as introspection or retrospection of our lives and the lives of our ancestors.

Most importantly, both—*divine and eternal truths*—are grounded in wisdom, experience, and the fundamental understanding that our possibility to sustain our pertinence as humans is wrapped up in where and how we perceive God in any defining moment. It is demonstrated in how we embrace, reflect, and react to adverse or favorable circumstances. After all, seeing in the darkness also means there is an essence of light (i.e., darkness cannot exist without light), and finding how to interpret our personal truth draws each one of us to a light within our spirit. Divine and eternal truth also play a role in how and what influences decisions, which also drives societies. Such truths are fundamental in finding and refining personal truths and clarity. Divine and eternal truth is a necessary morsel to sustain life within any experience. Focusing on personal truths can enrich the outcomes of an experience, especially when it aligns with things we cherish in our lives. When we concentrate on the divine and personal truths, we can use them to guide us through an experience. This can also help us make decisions that align with our values and beliefs, ultimately leading to better outcomes in most situations.

## About This Book

I am a spiritual director, an educator, and a woman of faith. I am not a theologian, nor am I trying to challenge or change the beliefs of anyone's religion. This anthology offers an exploration from the lens of spiritual directors, companions, and people of faith who sincerely desire to survey the application of wisdom as a paradigm for empowering, challenging, and changing perspectives within communities through sharing wisdom from different perspectives. It is an opportunity to see paradoxes for eternal and divine truth as a light that could open opportunities for relational change.

Secondly, this book is not for every reader. It is a book for those who desire to expand their internal vision of self as it relates to wisdom. It is for those who are engaged in the ministry of spiritual direction and soul companionship and those who desire to explore examples of how wisdom and truth are central to faith development. This book is for those who seek to expand the way spiritual companionship can be viewed in another context by looking for ways wisdom and truth play a part in exploring interior dialogue, promoting the need for deep listening, and then extending the dialogue to communities and applied within a social context. The book will also be helpful to those exploring spiritual formation and other areas of spiritual growth because a part of examining spiritual formation is exploring the fundamentals of wisdom and truth.

As a tool in spiritual direction and deep listening, these narratives and other prose forms within these pages can be read, synthesized, or explored as reflections for deeper conversations, individually or in small groups. These chapters can also show how questions, when formulated to reflect the concern, could become the beginning of finding wisdom and truth and lead to expansive conversations that can support healing. One of the ways this book can be helpful is by starting the conversation with discernment and questions of defining personal truths, then using the question at the end of each section to guide the reading for each chapter. This book is also an effort to increase understanding of the importance of eternal truths as an impetus for sustainable personal and social change. This anthology provides a practical application of truth and wisdom to contemporary issues, which can lead to systemic change. Eternal truths and wisdom are presented from various faith perspectives. In order to provide practical application to contemporary life issues, truth and wisdom are also viewed from diverse perceptions, situations, and experiences.

This anthology is not a treatise or study expanding, examining, or concerning the validity of eternal truths as proposed by Descartes's infamous *Meditations*, nor is it an examination or argument for or against Descartes's "truth rules" and Cartesian debates on God's will and eternal truths;[1] that premise and body of work, no matter how important and relevant, has been continually examined and argued by philosophers and theologians for centuries as phenomenological research. Instead, this book attempts to open simple conversations and extend an opportunity to explore how eternal and divine truths are applied as wisdom for contemporary times and used for further personal and community resilience and development. It is an effort to increase understanding of the importance of eternal truths as an impetus for sustainable personal and community social change.

While writing this book, I shared the names of some of the contributors with an acquaintance, who quickly asked, "*. . . but what do these people have in common?*" What they have in common are experiences and the need to express ideas about wisdom, truth, and divine truth that should be discussed, and, most of all, shared. The chapters are organized according to topics and represent individual opinions and perspectives on various issues from life. In developing the concept for this book, each contributor was requested to select scripture, sacred text, an experience, prose, or poetry as a way to explore wisdom and truths and then apply what has been explored to current conditions in society or an individual experience. There are points within the chapters where wisdom alone does not make the platform for change. It is the actions that are stimulated by wisdom that change the constructs. The chapters are connected with summaries before each section, creating transitions yet connecting the chapters to the various sectional themes.

---

1. Bruce, "Descartes's Method," 1–5.

Each chapter, including this one, has a section at the end, "Deeper Conversation/Deeper Listening," that provides opportunities to explore related questions. Some chapters also end with a spiritual practice that reflects the chapter and invites the reader to perform deeper reflection and opportunities to journal. The book is divided into six distinct sections. The sections are:

| | |
|---|---|
| Section 1 | Clarity of Purpose, Resilience, Courage, and Forgiveness |
| Section 2 | Identity and Spiritual Callings |
| Section 3 | Change Is an Inevitable Certainty |
| Section 4 | New Beginnings: A Clarion Call |
| Section 5 | Reaching for the Higher Ground: Human, Earth, and Spiritual Connections |
| Section 6 | Love, Hope, and Beauty in All Things |

The sections highlighted above are topical and represent ways the individuality of spiritual direction and faith formation can be transferred to a collective community.

Finally, the way of engaging traditional spiritual direction and faith formation and aspects of deep listening by nature is an individualistic examination of faith and interior life. Seldom is spiritual direction expanded into practices that can invigorate or inspire communities to explore alternative ways to connect and grow toward a change that affirms truths and wisdom as necessary components for spiritual growth and can affect community change. This anthology is designed to evoke questions. Questions drive us deeper into ourselves and help us connect with our most basic essence, purpose, and God's expectations of us. It encourages the reader to be aware, intentional, centered, and, most of all, present. It is through these steps we become aware of the power of truth and the power of wisdom.

## Divine Truth, Mysticism, and Contemplation

Divine truth always contains aspects of mysticism and contemplation. Growing up in a Baptist church, I learned to value community and the importance of seeking elders' teachings. My church was the center of my community, and I learned much about reading the Bible for more than remembering scripture. I learned the value of giving, receiving, dreaming of my future, and, most of all, the importance of a community engaged with justice and civil rights. From the earliest age, I remember how my church exposed me to lessons about valuing yourself as an African American in a White racist and dominant society that often sought to limit, short-change, and short-circuit dreams; these were lessons that would serve me well later in life. As a child, I never heard the words *spiritual practice*. It wasn't until much later in life, when I began to reflect on the concepts I was exposed to as a child and the impact such concepts had on the development of the inner spiritual life, that I was surrounded by wisdom and spiritual practices within my church community.

As an adult, I learned the value of contemplation as a spiritual practice and the difference between contemplation and meditation. As I matured, I saw wisdom in a different context. While I embraced the concept of eternal wisdom as lived experiences, I also began to understand that most experiences are reflective and could be an opportunity to be lessons that can be refined and applied over time. As I moved through life and widened my perspectives, I came to fully understand the Southern adage of "wearing life like a loose garment" or not taking on all aspects of life in a death-defying grip, as if it were necessary to my well-being to address or challenge the elements of every ilk as a way of living a whole life. In other words, I learned when to let go with trust in God; clearly evaluate before responding what was truly important to my well-being and the well-being of my community; and when I needed to address issues that required attention to do so with precise rebuttals. I concluded through such experiences that eternal wisdom is the inward experience carried by grace.

As I felt my change, I also learned the value of other ways of believing and engaging with the Holy. I began to expand my understanding of faith and explore various beliefs, such as Eastern Christianity, which views contemplation as literally "*to see God or to have the Vision of God*" or the "*state of beholding God*."[2] I embraced readings on mysticism and examinations of the desert mothers and fathers, where contemplation and self-examination were considered core values. Such readings ignited my spirit, and I soon learned to believe there is no one prescriptive way to enter into contemplation with God—wordless prayers, exaltation, praise, mediation, conscious adoration, music, prose, poetry,

---

2. Jeremy, "Contemplating the Face of Christ."

or continuous thought can be steps that lead to contemplation. Contemplation, after all, is a spiritual practice of being fully present—*mind, body, and soul*—to the Divine. While I understand the boundaries placed by mainstream tenets about the value of contemplation, I believe there is no one prescriptive or "right way" to enter into contemplative thought and contemplative prayer, which can lead to the presence of God. So, many times, how African Americans experience or express connections to the Divine are dismissed as practices because it does not follow the prescriptive manner that has become the accepted mode. The stories, music, prayers, and oral traditions that are part of my culture have been passed down from generation to generation, affirm communal resonance and the shared experience of core values expressed as eternal truths. I believe my ancestors saw contemplation and prayer as a direct connection to God, and they did not always follow the "rules" often touted today when describing contemplation. There is no way my ancestors, through the torturous way they survived capture, middle passage, enslavement, and beyond, did not use prayer and contemplation. Knowledge, silence, solitude, and awareness are necessary, appropriate, and valuable components for some people who use contemplative reflection. Still, for some people like me, who consciously honor my ancestors, these demands can negate the value of bringing my "whole self," which includes my heritage, cultural beliefs, identity, experience, and lineage, into a sacred space. I develop even more awe and wonder each time my deepening and understanding of the Divine grows. My faith has become perpetual at this latter stage in my life, and I still feel there is still much to learn and even more so to experience.

## Contemplation and Mysticism

Contemplation and mysticism are as old as time, and no religious group or faith has the complete answers to contemplation and mysticism or the exact precepts that will usher one into alignment with the Divine. There are elements of contemplation and mysticism in each of the mainstream religions. Suppose we allow ourselves to be open to exchange and interfaith dialogue without fear of compromising our beliefs? In that case, we can learn a variety of ideas from a variety of religious perspectives. To build an equitable and affirming community, we must enter into conversations with an affirmation mindset rather than a criticism mindset, ask questions that seek awareness, remain open to answers, and show genuine support. If we did, instead of remaining in suspicion, persecution, and skepticism, we would be on our way to community change, an expansive spiritual resolution, intercultural awareness, and building healthier communities.

If we examine the rudiments, contemplation and mysticism can be found in all indigenous people. From the Dagara of West Africa to the indigenous people of the Kággabba (Kogui) of the Sierra Nevada de Santa Marta, the Native people of North America, the desert fathers and mothers of Northern Africa, the Australian Aboriginal people, and countless other indigenous populations on every continent, can trace their beliefs about mysticism to centuries before the founding of Western religions. Writings by Malidoma Patrice Somé, Evelyn Underhill, and Zenju Earthlyn Manuel have highlighted the importance of contemplation and mysticism as a way to address our individual and modern societal concerns. Each of the five major religions has precepts supporting emptying or filling our souls to fulfill our destinies. Yet, we do not always see the connections between different faiths. Instead, we dwell in those areas that we perceive as differences, creating false measures of comparison and not allowing ourselves to affirm each other because we cling to notions that a belief other than our own could not be grounded in wisdom or truth. This leads to hierarchical thinking of good, better, or best, which also creates wedges between communities. One word that is often found in wisdom literature, regardless of faith, is *acceptance. Acceptance* that what is found within various religions will not alter our fundamental beliefs but will add to our knowledge and the richness and unity of the community. I question, especially regarding religious differences, how often and with what degree of genuineness we use acceptance when it comes to faith and religions that are outside of our own without resorting to labeling and mislabeling.

Contemplation and mysticism are essentially and intricately connected, yet the concepts are only partially interchangeable. I believe that not all contemplatives are mystics; still, all mystics are contemplative. I think the perceptions about these terminologies begin and end with how we perceive the term *mystic*. I'm always leery when someone initially introduces themselves as a contemplative or a mystic as part of their identity. In my recollection, Jesus, Buddha, and the Prophet Mohammad never started a personal introduction with "*Hi! My name is . . . and I am a contemplative and mystic.*" Yet, in our contemporary society, and especially among some spiritual directors, I have heard this quite a few times. Such pronouncements can appear questionable, and it really isn't about affirming the interior gifts or bringing to the conscious level who you are, which is a healthy exercise. I have also had several occasions where the same person who introduces themselves in that manner becomes surly and mean in the blink of an eye. How we treat people and see ourselves as beings who can discern the movements of God as the perfection of love in our lives is evident in contemplative actions and does not need pronouncements. Focusing on finding complete emotional resonance through contemplation, meditation, and prayer allows us to know ourselves more fully and opens us to God's purpose; this does not need human pronouncements. Over the years, when moving into a contemplative space, I have learned there is a shift from the awareness of self to a consciousness of alignment with God where words are unnecessary. I let go of provisional thinking, and prayer is no longer something I am doing; I am simply being in the presence of God. For me, this is being contemplative, an action that does not need explanation or an announcement of who you think you are.

## The Necessity of Eternal Truths

All disciplines, from science to philosophy or the performing arts, are based on an established set of paradigms or a structure of immutable truths. It is the same for our journey that we call life, which is built upon a series of truths. Carl Jung tells us, *"There are truths which belong to the future, truths which belong to the past, and truths which belong to no time."*[3] In viewing Jung's statement, we can surmise that, as humans, we can arrive at a juncture where truth becomes eternal and is perceived to be beyond time and space. At this point of recognition, we find the sustainability of eternal and divine truths and possibly the formation of wisdom.

It is safe to say eternal truths stem from time-tested actions based on faith, and divine truth emanates from the word of God. Throughout history, eternal truths have been constantly tested through experiences that have challenged and changed not only individuals but entire societies and cultures. As concepts, eternal and divine truth can occur at the confluence of belief and resolution because God's creation is within each

---

3. Jungian Center for the Spiritual Sciences, "Jung on Truth."

of us. However, it is essential to remember that both concepts strengthen our resolve as humans by reinforcing the need to examine the internal self against the external experience or how we "show up" in the world.

## What Is the Relationship between Eternal Truth and Wisdom?

In a world where we are conditioned to see the world in ways that reflect our experience, there is within each person an inert need for wholeness, unity, and alignment with what is true to the individual spirit. The need for the soul to be aligned with what is true is a part of our authenticity in our relationship with God, and it is an imperative for social connectedness to all beings. This internal alignment is where self-awareness and self-acceptance become integral and revealed at the heart of eternal truths.

In the direst of times, we may look to divine truths that can lead us to reexamine the essence of ourselves and the reasoning that propels our decision-making. At other times, examining our personal truths can refocus us and encourage us to question our fundamental beliefs about our faith or the promises made by God versus our experiences with society. At this point, we often have to turn inward, critique ourselves honestly, and pursue what is at the core of who we are. Frequently, it's at this point where what we believe and are willing to embrace becomes the most critical goal of our personal change.

While there are several ways to define truth, Saint Teresa of Avila gives us a simple yet essential definition for the truth, stating, "*Humility is truth. It is becoming aware of and accepting the truth of who we are.*"[4] Seeking the wisdom found only in divine truth promotes internal clarity in spirit and sustains our alignment with God and *Kairos*. Theologian and mystic Howard Thurman explains the moment of truth as the following,

> *When I become aware of the authentic meaning of an idea, concept, person, event and the bearing of that meaning upon my own life, I experience the moment of truth. There are, of course, in that moment elements that make for decision, elements that make for discovery, disclosure, revelation, understanding, insight, elements that make for dedication, for commitment,*

---

4. Caluag, "St. Teresa of Avila," §5.

*something that provides a structure in the light of which the life will be lived from that moment on.*[5]

In what can be considered the defining book of Protestant theology, *Institutes of the Christian Religion*, John Calvin opens with the line, "*Nearly all the wisdom we possess . . . consist[s] of two parts, the knowledge of God and of ourselves.*"[6] We can also find the paradigm supporting wisdom formation and divine and eternal truths from this premise.

## Get Wisdom, and with All Thy Getting, Get Understanding

Time and political changes cannot erase the history of a group of people when you understand and learn about the wisdom of a people. This is why keeping the stories and accurate accounts of historical developments within context is highly important. We seek wisdom and the applications of wisdom in many ways. The early writings of Aristotle identified five core elements of intellectual virtues:

*episteme* (scientific knowledge),

*techne* (technical knowledge),

*phronesis* (practical wisdom),

*nous* (mental agility and judgment), and

*Sophia* (conceptual or contemplative wisdom).

According to Ferrari, Kim, and Morris, there can be no such thing as someone who is wise without subject knowledge or without mental flexibility.[7] This application of mental flexibility also takes in the need for applying knowledge through experiences.

The University of Chicago's Center for Practical Wisdom has developed a repository of research on wisdom from several analytical perspectives. According to the Center's mission statement, "*by deepening our scientific understanding of wisdom, we will also begin to understand how to gain, reinforce, and apply wisdom and, in turn, become wiser as a society.*"[8] Wisdom literature has deeply influenced the writing of all

---

5. Howard Thurman Digital Archive, "Moment of Truth, Part 2," §9.
6. Calvin, *Institutes of the Christian Religion*, 1-2.
7. Ferrari, Kim, and Morris, "Interventions for Developing Wisdom," 193–210.
8. University of Chicago Center for Practical Wisdom, "About."

the major religions. As a cornerstone of most societies, foundational wisdom caused the development of institutions, influenced the growth of communities, and in general acts as a guide for developing the future. According to Staudinger and Glück, in lay terms, wisdom can mean many things, ranging from knowledge drawn from traumatic life experiences to intellect and rationality. Often, we reach for the future by examining our past for directions that inform our concept of wisdom, creating ways to explore our personal and societal change, expansion, and advancements.[9] Glück also sees wisdom as a form of genius that can be acquired through practice.

There are also several models of wisdom that support spiritual direction and formation application. One such model developed by Baltes and Staudinger is the Berlin Model of Wisdom, which is currently used to assess the level of wisdom using five aspects. This model is traditionally used to explore leadership and to quantify how wisdom is used in various contexts. The five aspects of the Berlin Model are:

- Rich factual knowledge (humanity and life)
- Rich procedural knowledge (how to deal with life's problems)
- Lifespan contextualism (understanding life contexts; changes over a lifetime)
- Relativism (awareness of individual, social, and cultural differences)
- Uncertainty (recognizing the limits of what we can know)[10]

The Berlin Model is most helpful in quantifying, identifying, and measuring responses from the various areas of wisdom. However, the most well-known theory and model of wisdom is Sternberg's Balance Theory, which focuses on the ability to apply wisdom as practical intelligence when making decisions.[11] According to Sternberg, wisdom is learned through experiences or tacit knowledge, which occurs during the hardest times in one's life. The Balance Theory relies on tacit knowledge, interests, and values to be used for the common good. Unlike the Berlin Wisdom Model, the Balance Theory relies on experience, which cannot be taught. It is the joining of personal knowledge and values that feed into a person's ability to balance personal knowledge with the values and interest

---

9. Staudinger and Glück, "Psychological Wisdom Research," 215–41.
10. Baltes and Smith, "Fascination of Wisdom."
11. Sternberg, "Balance Theory."

of others, as well as being able to choose the most appropriate response or action in a situation in order to serve the common or highest good.

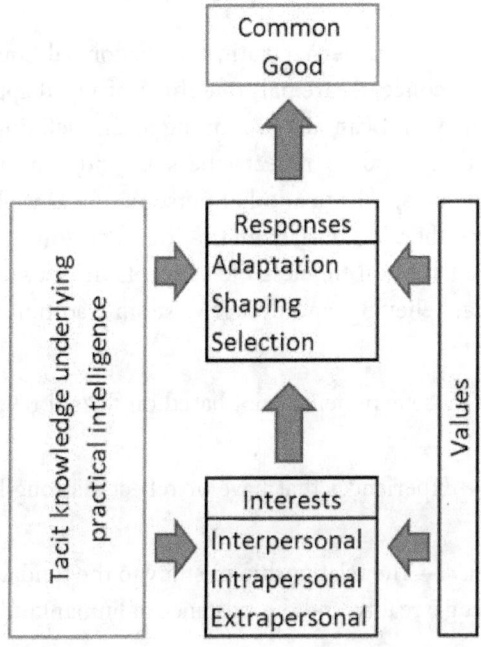

Tacit knowledge is used to balance Interests and Responses to achieve Common Good.

source: Sternberg (1998)

In examining wisdom, it is also important to examine identity. In identity theory, Erikson conceptualized that wisdom is developed as a form and results from personal maturation.[12] According to Erickson, this revelation also occurs when experienced through mastery of uncertainties involved in the later life crisis of integrity (i.e., acceptance of a life lived) versus despair (i.e., about paths not taken in life). Several writers who examine wisdom formats or the study of wisdom assert that wisdom

---

12. Jeste and Lee, "Emerging Empirical Science of Wisdom."

benefits from the systematic analysis derived from contextual factors and critical reflection and self-examination.[13]

## Combining Eternal and Divine Truth with Eldering and Wisdom

Essentially, divine truth, eternal truth, and wisdom, although individually explained as concepts, are part of a three-pronged approach to aid in spiritual clarity and can aid in refining and redefining individuals and communities. Wisdom reflects the soul and can enlighten, but most of all, wisdom speaks to another person's soul as well as the experience of one another. It is born from traditions, customs, backgrounds, and knowledge based on timeless life concepts. It is a sense of seeing, knowing, being, believing, and doing. Wisdom traditions can fall into several categories:

*Secular*—Those experiences not based on formal religion or belief systems.

*Religious*—Experiences that have or reflect a strong belief in God or Gods.

*Philosophical*—The relationship or study to the fundamental nature of knowledge, reality, and the existence of humankind.

*Cultural*—The relationship and experiences passed down intergenerationally or socially through related ideas, customs, social behaviors, and race.

While this list comprises only a few categories, these categories listed above are independent, but they can be combined to find intersectionality between each. There are also several fundamental aspects of wisdom, no matter how it is developed. Wisdom can also take the forms of situational or experiential. What can be experienced in life is only sometimes situational. Other times, it is a combination of experiential and situational. Wisdom, although enhanced by age, is not predicated by age. While elders are considered "experts" in life, their expertise depends on the extent of their individual experiences, the context of the experience, and, most of all, their discernment with God.

---

13. Baltes and Staudinger, "Search for a Psychology of Wisdom," 75–81; Staudinger and Baltes, "Interactive Minds," 746–62.

I once engaged with someone who expressed the desire to become a "very wise person." The desire was rooted in identity and the longing to be well respected within their family and community. This desire was connected to how the person admired their father as a "wise" person who was sought after in the community for advice on farming. This expression of desire surprised me because the person had done little to engage people with meaningful listening or truly valuing other people's perspectives. The person was known for offering unsolicited opinions on any subject, often looking for ways to "critique" (i.e., really criticize) without understanding or affirming individuality or respecting various perspectives on most topics. In most instances, conversations with this person were often an effort to gather information in order to control others. This person felt oppositional thinking, or demonstrating the opposite side, was appropriate in all situations. In retrospect, this person spent most of the time listening and looking for opportunities to correct others by telling others of personal expectations, citing the faults of others, offering dictates on how to live another person's life, or redirecting and interfering with decisions. This type of behavior is not wisdom; it is "hubris" and possibly narcissism. Furthermore, there is a delineation between becoming a wise, well-respected elder and being a well-read person, a source of practical knowledge, or merely opinionated. There is a difference between being an elder because of age and being respected for the aging process. There is a difference between becoming what is referred to as an elder and a "conscious elder." In other words, growing old only sometimes makes one wise. Conversely, being young does not mean there is always a lack of wisdom. Knowledge, a great deal of internal work, awareness of self, the desire for continual inner growth, never tiring of asking piercing questions, understanding the changes and newness offered each day, a tender graciousness in understanding the value in all people, taking an interest in supporting others, and most of all, actively creating a compassionate community contribute to making a conscious elder. According to The Center for Conscious Eldering, *The conscious elder intentionally seeks the internal teacher and connectedness with others, making them lifelong learners.*[14]

When all of these aspects are taken together, being a conscious elder creates unlimited opportunities for self-exploration and promotes opportunities for healing communities. These aspects can also set the stage for

---

14. Summarized from Center for Conscious Eldering.

exploring life-changing contemporary issues. Understanding the power of embracing wisdom and using wisdom and truth for systemic change can make a societal difference. While the term *eldering* may vary across communities, the one consistency in defining such concepts in eldering is the role of elders in society. The place of elders in any culture is revered, and the traditions of becoming an elder are often a hallowed process. This has been true since the dawn of time, regardless of culture or faith tradition. Being an elder also means the sense of belonging changes with time and experience. The place for an elder within a community often tells of the values within a community. However, being an elder that is respected takes more than chronologically aging and placement. It takes reflection, humility, discernment, and other attributes to rise to the standard of a conscious elder. After all, most people regardless of age are in the process of becoming an elder and eventually an ancestor. At any point in this process, we must decide what type of elder we want to be.

As a conscious elder, I have come to realize and embrace that I carry ancestral grief. Ancestral grief is not forgetting my ancestors and the lives they lived, the stories they left for our development in wisdom, and providing honor to their memories. It is a very weighty and unfortunate yet fortunate gift that some African Americans, Indigenous, and other minorities carry. It is ancestral grief that grounds me, aligns me, and reminds me of my life's purpose. As I live with my ancestral grief, it helps me to cope and identify injustices, especially in today's society, where White supremacy goes unchallenged and unchecked, just as it did with my ancestors. Keeping this memory helps support me in the way I choose to move in this world where, at times, where I live somewhere between *"Thank you, God"* and *"Help me surrender this to you, Jesus!"*

## Faith and Tradition

Divine truth and eternal truth are not limited to one faith, tradition, or culture. Each of the five major religions contains parables, documentation, and practical applications of eternal truths and conscious eldering that have stood the test of time. *"The most important teaching and tenet of Judaism is that there is one God, incorporeal and eternal, who wants all people to do what is just and merciful. In Judaism, all people are created in the image of God and deserve to be treated with dignity and respect."*[15] The

---

15. Israel Embassy, "About the Jewish Religion."

Qur'an commands Muslims to be honest with themselves and others. Islam also requires Muslims to be truthful in their words and actions, publicly and privately.[16] "According to the Talmud, one of the first questions a person is asked when appearing before the heavenly court after leaving this world is: '*Did you deal faithfully and honestly with others?*' (Talmud Shabbos 31a)."[17] Hindus must seek knowledge of the truth, which is seen as the essence of the universe and the only reality in life. According to the Vedas, "*Truth is One,*" but the wise expression of truth can appear in various ways.[18] In Christianity, Jesus represents eternal truth through his teachings and examples of how we are expected to live among ourselves and honor God's divine truth. Buddha taught that the embodiment of truth is aligned with beauty and how we care for each other and nature.[19] Within these pages are perspectives and representative voices on representative tenets from each of the five major religions, using contemporary situations, ideas, and commentary on modern life and how to apply beliefs about eternal truths. The contributors to this volume engage in many contemporary concerns. However, their primary goal is not to delineate and analyze eternal and divine truths from various perspectives or explore the merits of wisdom. Instead, the contributors use their faith and knowledge to explore contemporary topics, from the internal need for clarity, healing, and change.

## What about Wisdom and Its Relationship to Spiritual Direction?

Like most spiritual directors, I was immersed in Ignatian Spirituality and Quaker meeting styles during my training at San Francisco Theological Seminary. I appreciate using Ignatian desires as one of the fundamental training methods for spiritual directors. However, after I began to engage in spiritual companionship, I realized that there is a need to understand how spiritual direction has aspects that can be an opportunity to merge one's most profound truths with the lived experience of wisdom. It is also an opportunity to understand how wisdom is included and used in this melding. Spiritual Directors International (SDI) states

---

16. "Recite and Listen Qur'an Online."
17. Goldstein, "What Is the Real Meaning," §2.
18. Svoboda, "Four Degrees of Human Speech."
19. Shambhala, "Buddha Nature."

within the document "Comparison of Helping Relationships" in the Goal/Purpose/Why of Spiritual Direction section that an inherent goal of spiritual direction is "*developing and integrating one's deepest Truths; discover, attend to savor the presence of these Truths in everyday life.*"[20] However, there remains a gap in explaining how to achieve this goal, which is critical to developing spiritual understanding and deepening the inner context and values of spiritual direction.

Spiritual direction, by nature, is a solitary and individualistic examination of the interior person while in the presence of a director (companion/witness) and God. I was trained that the symbolic third chair is always present in any spiritual direction session (i.e., one for the directee, one for the director, and one for God). I was always curious if there could be a bridge between personal transformation and community change that was more explicit. Examining and building on truths and wisdom could be part of that bridge. Therefore, having conversations and understanding the interconnection between truths, Divine truth, and wisdom becomes a critical bridge to the sustainability of our perception of life and the creation of sustainable communities. When there is a personal change that is transferred from the interior to the community, outcomes of spiritual direction and faith formation have an impact on communities that have the possibility of coming full circle. This is why wisdom is more than knowledge. Wisdom requires integrating and applying knowledge, discernment, vulnerability to right or wrong, cognition of experience, sensitivity to change, compromise, and synthesizing perspectives broader than the issue that has an impact beyond the immediate community. As a collective, the contributors to this book are making strides to view how eternal and Divine truths are a part of all lives (whether acknowledged or unacknowledged), and these aspects are relevant in shaping and guiding spiritual practices as we develop mutual understanding. These and more aspects can be a part of spiritual direction and faith formation.

## Everything Starts with a Question

Engaging in the wisdom materials and truths has changed my approach to spiritual direction. Many years ago, I altered my format for engaging directees to a more Socratic engagement. I have always found that answers are always in the questions, and we need only to open up to God

---

20. Munger, "Comparison of Helping Relationships."

to discern how the question is a part of our life. After years of listening to directees struggle to find the core of their need to be heard and supported through deep listening, it became apparent the directee would benefit by taking time to pray, discern, listen, and formulate a question that reflected their need before we met. I developed a format that I call "K's Inquiry Method." In K's Inquiry Method, before each spiritual direction session, I request that each person send a question they felt was yearning in their spirit at least three days before our scheduled meeting. The questions should be carefully discerned. I then turn to prayer in preparation for the meeting, letting the question be the focus before God. The question could evoke, at times, for me to use an examen, lectio divina, poetry, or another form of verse related to the question as a place to start our focus. At other times, the question may move me to hold silent space. This method has never failed, and I have found that it works well and encourages the directee to turn to God not only for the question but to be more open to spaciousness during the session. Sometimes, the directee will use the same question in several sequential sessions. There are also times when the answer to the question will come over time, and in some cases, not at all. When this occurs, the conversation always turns to faith and how the non-answer aligns with faith. The directee always feels optimistic about the experience. I am always inspired to take one of the "sparks" from the questions to peer supervision for further self-exploration. The directee is strengthened by the knowledge that their spiritual question has been acknowledged and they have taken steps to open themselves to God in trust to further their faith. A realization soon arises that answers are often as complex as the questions and walking this path to engage with God is an undeniable spiritual awakening. The technique has allowed for a more focused session that helps us listen more passionately and deeply as we look to God for our truths.

Finally, when there is a shift to examine our internal compass as it aligns with eternal truth and is guided by a Divine truth within every aspect of life, combined with a healthy understanding and appreciation for wisdom, society and humankind can rectify and create an immutable change. Societal change does not take place in total isolation or a vacuum. It is a cumulative effort with participants from all areas of life with diverse perspectives, beliefs, and experiences. Toward the end of apartheid in South Africa, Archbishop Desmond Tutu is credited with saying, "*We must be ready to learn from one another, not claiming that we alone possess all truth and that somehow we have a corner on God.*"[21] Much about spiritual direction, soul care, and faith formation is about aligning the individual interior with the Divine. This book reflects truth, wisdom, and how we can learn from one another, taking what we know, changing about ourselves, and creating better communities.

## Deeper Conversation/Deeper Listening

1. What has been the role of wisdom within your personal life?
2. How is the role of wisdom reflected within your faith tradition?
3. How can a focus on developing and utilizing wisdom become a part of your community?

## Spiritual Practice

Pause for at least ten minutes. Think about the topics you have just read in this overview. What words or concepts are lingering in your spirit? What did you feel during this time? Take these feelings into a meditation or an opportunity to write a journal entry.

## Bibliography

Baltes, Paul B., and Jacqui Smith. "The Fascination of Wisdom: Its Nature, Ontogeny, and Function." *Perspectives on Psychological Science* 3.1 (2008) 56–64. https://doi.org/10.1111/j.1745-6916.2008.00062.x.

Baltes, Paul B., and Ursula M. Staudinger. "The Search for a Psychology of Wisdom." *Current Directions in Psychological Science* 2.3 (1993) 75–81. https://doi.org/10.1111/1467-8721.ep10770914.

Barker, Kenneth L., et al., eds. *NIV Study Bible: New International Version*. Grand Rapids, MI: Zondervan, 2008.

Barr, Robert E. "A Speculative Model of Christian Growth: A Melding of Matthew and Erik Erikson." DMin diss., Asbury Theological Seminary, 1984.

Bruce, Zachary MacKay. "Descartes's Method and the Role of Eternal Truths." Diss., UC Berkley, 2014.

Caluag, Tito. "St. Theresa of Avila: Humility Is Truth." *Lifestyle.INQ*, Aug 31, 2019. https://lifestyle.inquirer.net/344447/st-theresa-of-avila-humility-is-truth/.

Calvin, John. *Biblical Christianity: The Institutes of the Christian Religion*. Edited by Beulah Wood and J. P. Wiles. Fearn, Ross-shire: Christian Heritage, 2017.

---

21. Tutu, *God Is Not a Christian*, 160.

———. *Institutes of the Christian Religion: In Two Volumes*. Edited by John Thomas MacNeill. Translated by Ford Lewis Battles. Philadelphia: Westminster, 1960.

The Center for Conscious Eldering. https://www.centerforconsciouseldering.com/the-center-for-conscious-eldering/.

Descartes, René. *Meditations on First Philosophy: In Which the Existence of God and the Distinction of the Soul from the Body Are Demonstrated*. Translated by Donald A. Cress. Indianapolis: Hackett, 1993.

———. *Meditations on First Philosophy, with Selections from the Objections and Replies*. Translated and edited by John Cottingham. Cambridge University Press, 2017. https://assets.cambridge.org/97811070/59207/frontmatter/9781107059207_frontmatter.pdf.

"Desmond Tutu Quotes." Goodreads. Accessed December 6, 2023. https://www.goodreads.com/author/quotes/5943.Desmond_Tutu.

Israel Embassy. "About the Jewish Religion." Accessed December 11, 2023. https://embassies.gov.il/baku/AboutIsrael/People/Pages/Jewish-Religion.aspx.

Erikson, Erik. "Reflections on the Last Stage—And the First." American Psychological Association. Accessed September 16, 2023. https://psycnet.apa.org/record/1986-06118-001.

Ferrari, Michel, Juensung J. Kim, and Stephanie Morris. "Interventions for Developing Wisdom." In *The Psychology of Wisdom: An Introduction*, edited by Robert J. Sternberg and Judith Gluck, 193–208. Cambridge: Cambridge University Press, 2022.

Fullam, Lisa. "Teresa of Avila's Liberative Humility." *Journal of Moral Theology* 3.1 (2014) 175–98.

Jewish Sightseeing. "2004-12-02 Goldsborough Resign." 2004. http://www.jewishsightseeing.com/Dhh_weblog/2004-Blog/2004-12/2004-12-02-Goldsborough-Resign.Htm.

Goldstein, Warren. "What Is the Real Meaning of Integrity?" *Aish*, Dec 19, 2021. https://aish.com/565062172/.

———. "A Word of Torah: What Is the Real Meaning of Integrity?" *Detroit Jewish News*, Mar 23, 2023. https://www.thejewishnews.com/judaism/a-word-of-torah-what-is-the-real-meaning-of-integrity/article_526ade32-db27-52bc-ac89-c6de0273e743.html.

The Howard Thurman Digital Archive. "The Moment of Truth, Part 2, 1958 January 12." Accessed December 6, 2023. https://thurman.pitts.emory.edu/items/show/148.

———. "Thurman Research Resources." Accessed December 6, 2023. https://thurman.pitts.emory.edu/research.

Jeremy. "Contemplating the Face of Christ." *Orthodox Road* (blog), Sep 15, 2015. https://www.orthodoxroad.com/contemplating-the-face-of-christ/.

Jeste, Dilip V., and Ellen E. Lee. "The Emerging Empirical Science of Wisdom: Definition, Measurement, Neurobiology, Longevity, and Interventions." *Harvard Review of Psychiatry* 27.3 (2019) 127–40. https://journals.lww.com/hrpjournal/fulltext/2019/05000/The_Emerging_Empirical_Science_of_Wisdom_.1.aspx.

Jung, Carl Gustav *The Collected Works of C.G. Jung*. Translated by R. F. C. Hull. Edited by Herbert Read et al. London: Routledge and K. Paul, 1966.

———. *Jung Contra Freud: The 1912 New York Lectures on the "Theory of Psychoanalysis."* Translated by R. F. C. Hull. Princeton, NJ: Princeton University Press, 2012.

Jungian Center for the Spiritual Sciences. "Jung on Truth." Oct 4, 2023. https://jungiancenter.org/jung-on-truth/.

Kekes, John. "Wisdom." *American Philosophical Quarterly* 20.3 (July 1983) 277–86. https://www.jstor.org/stable/20014008.

Munger, Christine Luna. "Comparison of Helping Relationships." Spiritual Directors International. Accessed October 11, 2023. https://www.sdicompanions.org/wp-content/uploads/2022/02/comparison_of_helping_fields.pdf.

———. "For Those Seeking Connection." Spiritual Directors International Companions, Jun 2, 2023. https://www.sdicompanions.org/about/seeking-connection/.

"Recite and Listen Quran Online." Accessed October 11, 2023. https://read.quranexplorer.com/.

Shambhala. "Buddha Nature: A Reader's Guide." Aug 20, 2019. https://www.shambhala.com/buddha-nature-a-readers-guide-to-the-cause-of-awakening/.

Staudinger, Ursula M., and Judith Glück. "Psychological Wisdom Research: Commonalities and Differences in a Growing Field." *Annual Review of Psychology* 62.1 (2011) 215–41. https://doi.org/10.1146/annurev.psych.121208.131659.

Staudinger, Ursula M., and Paul B. Baltes. "Interactive Minds: A Facilitative Setting for Wisdom-Related Performance?" *Journal of Personality and Social Psychology* 71.4 (1996) 746–62. https://doi.org/10.1037/0022-3514.71.4.746.

Sternberg, Robert J. "A Balance Theory of Wisdom." *Review of General Psychology* 2.4 (Dec 1998) 347–65. https://journals.sagepub.com/doi/10.1037/1089-2680.2.4.347.

Sternberg, Robert J., Howard C. Nusbaum, and Judith Glück, eds. *Applying Wisdom to Contemporary World Problems*. Cham, Switzerland: Palgrave Macmillan, 2019.

Svoboda, Robert. "Four Degrees of Human Speech." Yoga International. https://yogainternational.com/article/view/4-degrees-of-human-speech/.

Tutu, Desmond. *God Is Not a Christian: And Other Provocations*. New York: HarperOne, 2011.

Tutu, Desmond, and Mpho Tutu. *The Book of Forgiving: The Fourfold Path for Healing Ourselves and Our World*. Edited by Douglas C. Abrams. London: William Collins, 2015.

University of Chicago Center for Practical Wisdom. "About." Accessed December 8, 2023. https://wisdomcenter.uchicago.edu/about.

Vedanta Society of Southern California. Accessed October 11, 2023. https://vedanta.org/.

# PART 1

# *Introduction:* Clarity of Purpose, Resilience, Courage, and Forgiveness

> *This section explores the importance of clarity as a guide to truth and purpose. Clarity is central to grounding people, meaning-making, fostering courage, and creating opportunities. It is also important as a concept in deciding how grace is a part of forgiveness.*

BUILDING A COMMUNITY IS a fundamental concept for survival. A community is the locus for developing and defining wisdom and seeing the world as a place with a purpose for each soul. Even in the face of danger, knowing who you are in relation to your potential can heal, change, and redirect your life. Embracing how purposefully, wonderfully, and creatively you can be opens up dynamic possibilities for furthering your being and opportunities for true belonging. In moments like these, we can choose to reveal and align with divine truth about the worthiness of ourselves in order to define and redefine our clarity. We can find clarity even in the direst of circumstances by connecting to a higher source within us and beyond our human convention.

One of the most salient eternal truths I have come to understand is people, regardless of how they are connected to you, will always find a way to define you. One of the realities of living is to learn how to express yourself with your own lens of clarity and purpose and not allow others to do this for you. The activist John Perkins is credited with saying, "*You don't give dignity; you affirm it.*" Nothing could be more authentic when it comes to affirming your being. It is essential to arrive at a space where we can hear the truth, see the truth, embrace the truth, and, most of all, be the truth. One-half of life is complicated by the intricacies we choose, and the other half is pathways we are compelled to follow. Either path is filled with the question of how you define and affirm yourself. Otherwise, much of our strength can be spent resisting, revisiting, or reinventing our identity. We must define how we design and create a space in life that may not be readily available to the outside society, and that space begins with the internal.

The following chapters explore the paths of several women. The stories in this section define the meaning of presence and how having a presence can change perspectives. The chapters provide insight into how cultural identity intersects with personal beliefs in making communities that exemplify the meaning of living in truth. The first chapter explores how an ancient woman of color exercises resilience and purpose by taking a stand to stand alone in the face of power; this is something each person can do today. Using only her faith and physical presence, she changes circumstances through her silent witness. In another chapter, a contemporary African-American woman connects to her inner strength and courage while relying on spiritual and biblical truths to heal and realign her to her truth path after a life-altering assault. The third chapter explores a need, especially among BIPOC women, to understand the power of loving yourself completely, addressing trauma by identifying the source, standing in your truth even if you must stand alone, and providing self-care, which is central to well-being. In retelling the development and founding of the Sojourner Truth Leadership Circle, women from various intersectional backgrounds are encouraged to explore the whole meaning of justice and clarity while reigniting resilience in a circle of trust. The section ends with a chapter that explores forgiveness as a process and how enacting forgiveness creates personal power and reinforces concepts about wisdom. These chapters bring forth the question, *Are we as humans more than our stories, or is it the stories of humans that define our identity and spiritual compass?*

# Chapter 1

# Unshouted Courage

Testifying in the Public Square

A. Vanessa Hawkins, PhD

*Vanessa Hawkins is a Presbyterian (PCUSA) minister and spiritual director in Durham, North Carolina. Her journey into spirituality was sparked during her seminary studies and as a mission partner at an Anglican seminary in South Africa. The seminary's approach to spiritual formation arrayed before her a rich tapestry of spiritual practices that moved her to pay closer attention to God's presence in her life. She received her training as a spiritual director from San Francisco Theological Seminary.*

*This chapter explores ways to value the voices of marginalized people and the role of faith, equity, and religion in helping to identify purpose. The chapter uses the biblical story of Rizpah to explore the essence of purpose and embodied wisdom that can inspire contemporary protest.*

THE STORY OF RIZPAH is found in 2 Samuel 21:1–14, and it is one of many short stories that depict David's actions as he establishes his reign as king. This tale begins with the revelation that Israel is amid a three-year famine. David is king at the time, but a bit of time passes before he becomes concerned about the drought. To end the famine, he eventually seeks the wisdom of a priest, who discloses that the culprit behind the famine was Saul. In Joshua 9, one learns that Joshua made a pact with the Gibeonites during the conquest of Gibeonite land. Posing as distant travelers seeking sanctuary, the Gibeonites tricked the Israelites into sparing their lives. Later, Saul ignored God's directive to spare the Gibeonites and exterminated many of them. To correct this wrong, David summoned the Gibeonites to determine how he could make amends for Saul's past actions. The Gibeonites are resident aliens—remnants of the indigenous populations. They are the "Other," although some of them have assimilated into the dominant Hebrew culture by the time of this story. They have fallen outside the Manifest Destiny contract between God and the Israelites and have survived on the margins of Israelite communities as laborers for the temple rituals. In this insider-outsider position, the Gibeonites have no authority to request the shedding of blood for appeasement. Only an Israelite can make that request. Yet, the text states that they requested the death of Saul's remaining sons. Saul's past efforts to exterminate the group can only be atoned by death.[1] The Gibeonite's request—*Hôqîa*— has several meanings. It can be translated as "ritual dismemberment," "to execute or hang"; "crucifixion in the sun"; "exposure with arms and legs broken"; and "to hurl down." In other words, a lynching takes place; apparently, this was acceptable in ancient Israel.

The negotiations are settled. David agrees to the state-sanctioned lynching, and the sons are provided as human sacrifices. Reparations for Saul's breach of the peace treaty is the lynching of seven sons. Their mothers are Rizpah and Merab—Saul's concubine and wife, respectively. This execution is designed to signify David's faithfulness to God and, thus, to the land's needs. It fulfills his obligation to appease God and do what is needed to ensure the land remains fertile. On the sacred ground, the Gibeonite high place, seven bodies were displayed for viewing those coming to or passing by the sanctuary.

So, I wonder whose interests are being served in the text? Are the Gibeonites sincerely requesting appeasement, or are they pawns of the Davidic establishment? Is David sincerely seeking to appease God or secure his kingdom? In his efforts to establish power, David began to fear the presence of Saul's remaining sons, who were coming of age. Is David's act of propitiation—appeasement—just? Is he only using this execution

---

1. The connections between blood guilt, famine, and infertility of the land are discussed in great detail in Kaminsky, *Corporate Responsibility*, ch. 5.

to claim his right to be king, and is he utilizing fear and terror as the organizing principles of his reign?

Saul's seven sons are collected, lynched, and left out in the open air for all to see. Rizpah enters the center stage to protest David's decision silently. Ultimately, one must decide if David hides behind the Gibeonites to exonerate himself and conceal the use of imperial power. Does this tale disclose the backhanded way that imperial powers use state sanctioned violence as an act of terrorism while also serving as a warning to any future resistors to the Davidic reign? Eventually, David acknowledges Rizpah's actions by collecting the bodies and ashes of King Saul and Jonathan and burying them. The saga ends. God is appeased and the rain eventually returns.

## Rizpah

We first learn about Rizpah in 2 Samuel chapter 3. She is one of Saul's concubines and mother to two of his sons. After her and Merab's sons are lynched in 2 Samuel 21 and left in the public square for any passersby to view, Rizpah takes refuge in the public square. In a sense, she squares off with David. Her actions have been interpreted as victim, savior, warrior, and pawn.[2] Her vigil over the dead bodies is a visible act of protest. This protest is a testimony given in silence. It is a reinterpretation and retelling of the oracle's message to God. The oracle stated that the expiation would appease God and rain would come. There is no rain. She stands with the impaled bodies as a witness to the viewers, David, and God.

Rizpah is referred to as one of Saul's *pileges*—a concubine, and she is identified by her mother's name. Yet Exum reminds us that she is a secondary wife.[3] She is a mother of two dead sons and five nephews, widow, mourner, secondary wife, and protester. After Saul's death, her life was in flux, and she lived in a context that was in flux as David tried to establish his kingdom. As a secondary wife, Rizpah's positioning is precarious. As a widow, she was already vulnerable. So in the future, what will happen to her remaining family members, for she is now a widowed concubine with no sons? Demonstrating *invisible dignity*, *quiet grace*, and *unshouted courage*,[4] Rizpah creates an altar, thus claiming sacred space

---

2. Fewell and Gunn, *Gender, Power, and Promise*, 161.
3. Exum, "Rizpah."
4. These are concepts coined by Katie G. Cannon in her book *Katie's Canon*.

within the Gibeonite's sacred space—their high place of worship.[5] Rizpah is discerning, and her silent vigil demonstrates that she is more than a grieving mother. She understands what is going on and comprehends David's true motives behind the veil of collaboration. After David fulfilled his obligation of ensuring the fertility of the land, he receded into the background and Rizpah took center stage.

Her silent witnessing exposes his political maneuverings and holds him accountable for leaving her sons and nephews unburied. She responds as one whose back is pressed against the wall, but she can't keep the truth of these actions to herself. She must reveal David's actions for what they are, so she testifies with nonverbal actions. She reinterprets the outcome of David's oracle by holding up a mirror to reveal the truth behind his deeds. There's more going on in this text than the narrator wants us to see, for surely Rizpah is not alone in this field during the harvest season. Throughout this ordeal, she never says a mumblin' word as she exposes the corruption of David. She takes center stage. She becomes the priest of this sanctuary, offering protection for the unburied dead. She stands in solidary with them for over four months. Surely, her witnessing is a communal act involving the support of friends, neighbors, harvesters, and strangers. Someone had to be in quiet solidarity with her—otherwise where did her food come from, how did she stay clean, who stepped into this sacred space when she needed to step away? She kept the bodies of her slain sons and nephews safe, while her community kept her safe. Eventually David hears about the vigil—words are whispered in his ear—and he realizes that he needs to get the upper hand on this matter. I wonder if an underground revolution was beginning to form.

David attempted to erase the memory of the house of Saul by erasing Saul's lineage. Yet David's trickery only served to ensure that the memory of Saul is enshrined in the community and land. Memory is both spatial and embodied. Rizpah's *"silence inscribes itself on her body. Her silence is ritualistic—internalized so that she can discipline herself in the act of memory."*[6] Rizpah's silence is also deafening. It is a powerful testimony that turns one's eyes to see the injustice perpetrated by David's unjust and violent actions.

> *Silence is a rich social space that can operate as a vehicle for either memory or forgetting and can be used for various purposes. . . .*

5. Walters, "To the Rock."
6. Melanchthon, "Reading Rizpah," 184.

> *The silence of Rizpah is overt with the absence of narrative and speech; but it is pregnant with meaning, with protest, resilience. It is a silence that is not easily forgotten or ignored; it enhances memory . . . . She wants to remember, and she wants to make others remember, and hence she turns to total silence. It is intentional, purposeful, and planned; the reason is to commemorate the incident and her children. She chooses silence, for it provides her the opportunity to be introspective and reflect, to commemorate, and it speaks louder than words.*[7]

To engage in testimony, Rizpah stands on the border between the public sphere and the establishment. "*Her vigil brought her into the presence of a community that was created and forged around the bodies of her dead children and her grief and her efforts to seek justice for them.*"[8] In this pregnant space, Rizpah uses her body and silence to construct a spiritual platform of contemplative resistance. This space is filled with the weightiness of her grief, and this grief burrows into the earth beneath her feet, the very spaces upon which the young men are impaled, and into the eyes of those witnessing her silent pleas for divine intervention. I wonder if, in this marginal space, she questions the Divine's role in all of this. Or maybe her testimony seeks to expose to God the truth about David and this situation.[9] What I do believe is that in this social space, Rizpah's quiet embodiment of love and compassion offers multiple interpretations of David's act of reparation.

## Testifyin'

Experience is a cornerstone of testimonies. Every Sunday, as a child I listened to testimonies for hours on end. In my home church, it was a requirement of conversion and was considered a sign of sanctification. Testimonies were the life and blood of my small church worship services. Whether in the pulpit; on the front, back, side pews—or even on the corner stoop—telling stories is an African American tradition. This early form of socialization has left its mark on me. They were a major formational factor in my denomination—the United Holiness Church. On its website, it states,

---

7. Melanchthon, "Reading Rizpah," 184.
8. Melanchthon, "Reading Rizpah," 181.
9. Hoyt, "Testimony," 101.

> *Originally, there was no desire on the part of the founders to establish another denomination, but they were forced out of organized churches because of their experience of holiness and their testimony of the Spirit-filled life. It became necessary for these persons who had testimonies of being saved, sanctified, and filled with the Holy Spirit, to have continuing contact with each other for mutual edification and comfort. As a result, many independent churches were established, and associations formed where people could feel free to seek God, not only to be genuinely saved, but also to be definitely sanctified.*[10]

For an hour or more, my church members would stand one after the other and testify to God's wonders and powers as God intervened on their behalf. I listened as, one by one, people presented their problem, recounted God's intervention, provided some type of biblical (re)interpretation of the event, and concluded with a praise report. People testified to God's intervention in their lives and gave evidence of their faithfulness through the disclosure of their response to God's presence.

Testifying is a subjective experience since it is based on an individual's understanding of the events being narrated. Testimonies rely on several sources: Spirit, Bible, self, context, and God. The Bible provides the stories, images, and framework for the testimony.[11] The Bible is a central feature in the life of African American churches, but testifiers constantly reinterpret the biblical stories that are foundational to their narratives. I am using interchangeably: testifying, testimony, and narration. I understand that there are differences between the terms. Testifying and testimonies are only one narrative form of expression used within the Black Church context, but for the purpose of this chapter, I am using the two terms interchangeably. Testimonies are one of the cornerstones of the Black worship experience through which people document their faith formation, (re)interpret biblical scriptures, reclaim their and community members' humanity, embody wisdom, and oppose dehumanizing oppression. It is a dialectical communal process between speaker, context, and texts told in story form and is sometimes presented in a circular indirect way. Most times people testify on their own behalf, but there are times when a testimony is presented as a "sign" or message (oracle) from God to the community of faith. I have witnessed many "God gave me a message for you," moments. These moments brought

---

10. United Holy Church of America, "Church History."
11. Hoyt, "Testimony," 93–94.

either words of judgment or praise for the community or a particular individual, or sometimes both.

Testifying is a contextual approach that "unmasks" structural forms of oppression as well as one's complicity in oppression. Telling them is powerful truth-telling moments, and truth telling is a complicated matter. It is a time of stripping away masks, hurts, anger, and fear and relaying to the congregation one's moments of vulnerability and triumph. Testimonies can restore dignity as individuals talk about a God who loved the people and who desired their emancipation. In my home community, they were stories told to and by people living on the margins of dominant structures of oppression. African American communities have lived with lynching as a state-sanctioned terrorism for centuries. Angela Sims, in her book *Ethical Complications of Lynching: Ida B. Wells's Interrogation of American Terror*, writes:

> *Quite often, individuals who subscribe to a tyrannical form of government do so to protect perceived points of privilege. In response to an 1897 opinion on lynching, the Rev. Norman B. Wood, a graduate of the Southern Baptist Theological Seminary of Louisville, explained what was accepted by many as a given in the United States. Wood stated correctly that "we have Anglo-Saxon law in our American code for the Anglo-Saxon civilization, which it is; and then for the new race of African citizens, the inauguration of African law in the form of lynch law." All too often, as Wood noted, this tendency to view America and Anglo-Saxon as synonymous perpetuated America's race problem.*[12]

Sims reminds us that every occupying force has its methods of intimidation. In the United States, lynching was one method. She describes lynching as a technique of terror utilized for social control to protect "perceived" White privilege. Sims supports her findings by examining the work of Ida B. Wells regarding lynching. "*Wells understood the dynamics of corrupt complicity that allowed lynching to become an almost unquestioned practice.*"[13] Sims reminds readers that Wells admonished Whites to "*seek creative ways to act on behalf of victims of violence in a society that often refuses to confront domestic forms of violence in a systematic and consistent manner.*"[14]

---

12. Sims, *Ethical Complications of Lynching*, 43.
13. Sims, *Ethical Complications of Lynching*, 45.
14. Sims, *Ethical Complications of Lynching*, 46.

This complicity to maintain privilege still exists today in the forms of racial violence, colorblindness, pseudo-multicultural inclusion, and other forms of denial. Emmett Till, an African American teen, was murdered at the age of fourteen in August 1955 for whistling at a White woman. Michael Brown—another eighteen-year-old unarmed African American son—was shot to death in August 2014 by a police officer. The brutality that Till and Brown encountered is a legacy of White supremacy that is built on *Othering* certain groups. Their mothers, Mamie Till and Lesley McSpadden, protested the deaths of their children that made visible the invisible ideological and philosophical principles of pseudoscientific White supremacy. This ideology governs the violence committed on Black bodies and constructs a rhetoric that *others* and demonizes minoritized groups. Till and McSpadden are mothers who mourned the death of their teenage sons in the public sphere. These mothers, as many others, challenge the belief that some folk matter and others do not. They, along with countless other women, cry out as witnesses for their children. Till and McSpadden followed their intuitive faculties and "*buttressed themselves against the dominant coercive apparatuses of society*" to mirror to the dominant society what they already knew but refused to acknowledge—"*America is sick.*"[15] Both mothers witnessed to the world the brutality of their sons' death. They testified to the humanity of their sons as a countermeasure against the ideological message of "Black brute." Their witnessing and testifying created a sacred space of transparency that the dominant public sphere masks.

> It was in their own "invisible institution," the "hush harbors," that the slaves were free to create "vehicles for expressing the spirit and gaining strength" to persevere; it was there that the field hollers, work songs, spirituals, and even the blues had their beginnings as the slaves rediscovered their own "sacred being through songs, rituals, music, and dance." The experience was truly spiritual . . . as we laid down our burdens, we became light. As we testified and listened to others testify, we began to understand ourselves as communal beings, no longer the kind of person that the slave system tried to make of us. Through our participation in these rituals, we become one. We become, again, a community.[16]

---

15. Cannon, *Katie's Canon*, 126.

16. M. Shawn Copeland quotes Dona Richards, *Implications of African American Spirituality*, 211 and 217, in Copeland, *Enfleshing Freedom*, 23–24.

As Rizpah laid her sackcloth of grief upon the "Rock," symbolizing her God, mothers of color across the centuries have laid down their burdens upon the same God. As Rizpah constructed a hush harbor upon the mountain on which her sons and nephews had been lynched, she silently bore witness in the public square. Rizpah's silent witness was a testimony that attested to the presence of God and Spirit. Can you see her squatting on the rock—gazing outwardly while searching inwardly—trying to make sense of David's actions?

Testifying requires going inward—to engaging in critical introspection. It is a looking inward and outward to critique life events and one's understanding of God's presence in the event and world at large. Testimonies can be *"beyond words"* in that one's critical reflection *"can be nonverbal ways"* of embodying one's witness to God's presence.[17] Many of the communal rituals shared in our congregations are non-verbal actions. Hugs on Sunday mornings, providing dinners for the sick, sharing the peace during worship, witnessing the sprinkling of water upon an infant's forehead—silent testimonies to the presence of God and Spirit. Testimonies are not told just for the purpose of speaking, but to encourage a change in the hearts, minds, and actions of the speaker and listeners.

## The Power of Testimony

Testimonies have a way of creating a dynamic space for investigation of sociocultural factors. We are influenced by our contexts. Rizpah's rituals on the mountain—as she beat away the birds, sat upon her rock of salvation, mourned the loss of her sons—were foundational to the construction of a sacred site of embodied grief. Testimonies have the power to transform us, our actions, and relationships. This is not just a pious form of confession where one walks away at the end with no sense of the way forward. People testify through songs, prayer, shouting/Holy Dance, humming, preaching, biblical interpretation, and silence. To tell one's story not only can be a persuasive moment filled with verbal expressions, but is also embodied via habits, actions, and one's very lifestyle.

There is a communal nature of testimonies. Thomas Hoyt, in his article "Testimony," explores the experience in hush harbors *"where storytellers similar to the African griots and priests testified to God's goodness"* in a way that connected one's African heritage to one's enslaved

---

17. Hoyt, "Testimony," 99.

reality.[18] The telling of one's story resembles a dance between the speaker and witnesses, which is similar to the call and response pattern of Black preaching. Other times, it materializes through lined singing which is another call and response format between a lead singer and the congregation. At times, a speaker would initiate a shout (or Holy Dance) that others would join in; it is a Spirit-filled and Spirit-led dance. There is always a witness to affirm the "truth" of the testimony by the clapping of hands or shouts of praise—"*Yes, Lord; alright Lord, um huh.*"[19] Embedded in this Spirit-led communal listening process is the opportunity for the community, as witnesses, to affirm the speaker's story.

## Conclusion

Testimonies are powerful in their silence. To testify is to bear witness; to give evidence to a truth. Look at Rizpah, throwing her mantle upon the rock of God and sitting in silent contemplation with the Spirit. Rizpah's silent testimony embodies the Spirit of resistance and hope that is needed for the thriving of marginalized communities. In that sacred public square, her silent protest is a testimony to the vulnerability of those deemed better dead than alive by oppressive establishments. Her protest is an act of social activism, informed by Spirit, and informing others of the plight of her loved ones.

Sharing one's testimony is akin to a spiritual practice. In one sense it is an examen of one's (or others') actions, words, behavior—held under the gaze of the Spirit. All that is required is guidance by Spirit, a willing and open heart, an ability to listen deeply, and to speak truth. The more you engage Spirit, the more you are (in)formed and shaped by her wisdom and thus, in turn, you strengthen your connection to her guidance. As a practitioner, one becomes a seeker of truths, new possibilities, and a deeper compassion for others. Rosetta Ross, in her book *Witnessing and Testifying: Black Women, Religion, and Civil Rights*, explains that testifying is "a way of life [that] meant living against the grain, living in conflict with and as a challenge to the status quo."[20] This intuitive connection to Source sharpens our lens so that we creatively, critically, and imaginatively expose acts of oppression and imperialism.

18. Hoyt, "Testimony," 93.
19. Ross, *Witnessing and Testifying*, 225.
20. Ross, *Witnessing and Testifying*, 225.

## Deeper Conversation/Deeper Listening

1. The United States prides itself on separating the public sphere from the sacred. How can you use your testimony to cross these mythical lines of demarcation and explore how your lived experiences embody both public and sacred dimensions simultaneously?

2. Exploring Rizpah's silent protest requires examination, imagination, and interpretation to discover the complex systems embedded in her social context. Reflect on those times when someone's quiet acts of resistance motivated you to reexamine your perspective on some past or current situation that marginalized others.

3. Wisdom offers opportunities to seek a life that is truthful to one's sense of self—how can the spiritual practice of sharing your testimony with others disclose your truths to you and your listener?

## Spiritual Practice

Testimonies have a way of creating a dynamic space for the investigation of sociocultural factors embedded in one's testimony. Our contexts influence us. Rizpah's rituals on the mountain—as she beat away the birds, sat upon her rock of salvation, and mourned the loss of her sons—were foundational to constructing a sacred site of embodied grief. Testimonies can transform us, our actions, and our relationships. This is not just a pious form of confession where one walks away at the end with no sense of the way forward. People testify through songs, prayer, shouting/Holy Dance, humming, preaching, biblical interpretation, and silence. To tell one's story can not only be a persuasive moment filled with verbal expressions, but also is embodied via habits, actions, and lifestyle.

Sharing one's testimony is akin to a spiritual practice. In one sense it is an examen of one's (or others') actions, words, and behavior—held under the gaze of the Spirit. All that is required is guidance by Spirit, a willing and open heart, an ability to listen deeply and to speak truth.

Take time to write your testimony.

1. Take time to still yourself and examine your life (you could also focus on the day's events).

2. Develop a timeline of important events and people that have impacted you over the years.

3. Outline why these events and individuals were important. Where were the challenges, the joys, the moments of growth?

4. Reflect on where you see God/Source/Spirit active in your life during these events or through these individuals.

5. There are several ways to develop your testimony: write in a journal, create a poem or a hymn, create an artistic drawing, or photograph a scene that best expresses your journey.

6. Share your story with others.

## Bibliography

Asante, Molefi Kete. "The Implications of African-American Spirituality." In *African Culture: The Rhythms of Unity*. Trenton, NJ: Africa World Press, 1996.

Cannon, Katie G. *Katie's Canon: Womanism and the Soul of the Black Community*. Minneapolis: Fortress, 2021.

Copeland, Mary Shawn. *Enfleshing Freedom: Body, Race, and Being*. Minneapolis: Fortress, 2010.

Exum, J. Cheryl. "Rizpah." *Word and World* 17 (1997) 260–68.

Fewell, Danna Nolan, and David M. Gunn. *Gender, Power, and Promise: The Subject of the Bible's First Story*. Nashville: Abingdon, 1997.

Hoyt, Thomas. "Testimony." In *Practicing Our Faith: A Way of Life for a Searching People*, edited by Dorothy C. Bass, 1–6. Minneapolis: Fortress, 2019.

Kaminsky, Joel S. *Corporate Responsibility in the Hebrew Bible*. London: T&T Clark, 2019.

Melanchthon, Monica Jyotsna. "Reading Rizpah across Borders, Cultures, Belongings . . . to India and Back." In *Bible, Borders, Belonging(s): Engaging Readings from Oceania*, edited by Jione Havea, David J. Neville, and Elaine Mary Wainwright, 171–90. Atlanta: Society of Biblical Literature, 2014.

Ross, Rosetta E. *Witnessing and Testifying: Black Women, Religion, and Civil Rights*. Minneapolis: Fortress, 2003.

Sims, Angela D. *Ethical Complications of Lynching: Ida B. Wells's Interrogation of American Terror*. New York: Palgrave Macmillan, 2010.

United Holy Church of America. "Church History." http://www.uhcainc.org/about-us/#.

Walters, Stanley D. "To the Rock (2 Samuel 21:10)." *Catholic Biblical Quarterly* 70.3 (2008) 453–64.

## Chapter 2

# For the Love of Black Women-Folx
## *or*

### On Caring for Us Hard and Well: Wisdom and Reflections from the Sojourner Truth Leadership Circle

Lisa Anderson, MDiv, MPhil

*Lisa Anderson is the director of leadership and founding director of the Sojourner Truth Leadership Circle. Lisa graduated from Union Theological Seminary (NYC), receiving the MDiv and MPhil with expertise in liberation theologies (Black, feminist/womanist, LGBTQIA), philosophy, and ritual practice.*

*I want to create spaces*
*where Black, mainly queer, although not always,*
*boys and girls know what it means*
*to feel God's aching, powerful yearning*
*and adoration for them in their bones.*

*I want to write the kind of things,*
*and spend my time helping anyone*
*with a dark, or otherwise uncommon body*
*to believe that the ordinary act of saving their own lives,*
*and showing up for the task "on the regular" is revolutionary.*

*I want to embrace the blessedness*
*of the intimate and the small,*
*and build my utopia in those spaces.*

*I want to cultivate beauty all around*
*and feel unapologetic in my embrace of this as a calling*
*of and for the faithful.*

*I want to be in a place that actually believes,*
*like Audre Lorde wrote,*
*that creating this kind of poetry is not a luxury.*

"Reflections of a Nerdy Black Queer Girl"
—Lisa Anderson

## History of an Idea

I REMEMBER THE CONVERSATION like it was yesterday. It was the summer of 2009, and I, along with a small group of Black feminist and womanist seminary-trained sister friends, were in the midst of imagining the focus for the next series of events for the women's leadership programming. We had been collaborating over the past season through our various organizations. Coming off of the modest success of our monthly church-based dinner conversations that highlighted the essential role Black women occupy in faith-rooted social justice work, our hope in the coming year was to find a way to go deeper than the standard emphasis on exploring the myriad contributions faith-rooted Black women have historically made to justice work could allow. To be sure, such conversations were always educational and inspiring, whether we reflected on the legacy of foremothers such as Rosa Parks, Ella Baker, or Fannie Lou Hamer or the impact of contemporary luminaries such as Dr. Prathia Hall, Dr. Melva L. Sampson, Bishop Yvette Flunder, and Dr. Wil Gafney were having on the world. The sense of connection to a collective story of Black women making change mattered, and we knew it.

And yet, as we huddled over our conference call lines—an unspoken sense that "we could do something more, that we could do something different" beckoned. *"What about a program on Black womxn and self-care,"* I announced. The ask dropped from my lips with less confidence than I actually projected. But the fulsome silence that followed my query felt decidedly invitational, so I pressed on. *"For as long as I can remember, I've always wanted to explore what it means to care about and for Black women in a world that historically has so little regard for us. What are the possibilities for radical personal and social transformation that might accompany* caring for us hard and well." The powerful words of one of my sheroes, Audre Lorde, immediately sprang to mind. *"Caring for myself is not self-indulgence,"* she proclaimed. *"It is self-preservation, and that is an act of political warfare."* An all too common, if not always deeply interrogated declaration, Lorde asserted that caring for and about Black women's bodies, minds, and spirits could upend the world as we knew it, which inspired me. Written during the height of her battle with metastatic breast cancer, I imagined this self-described "lesbian warrior poet" laboring on behalf of her own Black, queer flesh and inviting a world of like-minded siblings to do the same as an essential ingredient in her definition of what it meant to make a more expansive way for love and justice in the world.

These thoughts coalesced in my mind quickly, and as they did, I continued to think out loud with my friends. *"Everybody always talks about how hard Black womxn work. Our mothers work hard. Our grandmothers work hard. All the Black women we know work hard with the subjects of their labor, rarely focused on themselves or their own needs and desires. Is working hard for the primary benefit of others really why we were put on this earth? Is that really why God created us?"* Images of my own perpetually tired mother flashed before my eyes. The two and sometimes three jobs she worked to keep our family afloat, her unfulfilled dream of "wanting to do hair" in a salon of her own because her heart desired to create beautiful things, and most significantly, the persistent messages she received from family members and community that her reward for all her sacrifice might come someday—all these thoughts stirred my excitement.

My tone grew more insistent as I thought about my mother's sacrifices and the lack of care she received in the process against the backdrop of my own reality. Despite the educational privilege her sacrifices undoubtedly afforded me, I knew I was set on a similar path. The liberation framework of my seminary education notwithstanding, the FIRST and most consistent message I received from most of my mentors and all of the social justice folks I ran into was once again focused on the struggle everyone will demand from Black women. And at every turn, it was the tireless strength, the indomitable spirit, and the unwavering commitment of Black women that made the relentlessness of our labor seem natural, right, and even holy. "*Now, don't get me wrong, sisters,*" I concluded. "*I'm not saying the sacrifices we make for justice are not real or necessary. But when do we ever get to imagine a NEW WORLD—a world beyond the narratives and practices that relegate our needs to the bottom of every list, if they are considered at all? When do we get to imagine Black women cared for, rested, and well as an organizing principle and priority inside of a collective vision of the world made right?*"

I could feel the heat rushing through me as I uttered this long-held but unspoken sentiment. Long concerned that my secret desire to lean into what felt like a smaller and more intimate inquiry about the quality of care in Black women's lives would be perceived as trivial and outside the scope of what justice-minded theological thinkers should care about—I hardly let myself feel what I feel or know what I know. Namely, the power of Black women caring for and about ourselves is radical stuff. In a world that tended to disregard us at every turn, something inside me was so sure that Audre Lorde's description of self-care as "*an act of political warfare*" was precisely that! Political warfare against everything that had declared us invulnerable, unflappable, and magical to the point of feeling and needing nothing. Political warfare for the sake of being inside of our own needs—our desires—our own longing and creating whole new worlds from what we found there. The consent of my sister-friends to move in this direction was calm and immediate—as if to say, "*Haven't we all been waiting for this moment?*" As if to say, "*Yes, baby girl it is our time. It is our time!*"

## Manifesting the Dream

*We define self-care as a spiritually grounded
intention to respond to
God's declaration of the goodness of all creation
by honoring the one body, mind, and spirit given to us
by the creator
to do the work of love and justice in the world.*

*While the acts of self-care are ordinary
(getting enough rest and nourishment, cultivating financial
wellness, exercising, etc.)
disrupting the cultural narratives and societal pressures
that encourage women to sacrifice themselves for
any number of assumed greater goods—"the movement," "a
career,"
"religious and/or academic institutions"—is hard work.*

*—The Sojourner Truth Leadership Circle
creates a space for that discipline, and we believe
divinely mandated work of the spirit to happen.*[1]

Fast forward to 2022 and what has become the Sojourner Truth Leadership Circle (STLC) at Auburn Theological Seminary. It is the site where the battle I longed to wage for the care of Black women-identified folk a decade earlier takes place. Now four cohorts deep, STLC was founded in 2011 with an inaugural cohort of twelve Black women-identified leaders. So-called in honor of the abolitionist and feminist commitments of its namesake, STLC was created to cultivate the capacity of faith-rooted Black women activists who desired to organize their imaginations and their actions around their well-being. STLC is designed to develop an understanding that such orientation is integral to making a more expansive way for love and justice in the world rooted in the care and love of Black bodies, minds, and spirits.

Since its initial launch, STLC has evolved into a comprehensive initiative serving a community of several hundred Black women-identified faith- and spirit-rooted activists. From its inception, STLC was organized around the mantra *"self-care is a mandate for prophetic leadership"* and dedicated to the principle that *"movements for social*

---

1. Auburn Seminary, "Sojourner Truth Leadership Circle."

justice must no longer happen on the backs or over the dead bodies of Black women-identified folk."[2]

We make primary Black women folx desires for rest, pleasure, beauty, and love in their everyday lives. Our story-based methodology stems from these core values. Indeed, we believe that the desire of Black women to experience these things in the ordinary course of their existence is the birthright of every Black woman. Or put another way: we believe that the presence of God is revealed in and through the spaces where Black women love themselves hard and well and where they enjoin others to do the same.

From this premise, STLC gathers diverse cohorts of Black women into communities of mutual accountability with one principle goal: to help Black women imagine, build, and execute a discrete and time-bound self-care plan to express their hearts' desire. An intentionally practical and project-based goal, the reason behind such a focus is simple. In a world that deliberately and routinely practices disdain for and disregard of Black women, creating spaces where we can unapologetically cultivate the *holy habit* of centering their desiring hearts enables us to truly imagine a liberation beyond the limits anti-Black logic has placed on the imagination of us all.

Women work on "their plans" over nine months and are supported in their process with regular retreats, somatic rituals, leadership development, and individual and group coaching. They are also provided a no-strings-attached stipend to support their project financially. While developing a self-care plan involves a commitment of time and effort, the labor Black women perform is directed toward cultivating their own and their siblings' well-being and joy—story-hearing and -telling anchors the entire experience. As Black women explore the truth of their stories together, they begin to feel inside and underneath the supremacist logic that binds them. To be sure, Black women already have a keen intellectual knowledge of the extent to which such reasoning does not serve them. But the act of individual Black women FEELING into their fullness *together in the community* sparks a new way of imagining themselves as worthy of fulfilling their desire for care IN REAL TIME, one act at a time.

---

2. Auburn Seminary, "Sojourner Truth Leadership Circle."

## Our Sacred Text

We chose Toni Morrison's powerful description of the "Clearing" from her novel *Beloved*, which inspires and anchors this practice. The entire novel is a sacred text for the Sojourner Truth Leadership Circle. It is a story of Black folks navigating the afterlife of slavery—its trauma, horrors, hauntings, and the impossible life decisions Black folks were compelled to make still echo for so many Black folks now. We often recall the famous "Clearing" passage as an example of a community learning to value and fortify itself when, as Morrison writes of the White world outside of the Clearing, *"yonder they do not love us."*

Morrison's character Baby Suggs Holy is central to the theme within the Clearing. Baby Suggs is a preaching woman. Called by the divine and the yearning of her own "great big heart" to inspire the community to step into the fullness of its humanity, Baby Suggs Holy is a most unlikely carrier of sacred wisdom. But this disabled Black woman—she had a twisted hip caused on the plantation where she served—regularly retreated with the community of formerly enslaved folks in her town to a hidden place in the woods to impart the fundamental wisdom that *"in this here place we flesh; flesh that weeps, laughs; flesh that dances on bare feet in grass. Love it. Love it hard."* The scene Morrison sets is worth recounting at length.

> *In the heat of every Saturday afternoon, she sat in the Clearing while the people waited among the trees. After sitting on a vast, flat-sided rock, Baby Suggs bowed her head and prayed silently. The company watched her from the trees. They knew she was ready when she put her stick down.*
>
> *Then she shouted, "Let the children come!" and they ran from the trees toward her. "Let your mothers hear you laugh," she told them and the woods rang. The adults looked on and could not help smiling. Then, "Let the grown men come," she shouted. They stepped out one by one from among the ringing trees. "Let your wives and your children see you dance," she told them, and ground life shuddered under their feet. Finally, she called the woman to her. "Cry," she told them. "For the living and the dead. Just cry." And without covering their eyes, the women let loose.*[3]

The vision of Black personhood offered here fundamentally challenges the repressive ordering of Black existence demanded by the

---

3. Morrison, *Beloved*, 102–3.

White world. "In the Clearing" Black folk dance, they laugh and cry to the point of exhaustion and, in so doing, take ownership of their feelings and movements on their terms. This act alone represents defiance in the extreme, as bodies declared only fit for toil or disregard spend themselves in the service of their own needs and desires. But even more than standing in defiance, Black folks enact a grace-filled and disruptive love language in the Clearing—a love language that, as the novel unfolds, will empower them to come to the aid of the book's main character, Sethe, when the traumatic memory of the daughter murdered by her hand threatens to consume her. Baby Suggs rightly casts this embodied love language *as a way for Black folks to be with themselves and one another, with an integrity that exists before and beyond the White ordering of things.* With a tenderness and passion that mirrors what Baby Suggs is calling forth from the people she preaches:

> *Yonder, they do not love your flesh. They despise it. They don't love your eyes; they'd just as soon pick them out. No more do they love the skin on your back. Yonder they flay it. And O my people, they do not love your hands. Those they only use, tie, bind, chop off, and leave empty.*
>
> *Love your hands! Love them. Raise them and kiss them. Touch others with them, pat them together, stroke them on your face because they don't love that either. You got to love it, you! And no, they ain't in love with your mouth. Yonder, out there, they will see it broken and break it again. What you say out of it, they will not heed. What you scream from it, they do not hear. What you put into it to nourish your body, they will snatch away and give you leavins instead. No, they don't love your mouth. You have to love it.*[4]

The scene culminates when Baby Suggs and the community join together in a beautiful moment of mutual fulfillment; dancing, singing, and crying joyously.

Baby Suggs's words conjure the healing power of Black love as a response to their inherent freedom and worth rather than as a reaction to the murderous intentions of White supremacist society. This is to say, Baby Suggs helps people recognize that the love they practice there is in service to dignify the wholeness they already possess, despite circumstance or context. Before and beyond the limitations on Black life that

---

4. Morrison, *Beloved*, 103–4.

White supremacist systems and structures would place on them, there is a people called to love themselves *"regardless."* Before and beyond any abuse or violation, before and beyond any enactment of laws and customs that would make their love small, the Clearing is the space where Black people cultivate the capacity to know and be known, see and be seen, hold and be held, and to remember in the doing that being Black and being beloved TOGETHER is their birthright.

Of course, such knowledge does not remove the impact of White supremacist logic and culture on the individual and collective experience of the people. And the novel does not imply otherwise. After all, the Clearing is only a memory as the book opens, and every character in it struggles within and against the trauma and terrorism that the system as it stands would create for them. But it is finally the capacity of the people to organize themselves around the sacred and simple fact of their own full humanity that is transformative. The Clearing provided an occasion for that capacity to be acknowledged and nurtured. It provided an occasion for every Black man, woman, and child who experienced it to override the attempt to recreate Black humanity in the pernicious image and likeness of the false God of Whiteness. Instead, as Black people affirm the integrity of their BEING in the Clearing, they were positioned in the world beyond it to create all manner of counter-narratives and practices for the purposes of their own survival and even their own thriving.

> *I am often struck by the dangerous narcissism fostered by spiritual rhetoric that pays so much attention to individual self-improvement and so little to the practice of love within the context of community.*
> —bell hooks, All About Love: New Visions

## A Theological Framework

Such is the power of Toni Morrison's literary imagination, and why, when my sister friends and I first imagined a theological framework for the project, the Clearing emerged as holy writ and represented wisdom and truth. Black womxn folk, creating a space for us to BE TOGETHER in the fullness of who we are. That is the calling. That is the point. Black women folk create a clearing in the world each and every time we gather—a space at once within and beyond the confines of a world practiced in its disdain and disregard for us, but where we assume, assert, and act inside of the knowledge of our inherent worth, of our unassailable *belovedness*—that is the calling. That is the point. Black women and Black womxn folx learning how to create Clearings within our own souls—sacred well-springs that nourish and fortify us to struggle against whatever would undercut our fullness. But even more than this, Black womxn folk cultivate spaces of Clearing within our individual and collective bodies in order to imagine and give birth to new theological worlds. Black womxn-identified theological worlds carved out of the complexity of all we are, have been, and are becoming. That is the calling. That is the point.

## I AM Because WE ARE

And so, with all this, I return to our guiding mantra. "*Self-care is a mandate for prophetic leadership.*" Those words still resonate in the intimacy of our circles despite the worst offenses of the capitalist-driven "wellness industry." The commodification of self-care is often reduced to the idea that mani-pedis is the only societal way of displaying care. This, alongside the depoliticized tendencies of accepting prosperity gospel thinking and removing one's self from geographical areas considered urban, is a narrow vision for true love of self, after all—"*self-care is divinely ordained personal wealth attainment.*" It is these realities that have challenged STLC's vision from the start. And yet, deep accountability to Black futures is rooted in a collective and interdependent understanding of a human BE-ING being human has always grounded us. It is found in the word *ubuntu*—*I am because we are.* I look into the eyes of the siblings who come to us—Black womxn folk who represent, in the depth and breadth of their identities, all that we are—and I see it reflected in the possibility of the world we long for in what they create for themselves, in what we help manifest together.

Imagine her. She is a Black, straight, bi, or trans, a church elder without whom far too many younger ones would consider themselves of no account. She is dedicated to helping lead her traditional Black Church community to fully inhabit its call to become an affirming and loving home for Black folks. She thrives in this environment, AND her commitment has brought her to the brink of exhaustion. Imagine her plan to be baptized in the Jordan River; "*I'm traveling to the land where Jesus trod,*" she announces to her siblings—the certainty of her ministry and the intimacy of her relationship with God is that strong. Imagine the connection between the healing she will receive there and how that inspires how she retells the story of Christian tradition for herself and the broader Black community. She bears witness to the inherent continuity between Black lives and the liberation narrative that strikes at the heart of a decolonized Christian confession. She embodies a prophetic witness of new theological languages. *Ubuntu. I am because we are.*

Imagine her. She is what everyone is quick to define as a "badass sistah," and yet she is weary of standing strong in the face of the state-sponsored surveillance she has been under since the inception of her leadership. Her public persona of strength and courage is so fixed in the popular imagination that even her closest friends, including some Black women, encourage her to stay strong. "*But my soul is soft,*" she admits to her circle of siblings. And she wants us to know that it is her softness that really inspires her justice work. "*I am going to build altars to my gentleness all around me. I will say yes to this part of me because I know it's where my strength comes from.*" Imagine her filling her home with bouquets of flowers on a regular basis. Imagine her home overflowing with tangible reminders of beauty, sensual, organic color, and her capacity to claim tenderness as her birthright. Imagine her embodying that message alongside the declaration "Black Lives Matter." Imagine how her particular practice of softness helps other Black women release the stranglehold the performance of perpetual "badassery" has on their capacity to feel fully alive to the completeness and complexity of who they are. She embodies a prophetic witness of Black womxn's ease and gentleness. *Ubuntu—I am because we are.*

Imagine her. She spends most of her waking hours fighting to release Black children from the cradle to prison pipeline. The possibility of free Black babies is not difficult for her to conceive because God has blessed her with the power to dream vivid, revolutionary dreams. She regularly casts powerful visions from podiums and pulpits of Black children protected, exuberant, curious, and caressed into who they are and will become. Heaven on earth. But the work has become a twenty-four/seven proposition, where every table is a strategy table, every enclosure—a place to level a plan of attack against whatever would oppress our babies. "*A war room,*" as she was apt to say. Even her beloved home study, a space initially christened for rest and play, has become another space to toil and plan. She mourns the loss of it and ponders in the company of her sister-friends what it will take to reclaim time and space for herself. Imagine the power of a cohort surrounding her in prayer. Imagine them agreeing with her that "laying it down," from time to time, is precisely what God requires. "*God is not glorified by your chronic exhaustion,*" they remind her. Imagine her giving herself over to the process of "laying it all down," of refusing the grind that will never make us free, even when we tell ourselves it is for the sake of our own people. Her progress is incremental but steady, as both her calendar and her little spot on the upper floor of her family home are slowly transformed from "ground zero" to a more holy habitation. Fresh curtains adorn the windows. A bright, leather-bound journal and luxurious pen replace the laptop. A plush armchair and footstool replace the straight-backed office chair. And finally, an oversized framed photograph of her cohort siblings proudly displayed on the wall above her desk becomes an inspirational focal point. Imagine her welcoming Sabbath into her body week in and week out. Imagine her vision of heaven on earth expanded to include "Black women with our feet up." She embodies a prophetic witness of rest being rest as an attribute of the divine and Black women rest as what it means to proclaim, "We were created in the image and likeness. Black womxn." *Ubuntu—I am because we are.*

These are but a few of the stories Black womxn folk have shared. They represent the interplay between individual self-care experiences, the role of a supportive community to help birth the experience, and transformational insights that are central to all we do. And if that were all there was to recount, if the only wisdom to be gleaned were that the world is transformed for the better when Black womxn actively expand what it means to be human together refracted through the lens of the regard we extend to each, that would be enough. But it is finally the fact that we conjure together—a community of Black lives as diverse and as varied as we could have imagined—that matters most.

Imagine us. We are trans, cis, and gender non-conforming. We are queer, straight, bi, and intersex. Our bodies are able and disabled. We are Christians and Jews, Muslims and Buddhists, and Hindu practitioners of African traditional religions and spiritual beings. We practice and lead within traditional institutional spaces, on the streets, in the community, and throughout the African diaspora.

All of us are justice warriors whose action in the world is rooted in a love of Blackness and Black people. We understand that love is a spiritual calling and embed our practice of loving Blackness in the ordinary care of our own bodies, minds, and spirits. We privilege the frequently overlooked lives and experiences of Black women-folx in this effort. Our goal is to respond to the history of disdain and disregard, selflessness, and sacrifice too often visited upon us with reflection and action that not only works to dismantle supremacist logic but also creates Afro-futures of beauty, sustainability, and joy.

The results are myriad. But the calling, the longing, is of a piece. This is a call for the love of Black womxn. ALL Black womxn. All Black Lives.

## Deeper Conversation/Deeper Listening

1. Everyone can play a role in decolonizing thoughts and actions. What is your role in removing the mantel of disdain around self-care for women?
2. What can be done to promote spiritual direction as one unselfish act of self-care, especially for BIPOC women?

## Spiritual Practice

Think about the ways in which you can take better care of yourself; make a list. Write a journal entry outlining how you can achieve this list. Write a pledge to yourself about how you will make self-care a priority. Find a sacred verse or text that supports your pledge. Place this pledge where you can see it every day.

## Bibliography

Auburn Seminary. "Sojourner Truth Leadership Circle." July 5, 2022. https://auburnseminary.org/stlc/.

———. "The Tarrying Place." https://www.tarryingplace.org.

Morrison, Toni. *Beloved*. New York: Vintage International, 2023.

"The Papers of Toni Morrison. Princeton University Library Special Collections." Princeton University. Accessed June 11, 2023. https://library.princeton.edu/special-collections/exhibitions/papers-toni-morrison.

# Chapter 3

# Resilience, Strength, and Inner Power as Spiritual Practice

### Argrow "Kit" Evans-Ford, DMin

> Kit Evans-Ford is a certified spiritual director and the founder of Argrow's House of Healing and Hope in Davenport, Iowa, and Moline, Illinois. Argrow's House is a safe space where free services are offered daily for women healing from violence in the Quad Cities Region. She founded Autistic & Loved, LLC and authored 101 Testimonies of Hope: Life Stories to Encourage Your Faith in God and A Children's Book on Bishop Richard Allen: A Nonviolence Journey. Her distinguished awards include the Jacqueline Kennedy Onassis Award for Public Service Benefiting Local Communities and the Tom Locke Innovative Leader Award.

THERE HAVE BEEN TIMES in my life when I felt neglected by God. I questioned if God was still sovereign and if he had left or forsaken me. I can remember the day when that thought would impact the rest of my life. That day was May 13, 2008.

I was exhausted. The week prior, I had worked relentlessly with high school students by doing HIV and AIDS awareness campaigning in the community. In addition, I had modeled in a hat show on Mother's Day, rehearsing at evening practices for many nights. As a US Peace Corps volunteer, I filled multiple roles on the small island of St. Kitts in the Caribbean. After nine months of diligent work, which included health awareness efforts in the schools, outreach to local groups, mentoring high school-aged girls, daily teaching rotations, and participation in town and family events, I finally felt part of the Sandy Point community I loved. I felt comfortable and welcomed; this place was now my second home.

That Tuesday, after teaching HIV and AIDS education at the high school and remedial reading at the primary school, I headed home for a nap. I was tired, and I slept until 7:00 p.m. I usually go to Vivache dance class, but I decided to take the night off and not go to town for class.

I soon heard a gentle knock on the door. My Kittitian college friend Gary came over to use the wireless Internet. He is a bright and extremely promising young man. Unfortunately, the Internet was not working. So, instead, we watched my friend Mark's cooking show on the local station and talked about politics and the US presidential candidate Barack Obama until 10:30 p.m. As soon as Gary left, I checked the Internet connection. Oddly, it was now up and running smoothly. If Gary had known about the Internet, he would have stayed later to complete his work. *I wish the Internet would have been working. I wish Gary would have stayed.*

My nap gave me energy that I had not had for days. So, I turned the computer to YouTube and jammed to the sounds of great rhythm and soul music on replay while cooking and cleaning. As soon as the vegetables—my food for the week—were cooked, I turned on all the apartment lights to start my weekly cleaning. As I washed the dishes, I cleaned two knives, one small cutting knife, and one large butcher's knife; I placed them in the red dish holder to dry. The kitchen was now clean, my vegetables were in the fridge, and I was all smiles! I turned off the light in the kitchen, turned down the music, and started cleaning the bathroom. For some reason, as I walked by the small television clock in the living room, 11:35 p.m. stood out so that it looked like the numbers were in bold print. I entered the bathroom, and as I looked under the bathroom sink, I heard a strange cracking noise in the other room. I peered out of the bathroom, and the front door connected to the living room was wide open. I approached the door and immediately reasoned with myself. I thought, "*I did not close and lock the door when Gary left.*" I lived close to a mountain and felt the wind blow the door open. Without hesitation, I said, "*Yep, that is why the door is open.*" I truly believed that was the reason—until I closed the front door and turned the top lock. As soon as I turned the lock, I felt something was wrong. My instincts suddenly went on high alert. He was there. He jumped out as I walked toward the lightless kitchen. Unconsciously,

I held my hands up for protection. I will never forget—a mask, white tank, black pants, slanted eyes, hot breath, knife, and danger. I froze; he had a knife swinging before my eyes. A deep voice reverberated into the still air; he said, "*Don't scream, or I will kill you.*"

In the coming months and years, this event shaped my life in many ways and served as a point of reference even in times when I thought it should not. The aftermath was brutal; wrestling with both physical and psychological issues made me realize even more the preciousness of the gift of life. I began to seek support and help through therapy and other resources. I felt some sense of relief after the perpetrator was caught. I felt even more empowered because I was able to testify at his trial, where he received a sentence of forty-six years in prison. During the trial, I came full circle and realized God was still a very present help, and my spiritual center and my personal resolve became stronger. Through therapy, I found that I needed to lament what was lost in that encounter. Although the trial was over, I could not whisk past what happened and expect to be whole again without examining each aspect of what happened that night. Most of all, I needed to create a safe place to lay open my soul.

## Lament: An Expression of Grief or Sorrow

In the Isaiah 40 text, the people of Israel are tired. They are lamenting about what has happened to them. They feel neglected, used, and, most of all, abused. They feel as if God has abandoned them because of the torment they have endured for years by the Babylonian people. They feel alone and as if hope is gone. Lamenting offers the people of Israel the opportunity to have a safe place to cry, to acknowledge what they have lost, and to be honest with themselves about how their lives will never be the same. I felt the same way, too. Amid the lament, the writer of Isaiah 40 wants the people of Israel to push past their lament and see hope again. They are still worthy and a chosen people. Isaiah 40:29–31 reminds us, "*God does not faint or grow weary. He gives power to the faint and strengthens the powerless. And those who wait on the Lord shall renew their strength. They shall mount up with wings like eagles. They shall run and not be weary. They shall walk and not faint.*" Something good can be birthed out of pain. The eagle is used as a metaphor for strength and hope. It signified hope, and if they held on to the imminent redemption of Israel, the nation would be saved! Even though it seems like all is going wrong. The lesson in this passage made me realize that God has the power to direct all affairs concerning life, justice, restoration, and the world. Most of all, it made me realize God will not fail. With God, all things are possible. God is all-knowing, loving, and even has the power to rectify all things, whether large or small. I also learned there is no easy answer for suffering. I knew suffering would make one look inside for the interior connections and realize we already have a spiritual alignment with God, who holds all answers. We need to tap into that alignment as a source for our good.

I came to realize lamenting is necessary for healing. I began to feel the need to speak about my experience and what was lost and changed. Even today, the writer Nancy Raine's words still resonate with me as my own: "*Words seemed to make it visible. But, speaking, even when it embarrassed me, also slowly freed me from the shame I felt.*"[1] I took her wise words to heart and made them part of my truth. In the coming years, I learned that the more I struggled to speak about that night, the less power the trauma and its aftermath seemed to have over me, and my spirit began the process of healing. I focused on a writer named Judith Herman, who helped me to formulate the words I needed. In her writing, Judith Herman reinforced the importance of simply telling the story: "*Remembering and telling the truth about terrible events are prerequisites for the restoration of the social order and the healing of individual victims.*"[2] These words also become my eternal truth. To be able to recount unashamedly is a part of telling my truth, healing, and finding a new direction for my life.

## Questions and More Questions

There are varying interpretations of how people make sense of tragedy and suffering, i.e., questions of redemption, faith-testing, and sanctification developed within me. These questions and more are the same questions I initially had after that fateful night: *Why do we suffer? Why does it seem like God will not answer? Why do people take advantage of others? Why is there violence in the world?* The aftermath of my assault brought forth a variety of emotions and suffering. I wrestled with Post Traumatic Stress Disorder and how it manifested itself in my life. Like

---

1. Raine, *After Silence*, 23.
2. Lewis, *Trauma and Recovery*, 32–33.

the people of Israel, I wondered if God had forsaken me. After much grieving over what I had lost, and with the support of many people helping me to see God's love and God's intention for my life, I began to see redemption and sanctification differently. It took years to see how redemption applies to my life and the situation I experienced. Through this trauma, I had to learn how to find my truth amid turmoil. I had to find encouragement to see life beyond that moment, find my voice, and speak my truth to find healing. I found I could see a new ground, a new future, and a place for me after my traumatic experience. I gained knowledge about surviving and survival that I now share with other survivors of similar traumatic experiences. I embraced the image of the eagle as my icon, and it became a symbol of my healing. Remembering the eagle encourages me to face questions about that night, and sometimes I use the questions as affirmations, even today.

## The Value of Hope in Action

I found an even stronger conviction to use this time to help others like me. Ultimately, a sense of unbridled optimism comes after suffering and lamenting. A sense of resilience and overcoming can be more of a focus, especially when we make something good out of our pain. After years of therapy, returning to school, attaining another degree, and valuing the blessing of a supportive faith community, I started on a new path to study ministry. I opened Argrow's House of Healing and Hope. It was named after my dear grandmother, Rev. Argrow Margaret Warren, who was also a survivor of violence and a woman of compassion to many. Argrow's House is a safe space in the Quad Cities Region (which borders Illinois and Iowa), where free services are offered daily for women healing from violence and abuse. Services range from domestic violence support groups to therapeutic art, animal therapy, counseling services, spiritual direction, and more. Argrow's House is also a bath and body business where women healing from abuse create beautiful bath products that provide a living wage while working in a safe space that celebrates who they are. Every day, I make sense of my suffering when I can be present and support a woman who has survived violence with the resources she needs to move forward in her healing. My experience of suffering allows me a sense of empathy and alignment with others that causes me to be fully present, unlike before.

Resilience and strength are all about perspective. Looking at where I have been and the road that has brought me to where I am now, I have peace; this experience taught me to believe in the impossible and that healing is a process. My experience has increased my capacity to withstand, knowing recovery from difficulties is always possible with adequate support. I now know recovering quickly is relative, and sharing my truth is a necessary part of healing; sharing this story has taken me years. However, the writer of Second Isaiah was onto something when he used the eagle as a metaphor for resilience. This strong bird towers in the sky, protecting itself and pushing forward amid hardship and pain. As predators, they are seen as protectors and courageous; this is what I try to do as a facilitator to give hope to other women. As people of God, we can embrace the same resilience and spiritual center and take on the courage of an eagle, making it our truth. There will be hardships. However, when we connect to God as our spiritual center, God reminds us that he is a very present help, even in the worst kind of pain. "*But those who wait for the LORD shall renew their strength, they shall mount up with wings like eagles, they shall run and not be weary, they shall walk and not faint.*" And to that I say . . . Amen!

## Deeper Conversation/Deeper Listening

1. What purpose does suffering play in our life?
2. As a spiritual director, how do you support someone through suffering?
3. How can examining the role of spiritual truths play a role in defining how we view hardships?

## Spiritual Practice

This is a two-part spiritual practice.

### *Breathwork*

Choose a quiet space. On each of the following statements, whisper the mantra to yourself.

- Breath in: My practice is love
- Breath out: My path is peace
- Breath in: I honor my tears
- Breath out: I preserve the tears of others
- Breath in: I seek balance in my life
- Breath out: I am centered

Repeat as often as needed.

## *Seek Renewal*

It is often after trauma and dramatic changes that we seek renewal. Choose a time and place where you can begin renewal. Commit to this space as the most essential aspect that will allow you to connect, reflect, and renew. This can be done in a spiritual retreat, immersing yourself in nature, changing your morning ritual, making space for a nurturing weekly routine, or reading a spiritual text or daily guide. Find a supportive guide, companion, or spiritual director who can support you during this process.

## Bibliography

Lewis, Judith Herman. *Trauma and Recovery: The Aftermath of Violence from Domestic Abuse to Political Terror*. New York: Basic Books, 1997.

Raine, Nancy Venable. *After Silence: Rape and My Journey Back*. London: Virago, 2000.

# Chapter 4
# The Grace in Forgiveness

### Karen Simms Tolson, MS

*Karen is a spiritual director and educator with over thirty-five years of experience in teacher education, social justice program development, and community outreach. She has extensive experience working with local and national non-profit organizations, including the board of directors for the National Association for Multicultural Education (NAME). She serves on the Justice and Advocacy Commission of the Kentucky Council of Churches and the board of directors for Spiritual Directors International. She graduated from the San Francisco Theological Seminary, where she earned a diploma in the art of spiritual direction.*

Having memories is an essential part of living. As humans, we have the innate power to create memories that can last forever, just as we can choose to forget those things we desire to forget. The choice is always available and should be guided by what is wise, what is best, and, most of all, what is personally and emotionally healthy. Whether we like it or not, our memories will often shape our future. According to Chanequa Walker-Barnes, memories are not a set of *"neutral recollections"*; memories can be highly opinionated and, most often, incredibly impactful in shaping who we are.[1] Memories are, for the most part, time-related, situational, or people-associated events frozen in place. Memories are always filled

---

1. Walker-Barnes, "Myths about Forgiveness."

with emotions and encoded within our life circumstances. Memories are shaped or influenced by the events we experience and by our beliefs, biases, and feelings during the encounter. Our memories are also guided and infused by our cultural context, including opinions about truth and justice and how we interpret the world around us. Memories are essential because we can encounter various emotional challenges connected to memories, which also allows us to either repeat a mistake, dwell within the mistake, or learn a life lesson. Such challenges can lead us to face numerous questions ranging from rectification or excitement to regret and remorse. One such emotional challenge when it comes to memories is the question of forgiveness, which can be one of the most significant emotional challenges we face in life, both past, present, and future.

Alexander Pope may believe "*to err is human to forgive is divine*,"[2] but I prefer to believe forgiveness is intentional grace. Intentional grace is a display of compassion for ourselves as well as others. After all, not one person has the corner on hurt, and while we may be the victim today, we may play a role as the aggressor or the witness to hurt in another time. In the context of our memories, forgiveness plays a decisive role in our healing, allowing us to reconcile our perception of an incident while still regarding the memory and participating in our own healing. This is why I have always wondered where the concept of forgiveness originated. We know that babies are not born to hate, or cause hurt, and we learn during our lifetime how to hurt; this is not a dichotomy. We also know it is not within the scope of divine love not to forgive. Forgiveness is walking in the path of personal truth and deciding how there will be healing when there is a realization there is no other direction. Forgiveness allows you to remove the binders that prevent you from walking into a more positive future.

As Christians, we are constantly reminded of the sacredness of forgiveness and how Christ forgave. Chanequa Walker-Barnes, in her blog post "Myths about Forgiveness," relates that the Bible verses about forgiveness are direct and fall into two broad categories: God forgives us, and in response, we are to forgive those around us.[3] As Christians, we are reminded that forgiveness is at the heart of Christianity and the basic teachings of Christianity (e.g., Eph 1:7–8; Mark 11:25; 1 John 1:9; Eph 4:32, etc.). Quite simply, as believers, we are challenged to forgive without

---

2. Pope, "To err is human."
3. Walker-Barnes, "Myths about Forgiveness."

question—period. Furthermore, the Bible does not state that forgiveness is necessarily an immediate response but a directive we must follow. As a society, we are often reminded that emotionally and psychologically, forgiveness is usually about our personal growth, combining our ethical convictions and social experiences with our faith commands, which at times can be the crux of the challenge to forgive.

Forgiveness is one step in healing, and healing is always about the spirit enacting truth. The essence of forgiveness is not only intentional but a decisional truth. It is the question of how our truth aligns with a situation and the dictates of faith. Forgiveness is an exercise filled with lessons for anyone who cares to participate in "overcoming." Each of us has experienced something in life that requires forgiveness. Whether it is an act of betrayal, violence against our being, or aggression that changes our lives, we have all been there. When it comes to reacting or enacting forgiveness, the bottom line is that we will remember how we were affected by the actions of another, especially if the impact causes trauma, anguish, or pain to any degree. We will not forget the feelings, the emotions, and the experiences (whether we admit it or not) as a part of our lives. After all, to consider forgiveness is a process that swirls with emotions. Depending on the circumstance and stage of our life cycle and human development, we may also face the question of how we can forgive, or should we forgive, especially those things or actions that are egregious to the body, mind, and soul. Forgiveness is part of being in a community. When we decide to begin the process of healing, we play a definitive role in how we heal ourselves and how we participate in another person's healing.

## Can We Truly Forgive and Forget?

We hear and learn several sayings about forgiveness that I find troublesome. For example, the adage "forgive and forget" can be misleading in some contexts. I often question if we can ever honestly "forgive and forget" or if we should forgive some experiences, mainly if the experience caused a significant change in our lives or created physical and emotional damage. Secondly, sometimes, our desire to forgive and our capacity to forgive may not align with the emotional lens through which we view ourselves or the issue that caused us pain. While we may want to forgive, there are times when we must seek support to adequately process and integrate what happened before we can take steps to forgive and implement measures to heal. Forgiveness, after all, is an internal answer to a process that can include outward expressions. Many aspects affect our ability to forgive, including our worldview and the total reflection of our accepted and personal reality that caused us pain. Above all, forgiving and forgetting is more than reenacting, holding a grudge, or feeding memories. It is the release of a spiritual injury that is just as important.

Likewise, there is also the belief that if one forgives someone (or oneself in some cases) for a transgression, it is also assumed we will not think about it again, and this is not always an achievable action. Forgiveness can bring about a sense of closure, but it does not necessarily make the thought or memory disappear. The memory of the issue will frequently remain stored in the recesses of our minds. If we aren't supported and emotionally prepared, the memories of the offense at times may arbitrarily resurface, and we emotionally and mentally may revisit the occurrence, creating, in some cases, anxiety and trauma. Once we have decided to forgive, we must face the belief that if one genuinely forgives a person (or again ourselves in some cases) for a transgression, we will not think about it again; this argument is not always logical. The logic of pain cannot be fully described. It is like a pebble in water that has ripple effects. Unfortunately, there will be reminders in one form or another. Therefore, asking someone not to think about an event when the actions are wrapped up in hurt and traumas that detract us from our self-worth is neither healing nor logical.

Comparatively, the phrase "forgive and forget" is not found in the Bible. There are, however, numerous verses commanding us to "*forgive one another*" (e.g., Matt 6:14 and Eph 4:32), and not doing so hinders our relationship with God (e.g., Matt 6:15). The Bible also tells us that God places transgressions in the "*sea of forgetfulness*" (e.g., Mic 7:18–19). Still, I question if we can, as humans, do the same. According to Walker-Barnes, if an incident or experience is painful enough to warrant forgiveness, it is significant enough to be encoded within our memory.[4] Humans are "programmed" to store memories; we can and will remember things that hurt us. Unlike computers, humans cannot selectively delete, rewrite, or override words, actions, and memories. After all, betterment is a choice and not an option. The issue is how we will recognize and utilize the lesson from the experience to give ourselves the gift of freedom, progress on

---

4. Walker-Barnes, "Myths about Forgiveness."

the road to healing, and release ourselves from the bondage of recycling the experience; this is when there is a sign of growth and change in our perceptions and often our actions. This is also a sign of grace. It is one of the aspects that can be found in developing wisdom.

## Can Time Heal All Wounds?

Does "time heal all wounds"? Not really. Yes, time can do many things, but time does not always heal the most egregious aspects of life. The body remembers, the mind remembers, and, most of all, the soul carries the history of our lives. Forgiveness doesn't change the past, but it affects the present and transforms the future. Unfortunately, even when we feel we have progressed beyond the emotional parts of an incident, life will often send reminders of our experiences. It is at such times some experiences may become triggers. The way we process our feelings is essential, and I also know it is possible to change one's feelings over time, for the better or the worse. With practice, we can learn to recognize our automatic reactions to specific events and situations and choose how we want to respond. Through this process, we can change our feelings by consciously choosing how to react. This is part of healing and creates spiritual liberation. It takes time, intention, lamenting the loss, and embracing the love of the Spirit. After all, forgiveness depends on a person's current situation in life, willingness and emotional ability to explore spiritual and psychological situations, both large and small, and in a way that is appropriate to their needs.

## Applying the Bandage of Forgiveness Doesn't Always Take Away the Hurt

Forgiveness is a courageous decision that starts changes from within; it is a step toward finding the joy within. After all, our growth is not limited to external experiences; we expand from our internal compass and spiritual center through inner experiences. Sometimes, we view forgiveness as a one-time decision. But on the contrary, forgiveness may not be achieved in one actionable step. Depending on the situation, we may need to remind ourselves why we forgive many times over. Sometimes, our desire and capacity to forgive may not align with the willingness to forgive; the hurt is too great. While we may want to forgive, the process can be impeded before we have adequately sorted, examined, and integrated what happened to us. When faced with such crossroads, we must seek support and professional help through therapy, pastoral care, spiritual direction, and other qualified people.

## Different Approaches; Different Times

At times, there is generosity in the act of forgiveness, but there is also an emotional cost, depending upon the situation. When this occurs I call theses times "mercy moments." Moments that clarify how our existence can have an opportunity to align with God's expectations. It in such moments we seek solutions that at times may not have clear answers, but we seek them anyway. Until recently, forgiveness was something that was perceived as spiritual. Traditionally, addressing forgiveness as an expressive act was mainly left to the support of religious and faith communities, and the process was designed by denominations, religious leaders, and lay persons. In support of this position, it has been only within the twenty-first century that science and research have entered into the study of forgiveness and found that forgiveness also has health benefits. During the apartheid hearings, Archbishop Desmond Tutu developed a four-step process for forgiveness that included the following:

- Tell the story/narrative,
- Name the hurt,
- Grant forgiveness, and
- Renew or release the relationship.[5]

These simple and concise steps have since become more encompassing. Forgiveness can be complicated depending on the situation, and, psychologically, it has evolved into forgiveness training. In *Forgive for Good: A Proven Prescription for Health and Happiness* (2001), psychologist Fred Luskin writes, "*In careful scientific studies, forgiveness training has been shown to reduce depression, increase hopefulness, decrease anger, improve spiritual connection, [and] increase emotional self-confidence.*"[6] Luskin has since developed a protocol for forgiveness that includes specific steps and exercises that support the development

---

5. Tutu and Tutu, *Book of Forgiving*, 67–145.
6. Luskin, *Forgive for Good*, xi.

of prolonged physical, emotional, and spiritual healing.[7] While most research on forgiveness examines personal and interpersonal relationships, Everett Worthington, who spent his life investigating forgiveness on many levels, expands the research on forgiveness to include community forgiveness. According to Worthington, *"forgiveness awareness-raising campaigns that used methods such as public lectures, student newspaper articles, debates, panels, group discussions, and small-group education . . . helped community members replace negative thoughts, feelings, and behaviors with positive, generous, and loving ones."*[8]

Within the process of forgiveness as a spiritual practice, we can discern and examine responsibility versus accountability, offer compassion (to ourselves and others), and, where possible, begin the next steps in the forgiveness cycle, moving to reconciliation, restoration, and renewal.

As a spiritual practice, mindfulness is also used in spiritual direction when addressing forgiveness. It is a life-changing skill that enables us to be more present, fully aware, grounded, and compassionately attentive to our thoughts, feelings, and relationships. It works exceptionally well with those who are committed to addressing forgiveness issues. After all, mindfulness includes acknowledgment of emotions; emotions are central to humanity, and emotions are much more complicated than just a result of a social framework or social conditioning. Emotions are a combination of mental reactions, subjective experiences, physiological changes, and more. Therefore, deciding to forgive also requires healing, mercy, and recovery work. Most of all, it takes grace and time to reach an emotional resonance with a conclusion and definition of what peace looks and feels like. Forgiveness is transcendent to our inner voice and allows the Spirit of transformation to begin doing marvelous things to aid us in our healing.

## Forgiveness Does Not Always Include Reconciliation

Forgiveness doesn't require anything from the person we are forgiving. However, the steps leading to reconciliation, restoration, and renewal need the other person's conscientious actions. Reconciliation requires an admission of guilt and remorse from the offender combined with tangible actions signifying change and accountability. While reconciliation

---

7. Luskin, *Forgive for Good*, xii.
8. Worthington, Griffin, and Toussaint, "How to Build," §6.

is ideal when possible, it takes admission, acknowledgment, and professions of responsibility from the person who has committed the wrong. After restoration, the work begins to renew the relationship. Renewal is based on agreed-upon boundaries, and interaction will be established between the two parties. It is almost like starting the relationship from another perspective but with knowledge of the relationship's potential for the future. Most of all, depending on the situation, it is possible to remember the experience and forgive simultaneously; to do this, it takes time and the courage to take a long, loving look at self and where the hurt has led us. In some situations, the decision to remember and forgive is essential as a life skill to cultivate and makes it possible to protect ourselves in the future from similar occurrences.

I have found that forgiveness is too essential to my personal beliefs, self-care, and how I define inner peace to let forgiveness depend solely on reconciliation. Speaking the truth constantly shifts the atmosphere, whether it is acknowledged or not. Working toward the goal of forgiveness requires speaking the truth. There are very few times in my experience when an aggressor who has behaved poorly will spontaneously or willingly go to a victim, ask for forgiveness, and begin to take the necessary steps to reconciliation.

In most African-American families, there is a saying, "What goes on in the house stays in the house." Like other African Americans, I know this means you should not talk about anything that deals with experiences bound by emotions (right and wrong), egregious actions, family secrets, or take steps for healing outside of the house. Many African Americans cling to this "rule," covering various mental and emotional health issues ranging from ways racism is ever present to most issues in society to marriage issues and issues of emotional and physical abuse. Talking in this manner is an attempt to release the trauma that was ever-present in life. Secondary to this "rule" is the "kitchen table rule." This is a tradition where the opportunity to explore problems is discussed; it is a gathering of family and trusted friends (most often women) who offer advice, wisdom, or reflections on specific topics. It is a cultural form of wisdom sharing. The conversations are usually broad in scope, and the table was most often an intergenerational form of self-care. For people deracinated from their cultural heritage, the kitchen table became a form of council or circle of wise women and elders. The kitchen table rule can account for resolving issues using the wisdom of elders and others. It is also a foundational way a family can come together in compassionate sharing and a place to examine relatable wounds that were too often intergenerational.

There is no doubt that the "kitchen table rule" and "what goes on in the house . . ." beliefs are derived from generations of African Americans who probably developed these complex behavior patterns to connect, define, and protect the family unit. The "rules" were passed down through generations (again, usually through women) and were designed to protect what was sensitive and potentially dangerous. Such "rules" protected family secrets and family "business," but, at times, depending on the topic, the "rules" promoted shame. While I understand both of these concepts, and I have experienced these concepts, I also believe the concepts, depending on the situation, can hinder the support for problems that might need culturally appropriate therapeutic intervention. The fear of speaking a personal truth is common among women of all races, especially women who have faced racial oppression. But, if the reason for not speaking out stems from the "rule" that "what happens in this house stays in this house," then it might be time to decide if this rule still serves you or your family well. I believe that sometimes decades-old beliefs that no longer serve well should have an expiration date. After all, secrets can affect how families function, grow, survive, and thrive. As a community that has experienced the rawness and worse that a country can heap onto a group of humans and still survive, it is time to survey our personal and familial wounds. These are the wounds that bind us to intergenerational pain that has not healed. I believe there must be a recognition of original wounds, question how and where they originate, how the wound affected the paths of the family, and how, together and as a community, we can take steps to heal. Emotional wounds are portals, and they carry history that needs to be explored and used for the establishing of personal truth. They carry the history of how we got to a point in our lives and can help direct where we should go from there. Many times, the decision to keep secrets within the family makes for intergenerational trauma that impedes community health and perpetuates an unhealthy cycle.

## Healing, Forgiveness, and Boundaries

There was a period when I struggled with the forgiveness of a family member. The family member was loquacious and considered the "life of the party" type of person who mostly loved being the center of attention in any situation. However, my interaction with the person was quite different. When I finally began to talk about my concerns with this family member, I was met with exasperation by the individual and indifference by several of my family members; the lack of support went on for years and impacted me in many emotional ways. As I raised the issues more, the family member in question finally tried to apologize without accepting fault. The person wrote a letter full of "ifs" (i.e., "if I did this" or "if I did that"), which only compounded the situation. This person was supported by other family members who felt I should not "embarrass the family," or I "should just forget what the person does to keep peace," and most of all "just keep it within the family" or another way of saying "what goes on in the house . . . ." I eventually realized that standing in your truth will change your life. Standing in your truth will change how interactions occur with everyone involved, but most of all, it will change how you view yourself. Not acknowledging your truth creates turmoil internally and externally, impacting not only" self" but the relationships with all who witness or are close to viewing the discord that surrounds you. I have learned that all lasting actions of peace begin within; but it is hard to have peace when there is unheard and unacknowledged hurt, and we must start with an acknowledgment of when we are hurt in the unhealed spaces of our life, which is also the beginning of standing in our truth. It is hard to have peace when there is unheard turmoil within the heart, when someone feels subjugated and unhealed, and when sensitive issues go unresolved and turn to trauma. Instead of this being perceived as a wound in the village, it became "her problem." Trauma changes everything, including self perception. Through this experience, I learned that perseverance and standing alone in your truth honors the soul, and the importance of using your voice is everything when you are working to forgive. I realized during the process of forgiveness that not everyone, even family, may support and believe in the need for personal healing. The attitude of "carrying on" despite the hurt and the pseudo-portrayal of being the "strong Black woman" or the "sistah" that can withstand anything in all ways and all things is a myth. It takes away the opportunity to react to human hurt. It is okay to show your wounds; it is okay to show you bleed; it is okay to be vulnerable, especially in safe spaces and with the people and in the places that cherish us. I learned that forgiveness and healing are not for others; therefore, depending on the situation, the most important people in my life may not be included in the process. I also learned that the adage "what goes on in the house . . ." can be a form of revictimization and is not a healthy way to resolve anything.

It is important to remember that taking personal responsibility is not a time for pretentious acts, platitudes, and posturing, nor is it effective when ostensive conditional apologies are offered, which only compound the situation. I soon realized that the person I needed to hear a sincere apology from was incapable of taking responsibility or accountability for their actions. The person could not admit their "wrongdoing," making reconciliation, restoration, and renewal impossible. I also realized I needed to reassess how I felt about several family members, adjust my interactions, and add healthy boundaries with them as well. I also found that peace is not always at any cost, but the results of finding peace are worth it. While we live in times when "cancel culture" is the answer for anything and anyone that we find difficult, I realized that may not always be possible when it comes to family. Therefore, boundaries made for family members were carefully erected. Creating boundaries with family members meant I had to put my personal space of peace first. It meant not attending a Thanksgiving dinner or other celebrations and opting for time with people who valued me if I felt I was going to be challenged by another person's presence. I also found supporting myself with self-care, therapy, and spiritual direction was crucial to my emotional well-being. Establishing boundaries helped with my healing and learning it was okay to love some of my family from a distance if necessary. Access to me and my space became a privilege, not a right, regardless of who may seek it. Being able to forgive and move on is a responsibility we owe to ourselves, and I became a very responsible person.

Finding my center of peace with the issues, with the person and the family members who were not supportive, was long and arduous. It took clearing my heart, prayer, soul searching, and realizing this hurt could no longer be manipulated, strong-armed by outside and oppositional opinions, or allowed to define who I am. Heartbreaking ruptures in families are painful. However, freeing myself meant I needed to change the interactions with some family members regardless of what anyone in or outside my family thought or supported. It meant that I did not need to engage with that person on an interpersonal, let alone superficial, level. In my search for forgiveness, I realized that the offender did not need to participate in my forgiveness; it was a personal matter for my growth. I also realized that forgiveness is about finding the path and releasing the emotions that were barriers to my growth and perceptions about life in general. It meant redefining my voice and using my voice to be not only heard but understood. After all, we arrive at the future at the moment of any decision. Therefore, it is important to be wise and relentless investors in our own lives and our own decision making. Finding a heart for forgiveness is one of the most unselfish acts one can give oneself because it gives back a sense of power to the soul. I also found what Walker-Barnes ascribed when she stated *"that we can achieve forgiveness without reconciling."*[9] This is the eternal truth I have found in my situation, and that is the most I can ever hope for.

## Deeper Conversation/Deeper Listening

1. What are some examples of emotional challenges connected to memories besides forgiveness?
2. Can we properly process and integrate experiences before forgiving?
3. As spiritual directors and people who support others, what is our role when we companion someone who is refining how to forgive?
4. While this essay explores forgiveness on a personal level, can the same protocol be helpful on a macro level for such things as state-sponsored atrocities, discriminatory laws, or other acts that do not lead to equity, inclusion, and justice?

## Spiritual Practice

### *The Connected Heart*

This spiritual practice is one that can be done as a group or individually.

> If you are comfortable with this request, I invite you to offer your right wrist, palm up to the person on your right side of you. You will take your left hand with three fingers and gently hold the wrist of the person on your left.
>
> If holding the wrist of another person is something that is not comfortable for you, then I invite you to hold your own right wrist just in the area of your pulse.

---

9. Walker-Barnes, "Myths about Forgiveness."

Let's take a moment to settle in by closing our eyes and taking four deep breaths.

Repeat the following aloud:

"Behind the wrist that I am holding is a pulse and the beat of a heart that has experienced many joys, felt the warmth of smiles, connected with life on numerous adventures, and witnessed countless wonders. May we remember together today to be grateful for wonder.

"Behind this wrist is a collection of memories and dreams . . . some dreams are unknown, some dreams fulfilled, and some dreams yet to be fulfilled. May we be mindful of honoring memories and always seeking dreams.

"Behind this wrist is a soul and heart that might have experienced brokenness, moved through disappointments, love, and at times held space for pain. May we be thankful for the wisdom that is always a part of love and pain.

"Behind this wrist is a heart that still sees and seeks the wonder of the sacred and the works of the Holy. May we remember to honor our hearts as sacred spaces within ourselves.

"Behind this wrist are ancestors and all those who have gone before that we honor with our actions, deeds, and words. May we safeguard our sacred stories passed down through generations and the words we use."

## Bibliography

Bandura, Albert. "Commentary: 'On the Psychosocial Impact and Mechanisms of Spiritual Modeling.'" *International Journal for the Psychology of Religion* 13.3 (2003) 167–73. https://doi.org/10.1207/s15327582ijpr1303_02.

Garrison, Becky. "How to Find Healing by Connecting to Your Pre-Trauma Self." *Spirituality and Health*, 2014. https://www.spiritualityhealth.com/pre-trauma-self.

Luskin, Frederic. *Forgive for Good: A Proven Prescription for Health and Happiness*. New York: HarperCollins e-books, 2010.

Pope, Alexander. "To err is human; to forgive, divine." Brainy Quote. Accessed October 16, 2023, https://www.brainyquote.com/quotes/alexander_pope_101451.

Shapiro, Shauna L. *Rewire Your Mind: Discover the Science and Practice of Mindfulness*. London: Aster, 2020.

Tutu, Desmond, and Mpho Tutu. *The Book of Forgiving: The Fourfold Path for Healing Ourselves and Our World*. Edited by Douglas C. Abrams. London: William Collins, 2015.

Vangelisti, Anita L., and John P. Caughlin. "Revealing Family Secrets: The Influence of Topic, Function, and Relationships." *Journal of Social and Personal Relationships* 14.5 (1997) 679–705. https://doi.org/10.1177/0265407597145006.

Walker-Barnes, Chanequa. "Myths about Forgiveness." *No Trifling Matter* (blog), Jun 27, 2023. https://drchanequa.substack.com/p/myths-about-forgiveness.

Worthington Everett L., Jr., Loren L. Toussaint, and Brandon J. Griffin. "How to Build a More Forgiving Community." *Greater Good*, May 30, 2018. https://greatergood.berkeley.edu/article/item/how_to_build_a_more_forgiving_community.

# PART 2

# *Introduction:* **Identity and Spiritual Callings**

*This section examines the concept of wisdom and its connection to identity and overcoming adversity.*

> **After**
>
> After . . .
> Fear has had its way
> and denial has run its course
> and disillusionment has settled in
> and disappointment fades
> and the anger dissipates
> and the grief runs through you
> and the mourning season ends . . .
> All that's left is Love.
>
> —Jasmine N. Bellamy
> Ministry 101

FINDING YOUR WAY TO love and peace is the terminal destination in most spiritual decisions and experiences. And whether we acknowledge it or not, living is a spiritual practice. It is also a part of the rite of passage of life that we are born into innocence, mature into adulthood, grow by grace, become elders in training, and eventually take on the role of ancestors in waiting. During any of these interim periods, if we are blessed, we witness the gravity and manifestation of our ancestors' dreams—the dreams of change, hope, and thriving expressions of life in forms we cannot imagine.

An essential aspect of accepting and building change is how we see ourselves. I did not acknowledge or see the change in myself until I had several life-altering experiences. Each time the experiences caused me to pivot on my path and seek a deeper meaning to what happened. Depending on how we approach or view our perspective of history, most of us see our connection to significant life changes and challenges as a continuum rather than a period on some invisible and, at times, incoherent timeline that extends into infinity. We categorize our life into periods or stages that reflect our changes and growth often using the challenges as the reference. Then, all of a sudden, we are aging and, if we are lucky, maturing not only in body but spiritually. Viewing life this way has made me realize even more the brevity and scope we face with time as the only real constant that we can use as a measure.

We have become absorbed in presentation and performative actions that can be recorded through social media and often used as a measure of accountability or what is perceived to be the "best." It has become important to let our waiting audience know on the Gram or Facebook what we are eating, wearing, and who we are socializing with or doing each moment of the day. We wait with great anticipation for likes, thumbs up, and the approval of our actions. It has become a preoccupation that drives us to exhaustion and keeps us from focusing on the authentic within. We fail to recognize we have been given the most authentic invitation that we will ever receive, and we call it life. Only when we realize the invitation has already been extended will we be able to live authentically, taste it, contemplate it, and then actually open ourselves up to our personal best. We seldom recognize that our uniqueness is found within our DNA. When we realize this, the journey to becoming one with our intentions, our aspirations, and our actions can begin with clarity and lead us to more compassionate communities and the acceptance of change.

In most Western cultures, there is little reverence for aging. It is perceived to be something that should be avoided or deflected in deference to remaining young. Different from past ways of measuring aging, we now use social media as our timeline to mark the passage of time. We even have language delineating our timeline denoting early childhood, adolescence, teen, adult, and elderly that carry preconceived notions. We construct and organize our lives around these indicators, even in conversations and how we develop friendships. We tend to section our lives away from those who are not in our age group rather than integrating our lives with people of all ages. In order to build more substantive communities, we must consider how we live intergenerationally. In most indigenous cultures, the family includes those who are part of the past as well as the present. However, in the United States, we have taken on aging as something that needs to be separated from the community. Intellectually, we know that everything living is in the process of aging, but we seldom see aging as a spiritual practice. Seldom do we value the ways eldering presents wisdom. We do not question how we view belonging at all stages of life. In most Western societies, we do not usually think of ourselves as growing old until a seminal event occurs, such as the death of a parent or life-challenging events around a sibling or close friend; then, we take notice of our age and where we are on the life continuum. We tend to compare everything to youth and our younger and "better selves." We "shortchange" the richness of becoming older, wiser, and more steeped in wisdom because we mourn what has been lost in the transition to our current stage of life rather than embracing who we are at each stage of this progression, valuing the knowledge and wisdom we gather as we grow older.

The Buddha is noted to be among the first religious figures to teach the truth of the necessity of continuous change in a life span. Buddhism emphasizes the concept of impermanence, which is the idea that everything is constantly in flux and nothing is permanent. Buddhism also teaches that life is entirely suffering caused by attachment to continually change things. However, through living, one can learn to understand change and find peace by accepting life in its impermanence and aging as a spiritual change. The Christian worldview sees change as an inevitable but problematic process. In contemporary societies, we find that change is almost always attached to some form of power and control that spurs us to seek emotional resonance and spiritual alignment, especially in times of crisis. Our contemporary life is often spent going through times of "fix me, save me, change me" beliefs that are recycled according to need and situation but do not always serve us well. When I experience this behavior, I call it being stuck in the "spin cycle" of life.

In the following section, we meet writers who question these areas of reasoning by exploring the meaning and context of beliefs about wisdom.

Each chapter takes an exceptional method to explore how we seek and see change as a necessary part of life and the role of developing wisdom as central to identity and spiritual calling. The guiding question is, *Are lived experiences the only way we face, navigate, or explore change?*

## Chapter 5

# Black Cool, Wisdom Deep

### Eric Wilson, Minister, Spiritual Director, Poet

*Eric Wilson serves as the lead teaching minister of the University Church of Christ in Malibu, California. Wilson is a certified spiritual director, executive coach, and religion blogger for HuffPost. He is also an award-winning playwright and theatrical director. His work has been published and performed around the country, including the John F. Kennedy Center in Washington, DC. Eric is a spoken word artist with the 9 Beats Collective, an international group of musicians and thought leaders reimagining the teachings of Jesus for a new generation. Eric's work attempts to leverage contemplative practice, the arts, and soul care for the purpose of fostering social justice in the world. His book* Faith: The First Seven Lessons *was released in the fall of 2016.*

### A Catechism of Cool

THE CONTENT OF MY catechism was colored by the cool! As a child of the seventies, I was given a christening in cool. The living room in the home of my rearing, carpeted in purple shag, was a cathedral periodically graced with relatives who served as my patron saints. And all of them could only be described as cool. These were my intentional and sometimes my unintentional teachers on how to survive as well as thrive in the exile known as living as the marginalized in a space "a long way from home." Each one was a loud-talking, rhythmically walking, dressed to impress sage, offering wisdom on how to make it in the world antagonistic to your existence. And they were cool.

There was Uncle Tink, the patron saint of song. Here was a man who traveled Europe with the famed singer Bobby McFerrin in 1964 with a group called the California Jubilee Singers. Tink's coolness was made evident as he often allowed music not to come from him but through him. He was a man as generous with his care as he was with his tenor tone. He'd sing, *"Get on board little children, get on board little children, get on board little children, there's room for many a more."* There was Uncle Roland, a towering man with an inner stature that loomed even larger. He was to me the patron saint of hustlers. When asked about his many academic degrees, he would often quip about how his real education came from "matriculating on the street of Chicago." Saint Roland devoted his life to the education of children clothed in color on the South Side of Chicago and was willing to work deals, leverage resources, and hustle the most crooked politicians if it meant more Black and Brown children honed a penchant for reading.

That living room was often graced by my Aunt Kay, who carried the perfume and sweet liqueur of Orisha Oshun. Aunt Kay was a lover and was loved. I've often had total strangers who find out who I am approach me to let me know they loved and were loved by Kay. The regret of losing the opportunity to drink from her gourd stained their lips and furrowed their brows as they confessed their remorse to me, her occasional acolyte. There was always a gleam of nostalgia in their eyes that seemed to cut through the shadow cast by the sorrow of their loss. And she was cool.

My childhood home seemed to be a makeshift Mount Olympus located in the Near Northside of St. Louis. And these gatherings of my ancestors were filled with the incense smoke of cigarettes and the refrain from sacred hymns and canticles from Donny Hathaway, Marvin Gaye, Roberta Flack, and a cadre of jazz luminaries. My home was a sacred space where stories were told. It was a holy ground where plans were plotted. This was a place where wisdom was dispensed from the context of the cool amid the festivities of a Black bacchanal.

## Cosmology

Those brothers and sisters on Sesame Street were asking the right question. As they attempted to teach children the importance of community, they invited us in song to interrogate: "*Who are the people in your neighborhood?*" For them, this was a question drawing young folks' attention to the kind person who delivers their mail, toward the patient shopkeeper, or toward the safe people whom they could run to in a time of need. But from an ontological sense, this question of "*Who are the people in your neighborhood?*" is a question of cosmology. Who are the beings that have a direct impact on your lived reality?

From an African American ideological framework, our cosmology is made up of all those beings past, present, and future who influence the individual's as well as the community's flourishing and fecundity. This is a cosmology that includes the Divine manifested in various forms. This is a cosmology that includes ancestors of the past; that great cloud of witnesses. This African and American cosmology includes the children yet to be born. And all of those various beings have a direct impact on all of our lived experiences. All of which have the power to facilitate our ability to thrive in the midst of our exile. This is a framework predicated on our positionality in rhythms set by the caravan. A caravan with ancestors moving ahead toward home, as we, the living, follow behind, with those yet to be born steadily in pursuit. And all the while, there is the divine resting over and in us all. This is a caravan home. Leading a path of legacies left in our care. Meant to be gathered as we move. And that is cool!

## What Is Cool?

Cool is not hot. Nor is cool cold. Cool lies comfortable in the in-between of things. Cool is located in a liminal state. Cool is never found in the extremes but in the threshold. With one foot on the side of yes while the other foot is firmly on the side of no. And yet, cool does not waffle, nor does it vacillate in its bi-location. Instead, cool find truth within the tension of all things. And this is where cool's power and wisdom reside. Cool is a Black contextualization of the contemplative orientation. To encounter cool is to gain a glimpse of a non-binary positionality. It is where the truth of Jesus is found in the tension of being a lion and lamb. Where sanctification is understood by sitting in the tension of the same blood that stains is the same blood that cleanses. And heaven is found within the tension of the breaking out of the kingdom of God, found in the now and yet.

## The Exilic Heart

This has particular significance in the times we have found ourselves in. One of the redolent themes of the Bible that best describes the condition of the human heart these days is the theme of exile. We see the dynamic of exile through the Old and New Testaments. Adam and Eve, the exemplars of humanity, found themselves exiled. Exile was the natural consequence of eating fruit from the tree of the knowledge of good and evil. They become the picture of humanity's tendency to desire wisdom out of the context of the relationship with the giver of wisdom, who is God. This very human tendency naturally leads to exile. Noah finds himself and his family in exile. Abraham and Sara find themselves displaced. The children of Israel find themselves tossed about from one exile to another. While the Gospels, history, and Epistles of the New Testament find their blooming from the soil of foreign occupation. All of which leads to a deep desire for a space and place of being.

Upon this writing, our world is emerging from a global pandemic. The guttural reverberations of war and rumors of war echo off every wall that frames the corridors of power. The smoke, fire, and burning of racial unrest, xenophobia, heterosexism, homophobia, and transphobia fume everywhere. Leaving us with a sense of dislocation, disconnection, and disquiet. Many of us are living with an exilic heart. Psalm 137 sings over our exilic hearts. This psalm names our current heart hurt when it says in verses 1–4:

> By the rivers of Babylon, we sat and wept when we remembered
>
> There on the poplars, we hung our harps, for there our captors ask us
>
> For songs, our tormentors demanded songs of joy; they said, "Sings us one of the sings of Zion!" How can we sing the songs of the Lord while in a foreign land?

We would do well to ask John Coltrane, after the last note of "A Love Supreme" resolves, how we can sing songs of the Lord while in a foreign land. To ask Sly Stone, Nina Simone, or any number of African American musicians this question is to find the foreign land itself, with all the offense it metes out, can be a crucible of sacred sing if one can live in the tension of cool.

## Qoheleth Was One Cool Brotha!

Qoheleth, the great teacher of Ecclesiastes, was one cool brotha! Qoheleth means "gatherer." He was a gatherer of people and of wisdom. And to immerse ourselves in the wisdom book of Ecclesiastes is to participate in a gathering of souls, hungry to try to make sense of how we as individuals and as a community are going to make it together through this life. What are we going to do? How are we going to make it? How do we make sense of everything we see, everything life holds, and everything life sends our way? We haven't gathered here looking for answers to the smaller questions of life. But the big stuff! The big questions!

To enter into the passages of Ecclesiastes is to participate in a gathering filled with excitement and joy because its pages offer words from someone who has answers. Our excitement and joy grow as we meet the kindly author of the book, who lets us into a massive, well-lit lecture hall to meet Qoheleth, The gatherer of wisdom's truth. Yet, when we find our seats and direct our eyes to the front of the hall, all of the thoughts, questions, and conversation bleed away. Because sauntering onto the stage is Qoheleth. Dressed in a patchwork leather jacket of swatches of brown and tan, this cool brotha, with a look of profound indifference, writes one word on the board. And that one word is *hevel*! *Hevel* is a Hebrew word translators and scholars have had the hardest time trying to capture the meaning of in the English language. Much like so many of the words of the Bible, *hevel* has several meanings—"a powerful image"; "to talk about the fleeting nature and unpredictability of all of life"; "vapor or smoke." Meanings that are hard to capture in one English word and hard to understand with our current way of thinking.

Back in the lecture hall, the author says, "Ladies and gentlemen, I bring you Qoheleth!" And there is a smattering of clapping through the gathering because, with Qoheleth's cool indifference, we don't know what we are about to be made privy to. And with a vocal cadence like Richard Roundtree from a Blaxploitation film or a Black thought poet spitting a bar, he begins by saying: *Hevel, hevel,* everything is *hevel*! Some have translated this as "*meaningless, meaningless; everything is meaningless.*" While still others give these words the meaning: "*futility,*

*futility, everything is futility . . .*" And all of these translations are right. All of these translations are close. All of the translations get an aspect of *hevel*, but the definition is much more frustrating than just meaningless vanity or futility.

This word, *hevel*, Qoheleth keeps chanting as if he is Gil Scott Heron, is a noun associated with a vapor or mist. It is like that time you were thinking about a word, and it's on the tip of your tongue, but you just can't get to it! That's *hevel*. *Hevel* is a frustrating enigma. It is an exhausting puzzlement, and the more you keep reaching for it, the further it gets away from you. Qoheleth calls it a *"chasing after the wind."* You'll feel it. You can sometimes see its effects. But you will never catch up with it. That's *hevel*. And what is so frustratingly enigmatic and puzzling? What is as exasperating as chasing after the wind? Qoheleth says, "Everything!"

> *All things are wearisome, more than one can say. The eye never has enough of seeing, nor the ear its fill of hearing. What has been will be again; what has been done will be done again; there is nothing new under the sun.* (Eccl 1:8–9)

Qoheleth lets us know time makes everything *hevel*. Life's circumstances make everything *hevel*. And as we try to right ourselves from this first blast, Qoheleth says, in effect, I know because I've tried it. I have tried it all. I have had my share of pleasure in this life. I have gathered all of the wealth anyone would ever need. I have bought all of the stuff! Slept with countless numbers of partners! Drank my share of wine and sipped fame and status down to the very last drop. And after he did it all, Qoheleth says in Ecclesiastes 2:11, *Yet when I surveyed all that my hands had done and what I had toiled to achieve, everything was* hevel. It wasn't just meaningless, futile, or vain. But it was frustratingly enigmatic and puzzling.

We begin to get a bit edgy in our seats. And right at the moment we think about leaving, we sense the warm hand of God resting on our shoulders when we find out: Though time and circumstance make everything a frustrating enigma, God does make everything beautiful in its time. God places eternity in our hearts. God places a desire in our hearts to transcend all of it. And with the calming assurance from God, the wisdom of Qoheleth becomes abundantly clear. Wisdom doesn't come from life's certainties. Wisdom doesn't come from being sure about everything. We work so hard to maintain this image of safety and security and try to convince ourselves and others that everything's fine when it is not. While there is nothing wrong with wanting and working toward certainty, safety, and being sure, Qoheleth lets us know where real wisdom comes from. You can get "clever" from certainty, safety, and sureness. But real wisdom is found in the tension of things. Between the good and the bad. Between the hopeless and the hope-full. Between success and failure. Wisdom is found in how you live within the tension of things. God is seen clearer and feels richer within the tension of those things. Kingdom life is lived well when the people of God decide to show up in the tension.

This is the "wisdom of the cross" the apostle Paul discusses in 1 Corinthians 1:8. The cross of Christ is the greatest image of living well within the tensions of the in-between. On the cross of Christ, there is God willing to come down and sacrifice everything as Jesus hangs between earth and sky, sacred and secular, spirit and flesh, the holy and unholy, the pain and possibility, the beginning and end, and between life and death itself. As Qoheleth begins to leave the lecture hall, one of those gathered in the midst asks one final question: *Is life meaningful or meaningless?* The teacher pauses (because all wisdom is birthed from a pause. Wisdom is cast from the cauldron of still silences and "resting lulls"). And once the teacher's pause matures to its peak of ripeness, he restates the question given. "Is life meaningful or meaningless, you ask? My answer would be yes. It is meaningless, but Yahweh can make the meaningless meaningful-full. So just be cool!"

From Qoheleth to my ancestors, I have learned that "cool" is an act of resistance that will not let oppression have the last word. They have taught me cool is resilience. For to normalize the existence of life's tensions is to own the capacity to leverage what has been learned from said tension. The legacy passed down is cool and seeks not the either/or but the *tertium quid*. That third thing that reconciles all tensions as God seeks to reconcile all things.

God allows us to align ourselves with the caravan, traveling the circuitous path toward our heart's true home. And as we journey, we find a location in our dislocation. We discover a connection in our disconnection. We gather up for ourselves a profound sense of quiet in our disquiet. And with sacred moans before us, within us, and behind us sounding an invocation of cool, we find our space and place of thriving.

## Deeper Conversation/Deeper Listening

1. How does Wilson's definition of "cool" align with the meaning of an act of resistance in your life?
2. How does uncertainty build belief?
3. How do we normalize things that should affect us deeply? Is this an acceptable way to examine truth?

# Chapter 6

# My Jesus of Color

JASON VILLEGAS, DMIN

*Jason sees himself as inhabiting borderlands between culture and language. Born in Colorado Springs, Colorado, he was raised in a multiracial family. He has tried to reconnect and reckon with his European (Spanish, English, French, and Scottish) and Native American (Chichimecas) ancestry. He has called himself a "Methobapticostal," reflecting his Pentecostal upbringing, time in the Baptist Church, and eventual settling in the United Methodist Church, where he is an ordained elder—living out his vocation that at present is focused, like a funeral, in a service of death and resurrection.*

"I AM TIRED AS hell of all of these pictures of White Jesus," I thought as I walked around the small rural church I served. I was thinking about what we called in divinity school "The Scandal of Particularity," that God decided to come into the world in a specific context and to put in a particular type of skin. I thought about Jesus coming to the world as a persecuted minority, a Jewish baby born in the Palestinian town of Bethlehem to an unwed peasant mother. I thought about John chapter 1, which says that the Word of God, the way God decided to communicate their wisdom, became flesh and dwelt among us, moved into the neighborhood. I thought about how Jesus became indigenous to different places.

I don't think it is a sin for White European Christians to have painted pictures of Jesus indigenous to their context, but it is a sin when the blond-haired, blue-eyed Jesus gets lifted up as the normative expression of our Savior, a Savior born of Jewish heritage in Palestine. In the church that I was serving during the COVID-19 pandemic, we were wrestling with what it meant to be a church that was for two hundred years a rural, White, English-speaking congregation and only recently welcomed its first Black and Brown members, which were part of a growing Spanish-speaking population, mainly from Mexico. At that point, we were the only rural congregation in our denomination's annual conference. Our regional body of nearly eight hundred churches went from having only English-speaking worship services to including a Spanish worship service. I quickly learned it's very difficult to reckon with White images of Jesus that have always been in place.

But the church's demographic had changed, and we were trying to have worship in two different languages, and at least once a quarter, we needed a bilingual worship service. The images of Jesus needed to reflect that change, too. But everywhere I looked, White European Jesus stared back at me. The European-descended part of me could fit in with this. However, the half of my body with Indigenous ancestry longed to present the Latine migrant worshiping community with an image of Christ that dwelt among them: a Jesus of color. I prayed for something, anything, for some image of Jesus that looked different. And I mentioned this from time to time to the members of the church.

## White Jesus

We were worshiping in the parking lot in August 2020 amid the quarantine for COVID-19, and our Spanish worship service had started at the same time. Every week, I would stand in the parking lot, in English at one time of day and in Spanish at another, inviting people to worship from their cars as they listened to my voice and the music over a radio transmitter. One day, as I was preparing for worship in the church office, my eyes were greeted by a picture of the Lord, a watercolor painting on a faded piece of paper, enshrined with a burlap matting behind glass in a stained wooden frame. The painting of Jesus was actually two paintings, one panel being a close-up of his face and the other being his body on a cross. His skin was the color of coffee, the way I drank it in high school, about one-third cream and two-thirds coffee, and, looking into his eyes, I could tell he was Asian. The words drawn on the side of the panels were foreign to me, and in painted English calligraphy, in the bottom right corner was the word *Korea*. I realized that my prayer had been answered and that we had been gifted a Jesus of color. For months, I asked around, trying to find where the painting came from, and I never did. I displayed it on the walkway between the fellowship hall and the sanctuary. It was the first of a few pieces of culture representing the Holy Spirit breaking into the church in a different way.

We would go on to make two hundred yard signs during the quarantine that on one side said, "*You are not alone #HertfordCoTogether*," and on the other side said the same thing, except in Spanish. "*No estás sol@ #HertfordCoJuntos*." In November 2021, we took five youths to Pilgrimage, an event drawing nearly two thousand people from our annual conference together. These young women, with heritage from Mexico, the Pacific Islands, and Europe, made a banner representing our church to be part of the processional. The banner was a mixture of the North Carolina and Mexico flags, with the United Methodist insignia, the Cross and Flame, at the center. It was a symbol of how the church has room for all.

In July 2023, I moved from that church, and many multicultural, multilingual pieces morphed, struggled, or ended. The Spanish worship service died about a year before I was reappointed from the church, mainly because the Mexican migrant lay leader of the church and her family moved. Related to that was the reality that people are less inclined to show up to worship where they don't see themselves reflected, whether in the leadership or the physical space.

I am really trying to move beyond blaming people for problems. The apostle Paul, in Ephesians, talked about our battle not being against flesh and blood but against powers and principalities. However, when I see enshrined and enthroned the idea of White Jesus, this religious phenomenon can make people socialized outside of Whiteness feel subordinate in some way. Trying to talk about White Jesus and White supremacy to White people who have grown up in the church is difficult. I have heard a few people say it is as complex as telling a fish it is in water. How do you learn for the first time about something you have swam in your whole life?

I will admit that sometimes, in the midst of trying to explain this phenomenon, I have had failures of nerve and failures of courage. In the church I just wrote about, I was given immense grace to challenge the church, but so often, I failed to talk about the ways that Whiteness was at work. After being hurt early on by racism, I struggled to say how we needed to allow for culturally appropriate expressions of Jesus Christ in our midst. Things like praying for an end to migrant abuse had led to one-third of the church leaving, and the ringleader telling me it was because I was too political. The people who stayed probably would have heard me, but those who had left created a fear of abandonment—that the rest would go if I said too much. I share that story as a way to say that it is very important and also very difficult to talk about the proliferation of Whiteness in churches where the culture and the people have been steeped and grown in Whiteness. Most people know that European Jesus was "the Word" made flesh for their ancestors. Therefore, most White congregants do not see how this figure representing Jesus was warped into White Jesus, a symbol of oppression for non-White people.

The reason for resisting White Jesus is simple. He is not the savior of the world but an imposter. Yes, aspects of the Savior are present in White Jesus: the love for one's people, the redemption. But White Jesus is entirely devoid of a thing most important to the Lord Jesus Christ. White Jesus lacks that thing which we ought to pray for weekly, *"Thy Kingdom come, Thy will be done, on earth as it is in Heaven."*

It was the living wisdom of Howard Thurman that first gave me the language to see that Jesus Christ is always present with *"those who stand with their backs are up against the wall,"* as he writes in *Jesus and the Disinherited*.[1] James Cone gave me the language to see the Lord as the *"God of the oppressed,"* which is to say that in the United States, God is not a White man standing behind a pulpit but is an enslaved, possibly lynched Black body. I came to understand through these readings in the same way that they killed Jesus by hanging him on a tree; Christ shows up in the persecuted places of the United States when tortured bodies are hung from trees with the passive permissions of an empire built on exploitation. Christina Cleveland writes to her Patreon members powerful essays about the idol of "whitemalegod," who is not the Christ of our salvation but an imposter who has cosigned on to exploitation and taking away dignity from people made in the image of God. I deeply wrestle with how "whitemalegod" has entered the US and been enthroned and enshrined in historically White churches, which has played a part in violence done in his name.

As I have served a White denomination, I have deeply wrestled with this reality, even as I have prayed and dreamed about ways to challenge our

---

1. Thurman, *Jesus and the Disinherited*, 1.

members to follow the minoritized Jesus of color, who still shows up with people whose backs are up against the wall. I have been taught all my life to pray and talk through my feelings and struggles. Realizing the distance between the two versions of Jesus, I wrote White Jesus a letter.

## Seeing My Jesus

I never would have seen the ways that Jesus shows up with the oppressed if it was not for Black and Latino liberation theologians. Womanist writer Audre Lorde talks about the phenomenon in the United States where young people are taught and made to read European thinkers labeled as "classics" or the "greatest works of literature" although they have long since been dead. Students are also taught to adopt these European writers' worldviews without question and to use them in decision-making. She writes about how important it should be to teach about Black thinkers and philosophers who challenge these authoritarian ways of thinking and living.

I believe we are at a pivotal moment when we can see the flaws of the White church and White Christian America. As Robert P. Jones states in his book *White Too Long: The Legacy of White Supremacy in American Christianity*:

> White Christian Churches have not just been complacent; they have not only been complicit; rather, as the dominant cultural power in America, they have been responsible for constructing and sustaining a project to protect white supremacy and resist Black equality.[2]

As a United Methodist, I am not just trying to change the methods, but I am bearing witness to the fact that our method of church has died. We don't need it to be resuscitated or go back to how things were. We need new methods.

In my book *A Service of Death and Resurrection: Change and Hope in the Church* (publication pending), I talk more about this phenomenon, bearing witness to it from my context and experience. I reflect on our need for new methods, even as I am an employee of the old methods, longing for new ways of doing them, even while I reinforce the rules of the old ones. It is a paradox.

---

2. Jones, *White Too Long*, 6.

So many paradoxes exist—like the fact that my denomination was formed in the same year that the Rev. Dr. Martin Luther King Jr. was assassinated (1968), the same year in which the landmark fair housing was signed, when the KKK was still burning crosses; and we as United Methodist adopted as our logo the Cross and Flame (of the Holy Spirit). However, two things can be true simultaneously: more paradoxes. As a denomination, we have good ideas that do not always work out well. The United Methodist Church has one of the best church polities in the world because we have many layers of protection for minority church leaders and those who speak prophetic messages. But the problem arises that these same structures also protect what is harmful and make it difficult for us to hold ourselves accountable to a higher standard. Like an accidental typo I often make, the "united" has become "untied" in our church. Things are falling apart; the methods and their architects did not plan for what we're experiencing. We have such significant church structures that give immense room for creative imagination. Still, in this rapidly changing world, the fence around our life in the church has us grazing in grass that has dried and died, and we have a hard time moving on to greener pastures or re-fertilizing the growth that would occur within our existing ones.

## Change and Uncertainty

The Annual Methodist Conference 2023, our annual regional business meeting for the churches under the leadership of our bishop, provided a potent example of this challenge that we face: living in an old method while simultaneously yearning for a new one. We were at the height of experiencing a schism, with around 40 percent of our annual conference leaving with a mass exodus in January and a smaller one at our June meeting. We invited the esteemed pastor Adam Hamilton, pastor of Church of the Resurrection (COR), the largest United Methodist Church in Kansas City. He came and spoke to several smaller groups, including the young clergy group, from which I was about to age out. In the large group plenary, he talked to over one thousand of us, half laity and half clergy; he gave what I thought to be a compelling conversation for unity amid diversity of thought. Using text messages, he took polls from our smart devices. We voted to answer some questions about differences of belief concerning human sexuality. Over 90 percent of us said that both we and, in a separate poll, the churches we serve could live in a faith community with people who believe differently from us about human sexuality.

After that presentation, he shared several video clips from the movie *Jesus Revolution*,[3] which deeply touched my heart. This inspired everyone in the audience. This inspiration connected with stories of witness and testimony from COR, talking about its steep growth over the years, encouraging pastors from Hamilton's example to literally run after church visitors. It resonated very deeply with my own experience serving the United Methodist Church.

As my friends and I have reflected on this annual conference meeting, some of us have been frustrated by the paradoxes that were a part of the meeting. We were inspired and encouraged to move forward at a pivotal moment in the church's life. Still, we did not have creative examples connecting with the congregation's diversity. We were also frustrated that we would use the same method and thinking that has proven insufficient for the new generation of worshipers. I profoundly support using historical examples, but I question using the story of *Jesus Revolution* as our inspiration.

This example makes sense to me because most of the power in the church is held by aging "Baby Boomers" who came of age around the time of the historical Jesus Revolution. Even if they were not hippies or living rustic lives, they would have seen the "Jesus freaks" that were portrayed in the movie. One of my friends said that watching this movie clip felt nostalgic for a moment and that he's not sure it ever happened in our Methodist church. It felt self-congratulatory and challenging, even while it did not make us get out of our comfort zones to try to engage in a way that aligned with the cultural backgrounds of our changing congregations.

While some of the White Baby Boomers in the United Methodist Church may been hippies, most of them probably benefited from the G.I. Bill or from some government programs allowing them or their families to have subsidized housing, which was intentionally not available to Black people in the United States because of White supremacist laws. The irony of the *Jesus Revolution* for some White Christians is that they voluntarily gave up lives of luxury for a time, only to return to those deep places of privilege to become the wealthiest generation in the history of any nation

---

3. Netflix, *Jesus Revolution*.

in world history. Watching the *Jesus Revolution* video clip felt like an invitation for older White power brokers to make space in their places of power for other people who are different to come in and use the area as it exists more than it felt like a challenge to change from one method to another that is more encompassing. Even though the conversation resisted steel religiosity in favor of inclusivity and welcome, it did not address the White supremacist roots that still must be excised.

I wonder what it would look like if instead of watching a clip from *Jesus Revolution*, we watched a clip from a Spike Lee movie about the Black struggle for liberation or if we watched a clip from either a documentary or film about Latin American migrants going to "El Norte" with profound faith and hope. Rather than returning to lift up successful examples of a method that is proving in most places not to work in the age of secularity and postmodernity, what if we lifted up examples of the historical Black church, witness of "hush harbors," and "base ecclesial communities," like Brandon Wrencher and Alexia Salvatierra write about in *Buried Seeds: Learning from the Vibrant Resilience of Marginalized Christian Communities*.[4] One of the lessons taught to me in recent years is that the wisdom we need for moving into the future does not exist in a practiced paradigm inherent in the historically White church.

Specifically, we need to name the places where our method is dead, even if we do not have the energy or resources to change the way those methods function legally. Families who have walked with an elder through Alzheimer's or dementia know what it is like to journey with someone dead yet alive. The salvation in these moments comes in both grieving the death of what has been while also celebrating the presence of life, that respiration still happens, and that spirit is still exchanged with the lungs. Our previous message may not be helpful and moving like it once was. Regrettably, it is still breathing.

White church methods and members struggle to name death, I believe, because death is the ultimate loss of power and control, and these are two historical hallmarks of Whiteness—power and control have always existed. For example, the idea of racialized identity was created to control others, which creates an inherent shame. When shame turns inward, it becomes anger. However, the church does not take responsibility for being the nucleus of the anger. The Christian church does not take responsibility for the negative results of colonization, which stripped cultures and divided families. Instead, there have been throughout history efforts to change the narrative to reflect only one narrow perspective. If we look at

---

4. Salvatierra and Wrencher, *Buried Seeds*.

the death of our method of the church through the lens of the spectacle of Holy Week—when Jesus triumphally entered Jerusalem, spent time with the people, celebrated the Last Supper, was crucified, died, and was buried, and then was resurrected—we find parallels to our life in the church and the role the church has played throughout history.

Our method of church has endured or will endure a good Friday. Our comfort zones, way of gathering resources, way of growth through open doors, our assumptions of homogeneity, and our ability to communicate with others quickly—it is all dying or has died. Those of us who are most institutionalized will be like the disciples, paralyzed in fear, and at least with our emotions and vulnerabilities, locked in a house, even though we have heard that resurrection is coming. Those who have been taught to provide answers to prove their competence as religious professionals may find themselves in desolation and exile. This is the space of Holy Saturday, having seen the death of what we have known, not knowing if resurrection can come, dreaming of resuscitation, dreaming that things would return to the way they were.

It is in this pivotal moment that historically White churches must realize that they are not alone in Holy Saturday, that, historically, their expression of church has caused crucifixion and moved other Christians into that space, and that ethnic and racial minority churches have long survived in the area of Holy Saturday, unsure if or when resurrection will come. This is the wisdom I have learned from the *Latine* church, which has long lived in the space of Holy Saturday.

If the spiritual wisdom of Howard Thurman is true, the Lord is present with those whose backs are up against the wall. If the words of James Cone ring correctly, then it is true that the Lord Jesus Christ is not a White man but, in the United States, has been a lynched Black body. Suppose it is true that we do not serve a God of the empire but a God whose kingdom comes at the margins, on earth as it is in heaven. In that case, we will find our footing in Holy Saturday as we who serve historically White churches become disciples of the Black church and other historically oppressed expressions of the faith. If we have followed White Jesus, we must repent and follow the Jesus of Color, the Body through which God chose and chooses to enter the world.

Even though we have our endowments and ways of ensuring power and resources for our progeny, we must not hold onto these things, trying to maintain a semblance of control. We must not rush through the question of death but sit in it, for it is in letting go that we find freedom. We cannot see life by seeking it. We cannot find the next instance of the church by putting all of our energy into it. We must follow Jesus into other places. For it is in giving up our dying method that we will find it. In giving up our lives, we will be reborn to whatever everlasting life may look like. Thanks be to God.

## Deeper Conversation/Deeper Listening

1. How can the church redefine itself to include the voices that are a part of the contemporary congregations?
2. How can the lessons outlined here be used in a spiritual direction?
3. Have you ever experienced being the "other" within an environment? How did this experience impact your perspective about yourself and your commitment to developing a community? If you have not experienced this environment, what can you do to improve such situations?

## Spiritual Practice

In moments of profound change within our institutional church, find a quiet space and visualize a fallen tree in a tranquil forest. This tree represents the elements that have come to an end, like traditions and structures. Embrace the idea that from this death, new life emerges, just as the fallen tree nourishes various organisms and allows sunlight to shine through. How might this help you accept the demise of institutional things that once stood tall and powerful, like a tree in the forest? Where are you seeing new life?

Return to the present with this awareness, finding hope and resilience amid the evolving landscape of your institutional church.

## Bibliography

Jones, Robert P. *White Too Long: The Legacy of White Supremacy in American Christianity*. New York: Simon and Schuster, 2021.
Netflix. *Jesus Revolution*. USA, 2023. https://www.netflix.com/title/81629410.
Salvatierra, Alexia, and Brandon Wrencher. *Buried Seeds: Learning from the Vibrant Resilience of Marginalized Christian Communities*. Grand Rapids, MI: Baker Academic, 2022.
Thurman, Howard. *Jesus and the Disinherited*. Boston: Beacon, 2022.

## Chapter 7

# The Authentic Self and Desire
## Listening to the Voice of the Heart

### Deborah A. Wade, Spiritual Director

*Deborah A. Wade was born and raised in the Roman Catholic Church and became very aware of the spiritual nature of her being from a very early age. God continued to call her through various avenues and ways to listen to people of faith. These listening avenues were not only in the hallowed halls of the house of God but in the supermarkets, shopping centers, and gas stations where people needed to be heard by someone, and God would tell them—"... go, speak to her." She holds certification through the Ministry Formation program of the Archdiocese of Louisville, a two-year program of ministry works and faith formation.*

I came across a quote from Jim Morrison, lead singer of the Doors, a group that was popular during my high school days, that called me back time and time again. Jim stated that:

> *The most important kind of freedom is to be what you really are. You trade in your reality for a role. You trade in your sense for an act. You give up your ability to feel and, in exchange, put on a mask. There can't be any large-scale revolution until there's*

> *a personal revolution on an individual level. It's got to happen inside first.*[1]

There must be a personal revolution on an individual level . . . it's got to happen inside first. This makes me aware of how our lives are a journey, and we are called to come home where we are called to be, in our own Spirit and our world. It sometimes takes a lifetime to find your true heart's desire and then live out of that desire, but the journey is worth it. Each of us has experienced more than once how society has encouraged us in our lives to don a mask that hides the true self and heart of who we are to be in life. It is a form of playing hide and seek with our inner voice and our inner spirit.

Society, family units, schools, jobs, and institutions all encourage us not to live unique lives but to be authentic. We are encouraged to "fit in," or "don't ask questions," and, above all, to "not rock the boat." The masks that we can don—our personas—are an unauthentic way to make it in life that can cover many real aspects of ourselves and are all about getting by, looking good, and not having people find out the "bad" stuff about us that we don't want others to know about us. This can lead to us focusing our time and attention on what we think is wrong with us and what needs to be fixed. Self-criticism can lead us to believe we are not good enough to do what we are called to do in the world and live into our calling.

And, then, there is fear. The African American poet Paul Lawrence Dunbar states in his poem "We Wear the Masks" that "*We wear the mask that grins and lies. It hides our cheeks and shades our eyes—this debt we pay to human guile. With torn and bleeding hearts, we smile . . . from tortured souls arise.*"[2] Fear is one of the greatest barriers of being authentic to ourselves. Fear to be who we are called to be, to say what we mean, and to live our lives honestly and totally. So, how does one remove the mask? What is the spark that can lead one down a different journey—a journey of living what is in your heart and living the truth?

## So, the Journey Begins!

There seems to be an invitation in the restless way we may become from time to time; it may be in the way we keep ourselves too busy so that we cannot look at the "real" in our lives; it may be the sense of truth that

---

1. "Jim Morrison Quotes."
2. Dunbar, "We Wear the Mask," ll. 1–4, 11.

we carry with us but never voice—not even to ourselves let alone our closest friend.

The journey begins primarily in two places—one is in the heart, and the other is in the spirit/soul. The heart, for me, is where one will find one's true self. The soul is so much a part of the Divine that you are true co-creators with the Divine. One's true self is always there, still developing and unfolding more daily as we live. My journey began when I started to think differently about my ministry of spiritual direction. In my experience, my teachers taught what I believed about God/Jesus/Holy Spirit/Divine/Spirit/Universe. Still, it had nothing to do with church building, kneelers (who at the time were regulated) as being essential to pray, or what prayers you said when and how. I had to discover that everything has to do with eternal love; it is the love I feel when I connect to the Divine/Holy One/Spirit/Universe, a love God has for me and all those around me. Though I initially felt this way, it was hard to form and express in words and speak those words. Many issues were hard to describe initially, but the journey had begun for me with the nudge, a whisper, and the restlessness found in the invitation.

Through listening with my heart and Spirit, I began to develop a voice through the process of spiritual direction. Through the movement of the Spirit, one can connect to the VOICE in the heart of a person and the heart of the Spirit of God within that person. It is the spirit of the Divine's movement within us and our listening hearts. The Divine's spirit—no matter how one names that Spirit—is the voice that is heard in our hearts. It is the everlasting invitation to know your very self.

In the journey, we, as spiritual directors, encounter ourselves and our directees with the invitation to look deeper. The journey helps us as directors to become aware of and recognize our own masks and why it is so critical, as a director, to remove our masks first. It is only through mask removal that we grow as a conduit in helping the directee remove the mask they wear. When we can show our true selves without worrying about what they may think of us, we can listen and hear the spirit of God/Divine within the directee before us and within ourselves. In listening to that whisper of truth that the director shares with you, the director begins to remove the mask. In listening to that voice of the spirit and the heart, the exploration of the heart, soul, and spirit of the directee begins a journey to self.

The voice of the spirit in a direction session with a directee must be honored and held as sacred. When a directee begins to trust the relationship is when the true voice—the authentic voice—is spoken—and it may be only one word, it may be a whisper, but in that whisper or that one word lies the breadth and depth of God/Divine for that person. The depth can be unimaginably unfathomable, and the breath can take a lifetime to approach. During a session, it is essential to listen to your heart, your spirit, and your soul to hear what is being said by the directee. Knowing your own "stuff" is critical, so you will not mistake it for the director's outpouring.

Before you can honestly know the Divine/Spirit, you must know yourself, the person you are, the unique creation of a loving Creator. We all have a journey into the true self, the person the Divine wants us to be and hopes for us to become, the man or woman made in the Spirit/Divine's image and likeness. In continuing the road of discovery, look for ways in which the Divine acts in our lives and helps us discern what is of God/Divine for each of us. These ways can be likened to the footsteps of the Divine. These footsteps help us reflect on the subject of the experience shared in a session to help the directee to discern their authentic self.

In the role of a director, we help the directee discern their experience by asking questions and listening to the directee's heart. The questions are not to be formed to the glory of the director's intelligence but created by the director's connection to their heart and spirit and holding the sacred space in which the directee can experience a deeper humanity, experience service to others, experience compassion and a deeper relationship with themselves, and the move of God. The Divine/Spirit in a directee's experience can act with compassion, truth, justice, responsibility, and respect. In holding space in these ways with the Divine/Spirit, we can see the movement of the Divine in the lives of the directees.

In closing, here is a quote from Ginger Bowler, PhD, from the book *Listening and Communicating with Energy*. Ginger states that:

> *Life is a journey of the soul. So, everything we do, think, feel, and believe is a part of our soul's journey to find out what it is trying to find: lasting happiness, unconditional love, God. The ego thinks it is not so cool to seek God. Most egos want power, money, fame, but all egos want control, absolute and unquestionable control over your life and over the way others think of you. The ego's job is to survive and to control. Anything that the ego considers itself to be is what it will attempt to control and protect, such as a job, a reputation, a title, status in society, a new car, a relationship, control over other's religious beliefs, or even a watch. Moments of being in the real self include being in touch with the real self that yearns to experience God in the eyes of a friend, in the laugh of a*

companion, in the feel of the wind and the beauty of a flower or the face of a love one.[3]

This, my friends, is truly being in the presence of the authentic Self.

## Deeper Conversation/Deeper Listening

1. What are some of the masks we wear, and why do we wear them?
2. When do you feel the most inauthentic?
3. How can we reveal the authentic self?

## Spiritual Practice

One spiritual practice I do daily is what I call the Gratitude Prayer. I find this to be a powerful prayer if spoken aloud and when you are alone, so that there is no reservation in a person's proclamations.

Take a moment to quiet the mind by closing your eyes and taking four to five deep breaths. After calming your mind start by saying *"Thank you God for my blessings."* Then I begin to cite those things that are blessings to me. I make sure I include tangible and intangible things such as feelings and emotions.

This act of thanking God, or whatever a person calls the Divine, can be done silently or by speaking out loud what you are thankful for. The prayer has no time table. The prayer doesn't have a quota. It is spoken or proclaimed as long as the person has things to thank God for. The items can be actual things that have occurred in the person's life or things a person is saying thank you for their coming.

The prayer is ended by just saying *"Thank you God for all the blessings you have given me and continue to give to me each and every day. Amen."*

## Bibliography

Bowler, Ginger. *Listening and Communicating with Energy.* Madison, WI: Focus on the Light, 2000.

Dunbar, Paul Laurence. "We Wear the Mask." Poetry Foundation. Accessed December 29, 2023. https://www.poetryfoundation.org/poems/44203/we-wear-the-mask.

"Jim Morrison Quotes." Goodreads. Accessed December 29, 2023. https://www.goodreads.com/author/quotes/7855.Jim_Morrison.

3. Bowler, *Listening and Communicating*, 31.

# Chapter 8
# Journeying to Our True Nature

GRACE J. SONG, PHD

*Grace Song is an ordained Won Buddhist Kyomunim, meditation teacher, and advocate of interfaith dialogue. She's the Won Buddhist Studies Department Chair at the Won Institute of Graduate Studies. Grace is a member of the Philadelphia Mayor's Commission on Faith-Based and Interfaith Affairs, Steering Committee member of the Won Buddhism to the United Nations Office, and a board member of The Society for Buddhist-Christian Studies. Grace holds a PhD in Won Buddhist studies from Wonkwang University, an MA in East Asian philosophy from Seoul National University, and a BA in religious studies from the University of Toronto. Her writings and online teachings have been featured in* Tricycle: The Buddhist Review Magazine *and Buddhistdoor Global. She is committed to embodying the truth of interconnection and invests her time putting into practice her belief that renewing society starts with renewing our inner lives.*

MOTHER NATURE, IN ALL of its forms, never ceases to amaze me and teach me valuable life lessons. The rising and setting sun, equally shining its rays for all people without discrimination, dancing leaves falling to the ground in autumn without clinging to the branches, and the moving air entering and exiting my body to assist in my moment-to-moment existence. Following my ordination as a Won Buddhist *kyomu* (Won Buddhist ordained devotee), I met spiritual teachers who personified

Mother Nature's virtues. They spoke with care, acted with wisdom, served with compassion, and treated others as if making a gesture to buddha. These teachers understood that practice was life and that life was practice. One of my teachers would sit down with me and explain that the path to enlightenment did not need one to give up the world to devote one's life to alleviating personal suffering. Instead, walking the spiritual path meant being present *in* the world and seeing each challenging situation as an opportunity for practice. "*Do you remember that friend who gave you a hard time?*" my teacher would ask. I nodded. "*She's your buddha.*" The following stories are moments shared with my Won Buddhist spiritual mentors, the inspirational teachers who helped shape my practice, vision, and views about faith and practice. They taught me the true meaning of being human and embraced me with pure loving-kindness. Upon reflection, I sometimes wonder what seeds were planted to make us meet in this lifetime possible. I'm forever grateful for their wisdom, compassion, and authenticity.

## Our World Is a Living Scripture

I distinctly remember the first time I met Ven. Beoptawon, one of my first spiritual mentors in Korea. Her petite and rotund frame complemented her strong features, which often intimidated students. She taught with a strong voice, and her explanations were always clear and lucid, free of flowery speech.

During one particularly memorable summer, I had the privilege of studying with Ven. Beoptawon in her small room in a residence for retired female clergy. Whenever I entered her quaint room, a plate of fruit or hot drink would await me on a small, round, glass-covered table. As I would eat the fruit with a small fork, she would occasionally tend to the flowers by her window or clean the floor with a damp rag.

One day, Ven. Beoptawon motioned for me to peel the skin off some fruits that she had piled in a wooden bowl. As I began to peel a Korean pear, she said, "*Did you know that each fruit has to be peeled differently?*" I looked at her as if I understood her words but proceeded to peel the fruit without putting much thought into it. My only goal was to separate the skin from the fruit. "*Each fruit,*" she said slowly, "*follows its own principle. Some skins are thicker than others and should be peeled more deeply; otherwise, a bitter taste will be left in one's mouth. Conversely, other skins* are thin and should be peeled carefully so that none of the fruit is wasted." "*The world is a living scripture*," she would often say enthusiastically. "*Don't relegate the teachings to scriptures or books.*" Her words echoed the words of Founding Master Sotaesan: "*If people look at this world in the right spirit, there will be nothing in it that is not scripture. When you open your eyes, you will see scripture; when you listen, you will hear scripture; when you speak, you will recite scripture; when you act, you will apply scripture.*"[1]

Ven. Beoptawon urged me to connect with the world around me through all of my senses and view life as a living school in which lessons are imparted. Reframing the world in this manner helped me reimagine relationships between humans and explore the reasons for our transgressions and suffering. Moreover, it pushed me to investigate universal principles and intricate relationships between the universe and its many evolving parts. She would remind me, "*Our lives have a profound and inescapable relationship to human relationships and universal principles, so the world is an open scripture.*"

This reminds me of a story in the scriptures. One day, while reading the newspaper, some disciples argued the pros and cons of current events. The Founding Master heard them and said,

> *Why do you talk rashly about matters that are none of your business? A person with a genuine outlook does not talk lightly about others' pros and cons. Even while reading the newspaper, the proper conduct for practitioners, and the way to gain true benefit, is to examine carefully in what you read the root cause and the good and bad fruitions that result, taking them as mirrors for one's future conduct. This is an approach for illuminating the one mind by penetrating all dharmas. For a person who reads newspapers in this spirit they will become a living scripture and source material for wisdom and merit. Otherwise, one will only become good at critiquing other people's pros and cons contentiously and glibly, thereby falling easily into the abyss of transgression. You must be extremely careful about this.*[2]

In life, we all hold numerous preferences, opinions, judgments, and criticisms of certain people and situations. Additionally, we circumvent challenging circumstances and dodge those who bring out the worst in us. In times of distress and pain, we turn to texts brimming with wisdom to navigate through the unavoidable challenges life

1. "Chapter 3 Practice: 23," *Doctrinal Books of Wŏn Buddhism*, 180.
2. "Chapter 4 The Way of Humanity: 35," *Doctrinal Books of Wŏn Buddhism*, 236–37.

throws at us. However, what if we considered these perplexing external circumstances as living scripture?

In the process, we would understand the principle of cause and effect and how certain choices result in particular outcomes. We can utilize these moments to reflect on our intentions and actions. For example, we can inquire why a limitless paradise is opened when one does what is best for oneself while simultaneously doing what is best for others. We can also investigate how someone who harms others in pursuing their happiness ends up committing numerous transgressions and suffering.

A story in the Won Buddhist scriptures recounts a time when a wealthy man, after saving his poor neighbors by releasing some money and grains in a famine year, kept wishing he would be eulogized for his virtue. The villagers conferred and erected a stele, but the man was still dissatisfied, so he spent more money to erect a new stele and construct a huge stele pavilion. The villagers thought his actions ludicrous, so there were many criticisms and disparaging remarks made. Kim Kwangson heard about this and presented it during a conversation session. The Founding Master listened and said, *"This is a living scripture about warning people who compulsively seek honor. Although that person did this deed to enhance his reputation, didn't he lose even his previous reputation, not to mention enhancing it? Thus, a foolish person seeking honor only damages it instead; a wise person does not intentionally seek to be honored; instead, merely by performing proper actions, great honor naturally comes to him."*[3]

Life's challenges often push me to return to the written scripture to rely on the words of the masters. Ven. Beoptawon wasn't discouraging me from studying the scriptures; rather, she explained to me that the purpose of the written scripture is to provide us with tools to navigate the myriad human affairs and universal principles in the scripture of our lived experience. The written scripture helps us use our minds effectively, which is the fount of blessings and wisdom. They say that each of us is part of the infinite universe, contributing to its perfection. When we view the world as an open scripture, we are partaking in writing our life scripture. Each time we are aware, awake, and mindful, we can change the trajectory of a situation for the better—not only for ourselves but also for others.

---

3. "Chapter 4 The Way of Humanity: 54," *Doctrinal Books of Won Buddhism*, 249–50.

## Great Work

I often wonder what I would ask my father if he were alive today. To be honest, I feel like I barely knew him. I know that he would go to the library every weekend to borrow books, which he then read on the couch, spending hours pronouncing the unfamiliar words aloud. He favored doughnuts to cake and enjoyed tackling complex arithmetic problems. But if he were sitting next to me right now, I'd ask, "*What brought you joy growing up?*" "*Tell me about your high school years.*" "*What were your parents' names?*" "*What was it like to be the lone Korean architect in a field dominated by White people?*" As an adult, I wonder what went through his mind when his daughters no longer feared his authoritative voice and instead sought affirmation and admiration from their peers. Did he feel invisible? What anxieties kept him awake at night?

His eyes were frequently filled with dread and fear, and I knew it was for us: he was afraid we wouldn't be prepared for the outside world. To safeguard us, he redirected our attention from any exterior danger to our inner potential. Even if we couldn't change our external circumstances, he helped us have faith in the profound truth within. "*There's nothing you can't do,*" he would reassure us. "*Never totally rely on your husband, especially financially.*" "*You must have your own career and make your own money.*" "*Repeat, repeat, repeat, don't skip a day.*" Whenever he thought we'd strayed, he'd throw us pearls of wisdom. There was no room for error in his life since there was little to fall back on.

Two things inspired my father: his faith and the guidance of his spiritual mentor, Master Daesan, the Third Head Dharma Master of Won Buddhism. When my father felt stifled by a lack of words, misunderstood, or ignored by society, he turned to something transcendent, something greater than himself. He journeyed deep to discover a realm devoid of contempt and derision. No one could defile this spiritual sanctuary, as he was the only one who could reach it. Without a doubt, my father's greatest source of consolation was his yearly trips to spend time with his spiritual mentor.

All year long, as they worked, my parents would save up for that flight to Korea to spend two weeks with Master Daesan in the summer. "*Why do we have to go to the country?*" my sister and I often asked. "*Can't we stay in the city? There's nothing to do, and there are too many mosquitoes!*" My father would just give us the "death glare" and say, "*You're going!*"

At least when we arrived at the retreat center where Master Daesan stayed, the *kyomus* would warmly greet us. My sister and I would receive sweets and tiny yogurt drinks. As soon as I consumed the treats, I felt nothing but gratitude. The *kyomus* treated all their guests like family, and one would always give up his sleeping space for us. Just like everyone else, we would begin a period of fixed-term training. Whether from Toronto or Miami, you ate the same food and participated in the same activities.

Master Daesan appeared to me as a grandfather at times and a great teacher at other times. He seemed so carefree, going with the flow and paying no attention to any particular person. I also learned that he was extremely observant. Some summers, Master Daesan's third daughter would also come with her family from the United States. She has five children, so we spent the days playing together, collecting rocks, making up games, or simply running around the grounds. One time, Master Daesan must have sensed that we were bored, so he told one of his attendants to take us to the movies to see *Jurassic Park*. We were pleasantly surprised and immediately hopped into a minivan. It was a rural theater, so the right side of the screen was blurry, and the dubbed voices were out of sync with the characters' mouths. But none of this mattered to us; we were just glad to be skipping training. We munched on peanuts and dried squid because the theater didn't sell popcorn. In that moment, I felt Master Daesan's compassion, concern, and care.

Throughout our time at the retreat center, Master Daesan encouraged us to work toward building a harmonious world. "*You have to do great work!*" he would always say. I found this paradoxical because we were always in the countryside, staying in humble houses, sitting on rocks, pulling weeds, and eating food from metal trays. "Great work" seemed like something you would hear about in a fancy hotel conference room filled with CEOs and business owners. We were just a bunch of working-class families and students. Thinking about it now, however, I realize this is the greatest strength of Won Buddhism. We're still a relatively obscure religion, but we have a grand vision. And most significantly, we have a road map—one that's clear, concise, and realistic. We have to make it happen. So, when Master Daesan said to us, "*Go out and do great work*," he planted seeds of faith and hope. He believed every single one of us was precious and had the potential to guide all sentient beings from the bitter sea of suffering.

In the founding years of Won Buddhism, people must have wondered similar things to what I did as a kid. A bunch of farmers, mostly illiterate, being told that their sincere faith and practice moved the heavens and that, if they put some rice aside and quit drinking and smoking, they were contributing to a world mission. Who would've thought? Now I know why my father saved up every year to spend two weeks in rural Korea. After those two weeks, he left feeling like a living buddha. After those two weeks, his spiritual vow grew stronger. No matter how hard it could be as an immigrant in Canada, he could endure those problems because he had deeper faith, a stronger public spirit, and greater compassion. Moreover, he now had a strong vision of what he needed to do. He knew that his work as an architect, however small, contributed to a greater mission.

## Beginner's Mind

Whenever I hear the word *leader*, I think of a tall person in front of a large crowd or a person walking ahead of others. Sometimes, I visualize a conductor holding a baton, a person sitting at the head of the table, a judge holding a gavel, or a coach blowing their whistle. Over the years, I've learned that leadership in the spiritual world looks very different. A true spiritual leader doesn't necessarily stand at the front, walk in front of others, or sit at the head of the table. A true spiritual leader keeps a beginner's mind. They're never at the top because they know there's always room for improvement. As a result, they are both a teacher and a student.

I think one of the reasons my faith in Won Buddhism grew deep was because I learned it through stories told by my father. He wouldn't sit me down with the scriptures but instead would retell stories of his teachers, and I would watch his eyes light up. His stories taught me that true spiritual teachers don't just talk; they put their words into action. This, then, is the greatest strength of Won Buddhism: we are a community of active Buddhas—not just living Buddhas, but active Buddhas.

At one summer retreat, I met a Won Buddhist temple member who attended one of the temples where Ven. Baek Sangwon worked. "I'll never forget her," she said to me. "Why?" I asked. She replied, "Because she lived differently." "How so?" She then began to share a story. "I lived in the neighborhood and passed by the temple several times. I would always see this old woman working in the garden—a very small woman. I assumed she was a grandmother and a member of the temple because she looked so plain, and her clothes were dirty from gardening. A few months *later, I decided to attend one of the Sunday services. I arrived a bit early and sat with the other members. When it was time for the service to start, a small woman wearing a clean, bright white robe walked in with her hair neatly pulled back, and she stepped up to the lectern to speak. You couldn't imagine my surprise when I realized it was the same woman working in the garden. It was like meeting two totally different people. For some reason, this moment will never leave my memory. She taught me that work and practice are not two."*

As she told me this story, I pictured this senior minister in the garden one day, then in front of the lectern giving a sermon the next. In Won Buddhism, we're trained to see that work and practice are not two. Buddhadharma is daily life. Daily life is buddhadharma. This is possible through spiritual training. We witness this in our Won Buddhist elders, who show us that Won Buddhism is a living religion.

When you put our teachings into practice, you are never done. Won Buddhism teaches that life is a work in progress and the path is the goal. For us, the world is a living scripture, and every place is a training ground. Authentic spiritual teachers are not people who walk around with halos over their heads or have some distinguishing physical features. They might resemble your grandfather, neighbor, or the old lady hunched over gardening in her front yard. Where does this motive force come from? It comes from a deep and wide spiritual vow that grows as we become one with our teacher. True leaders always have a teacher or mentor. The founder of Won Buddhism, Sotaesan, found his teacher after reading the Diamond Sutra. He wrote, "*Sakyamuni Buddha is truly the sage of sages. Hence, I adopted Sakyamuni Buddha as my original guide.*"[4] This passage struck me because Master Sotaesan acknowledged that someone had already become enlightened about what he had awakened to.

As I continued reading the scriptures of our masters, I noticed that every one of our great teachers acknowledges their teachers. You will never hear a true teacher talk about "their" teaching. They will always refer to their masters. True leadership is not about where you stand, who you know, or what you wear, but how you make the teachings come to life—in this way, gardening becomes just as important as leading a Sunday service. True leaders maintain the beginner's mind by constantly training. They know that practice is not something they'll one day grow

---

4. "Chapter 1 Prologue: 2," *Doctrinal Books of Wŏn Buddhism*, 105.

out of; it's a life-long journey. The journey is never done alone, but in the presence of good mentors, we keep it in our minds and hearts.

To our mentors, we give a deep bow of gratitude—that they were able to express something inexpressible to make it relevant and practical for us today so that we can live happier and more meaningful lives not just for ourselves but to better serve others. My wish is to maintain the beginner's mind and train passionately, learn continuously, teach compassionately, and live fully.

## The Sky

Wisdom manifests in many forms. Spiritual mentors have played an important role in my life as an ordained devotee. They've held me through difficult situations and directed me to brighter paths when I felt lost and confused. When they scold me, there is no transfer of anger, only love. Perhaps the greatest gift has been learning and experiencing that innate wisdom exists in each of us. When the inner chatter subsides, and the involuntary banter dissolves, the bright light of wisdom shines, and life is lived with more clarity and kindness. The world is a living scripture, full of lessons and opportunities for practice. If I'm courageous enough to shine my light inward and become one with myself, an incredible thing happens: I begin to feel one with others.

Wisdom is embodied in my practice. Our mind mirrors the sky, with our thoughts and emotions forming the clouds. On some days, these clouds are light and fluffy, filling us with joy. On other days, they loom large and dark, bringing storms of thunder and lightning, leaving us in turmoil. Yet, through it all, the sky's true nature remains untouched. It cannot be made cleaner or more sullied. In moments of sincere meditation, we have the opportunity to glimpse this clarity of mind. It is in these moments that we come closest to our true selves, boundless and immense.

But when we identify with the clouds and transitory personalities it's easy to feel isolated, as if there's a distinct separation between ourselves and everyone else. This mindset traps us in a cycle of self-centeredness. When we touch the nature of the mind—our true nature—then we see that we're all completely connected. It's not about possessing a fragment of the sky as "mine" and another as "yours." Understanding our deep connection, we realize that the kindness, respect, and love we seek from others are the very things they seek from us. This realization stems from recognizing that, on a fundamental level, there is no distinction between us and others.

## Deeper Conversation/Deeper Listening

1. What are some of the interconnections we have but do not always recognize?
2. How can we shine our light inward?

## Spiritual Practice

In the serene journey of spiritual practice, seated meditation stands out for its simplicity and accessibility, inviting all who seek inner peace to begin with just a few straightforward steps. The process starts with the preparation of your space, laying out a mat where you can sit comfortably in a cross-legged posture or sitting in a chair, ensuring your spine and head are aligned as if reaching toward the sky. This initial posture sets the foundation for your practice, grounding you physically and spiritually.

As you settle into this posture, your focus shifts inward to the elixir field, located just below the navel, drawing all your strength to this central point without clinging to any thoughts. The act of centering yourself here helps in gathering scattered energies, especially when distractions arise. Maintaining a smooth and rhythmic pattern of breathing enhances this focus, with a slight emphasis on longer inhalations and shorter exhalations. As you breathe in, let your lower abdomen gently expand; as you exhale, softly draw your lower abdomen back toward your spine, engaging in a rhythm of breathing that is as pure and effortless as that of an infant. New practitioners might encounter physical discomfort or intrusive thoughts, but these are merely obstacles to acknowledge and gently overcome without frustration. Itchy sensations or the feeling of ants crawling on your skin are natural signs of increased blood flow and should be left unaddressed to maintain the meditative state.

Above all, the journey of seated meditation is one of inward exploration, avoiding the pursuit of extraordinary experiences in favor of a profound, steady presence. With consistent practice, the boundaries between self and others, time and place, begin to dissolve, leading to a state of deep tranquility and nondual awareness. This culminates in a blissful experience of unity and peace, a testament to the transformative power of meditation in the realm of spiritual practice.

## Bibliography

*The Doctrinal Books of Wŏn Buddhism.* Won Institute. Iksan: Wonkwang, 2016.

# PART 3

# *Introduction:* Change Is an Inevitable Certainty

*This section examines how faith and spirituality relate to political and social change and how it's a spiritual practice to respond to that change.*

I'M WRITING THIS MANUSCRIPT when the world is on a collision course with itself. We have become divided on issues of humanity and the importance of where and how we decide the value of human rights, the importance of being good stewards and caretakers of the ecosystem, and the maintenance of human dignity. The creation of wars and conflicts based on notions that compromise humanity while highlighting heroism is no longer considered outrageous. White nationalism, with its historical and systemic use of racism as a pattern of oppression, is once again being used to justify political, social, and religious actions and reactions without opposition and resistance. The ones with the loudest platforms, often having the least validity but the most to say, are arrogantly resurgent without appearing to bear the consequences of their words or actions. With lesson after lesson, we have not fully learned we cannot oppress people, create social and political conditions that endanger lives, arrest our way to regulatory safety, and expect to create a peaceful world or society. It gives even more meaning to the wise words of Fannie Lou Hamer, "*Nobody's free until everybody is free.*"[1]

The rights and limitations to freedom are becoming questions just as much as how we value each other and how we sustain life. There is a never-ending news cycle of violence against Black and Brown people that is being compounded by cadres of menacing mob-minded campaigns that place targets and ignite the simmering anger that has always been just below the surface of White conservative society. It is palpable and has spread throughout the world. Anti-Semitism, hatred, and oppression against Palestinians, Africans, African Americans, Latinos, Hispanics, and Asians are rampant. Questions of the legitimacy of intersectionality, the right to explore and teach equity and inclusivity, and bashing the legitimacy and rights of the LGBTQI community have become legislative fodder. Intimidation, fear, and violence are bubbling over, yet we do not see a spiritual connection to all of this. In some spiritual direction and faith formation circles, there is ingrained disbelief that the political and human rights issues are not something that the proverbial "we" should engage in or the outright declaration that this is not a subject for spiritual direction, faith formation, or soul care. If this is the claim, then it is time to reexamine our purpose and why we are deep listeners to issues of the soul when the pain that is emanating from the current state of affairs is a soul issue.

At times like these, we have several choices, and we, as people of faith, have the obligation to make choices. We can retreat and deny our involvement or relationship to such issues, claiming a higher moral ground of solitude; we can sit in judgment and offer intellectual exchanges that do not provide direction for resistance and action; or we can choose to face the truth and examine what we believe to be true about ourselves, what we affirm within the scope of our faith, and what we are willing to do or sacrifice to begin the steps to community resonance and healing. Whether we are prepared or not, political issues and global unrest will land within the perimeters of self-care and spiritual companionship. Seeing the world around us change and how we respond to change is upon us. Most of what is happening is occurring is based within what I call "*WAAF-ing,*" or *words, actions, anger, and fear*. Every deliberate ill will and hateful action emanates from something that is said and believed, placed into action or reaction, resulting in anger and furthering fear, "*WAAF-ing.*" History

---

1. Brooks, "'Nobody's Free Until Everybody's Free.'"

has taught such actions end communities and civilizations, yet there is persistent disbelief that it will be different this time. Hate has always been more of a noun than an adjective. But *hate* is on the verge of becoming an "acceptable" verb that is acted upon because of the lack of wise voices denouncing and demanding better of ourselves, our friends, our families, and our leadership, accepting nothing less.

For me, recognizing the need for peace and the value of life is the beginning of faith in action. Not sitting in silence, hoping for change. We can find grace, hope, and mercy within the mystery I call God. In such times, these elements will guide us into peace, which can lead us to grace; it can lead us to actions and resistance as a spiritual practice within our communities. Having grace makes us acknowledge the value of life. In truth, all grace is prevenient—we cannot move toward God unless God has first moved toward us, and God is always with us. We go within to commune and connect to God, who is always available and ever-present to move toward us even as we see the worst in ourselves or the best. To understand the connection between grace as a prevenient aspect in defining wisdom, we must realize this is a requisite to identify a deeper connection to one's self and the divine. We have an enormous opportunity and ability to see the vastness of the world's interconnectedness, even in the most minute aspects of life to the most overt occurrence. We can take the best of wisdom from various aspects and create harmony even in the midst of chaos. Out of dissonance, we can always find our way to harmony; it takes time, attention to the details, and, most of all, clarity of purpose.

Faith has always been a historical guidepost for sustaining change in society. In times like these, the twin packages of faith and uncertainty and the companions of hope and mercy must dwell together. It is essential to embrace the experience of uncertainty and question the unknown as a path to more assertive faith that will propel you from the sidelines into taking a stand. It is from such experience that we realize what truth is. An old idiomatic expression states, "Faith and its object cannot be separated." In other words, faith is a companion to our being and integral to our growth, but only if we allow room and acknowledgment for faith. It can be an aspect of how we connect to things that are critical to life. A part of faith is the practice of seeking and holding on to truth, and our faith expects us to place what is true into practice and not become stagnant or complacent witnesses to all needs.

We grow in faith through several ways, including but not limited to uncertainty, experience, and witnessing. Each of these aspects correlates to developing wisdom and seeking eternal truths. It is through this method of examining and reexamining we focus and refocus on our relationships with God. Unfortunately, in this day of "fast food" consumption and "cancel culture," we can miss opportunities to witness the vastness and interconnectedness of our various experiences. In some ways, we have become dismissive rather than seeking and examining the particles of life as well as valuing the experiences of others, especially the wisdom offered by our conscious elders, as a way of enriching our changing communities.

One of the most significant examples of faith, eldering, and wisdom in action is the story of Abraham. In *Fear and Trembling*, Kierkegaard's most famous work, Kierkegaard explores Abraham, who has become known among his followers as *"the father of faith."* Kierkegaard draws inspiration from the story of Abraham's experience when God commands the sacrifice of his only son, Isaac, at Mount Moriah. In this situation, it is essential to remember that while God calls Abraham to perform such a drastic act, God has also promised to make a great nation from Isaac's descendants. This makes the situation even more difficult for Abraham. It took faith for Abraham to follow the directions of God; it took faith to know, regardless of the outcome, God would always illumine Abraham's path and continually define his faith. It took the wisdom of experiencing God's faithfulness for Abraham to believe God would provide the answer and reason for the sacrifice. What was tested was Abraham's resolve to follow God's directive and wisdom. I wonder, from this example, about a modern-day person like Abraham. I wonder if we really have the foundational trust it takes to believe there will be good if we have the resolve to follow our hearts, the resolve to take action, and true intentions. Too many times, we become aspirational for a goal rather than committed to what it takes to follow through, like Abraham. I am sure Abraham had questions about the provision and the sacrifice that he was asked to make. The difference is he followed the directive; he lived into his commitment; it was about his relationship to the Divine. In my time as a director of equity for the Kentucky Department of Education, I became somewhat leery of people who wanted to be included in leading charges on racial, social justice, and political change, especially people without an experiential background, previous examples of commitment, let alone substantive and adequate preparation and training in relative subjects on diversity, equity and social justice theory. I am even more leery today, with the various iterations of DEI training being manufactured under different names for monetary gain and placed in the hands of people who are only committed as far as it does not inconvenience them. I truly believe in the wisdom of being careful about who and how someone comes late to the table when the table has been there all along, exploiting how to change without understanding the necessary context of need. When this happens, the truth of who they are will always show in the details and the outcomes.

In the following chapters, the contributors explore how change is the consistent element of growth and a critical role of faith. These chapters also examine the relationship between social and spiritual responses to political and social change. The contributors explore how responding to such change is an opportunity to strengthen faith. However, faith combined with discernment, when faced with the most destructive goals of racism, toxicity, misogyny, homophobia, and destruction, can be an opportunity for a new beginning that values all people. French philosopher and mystic Simone Weil said, "*To be rooted is perhaps the most important and least recognized need of the human soul.*"[2] Human unrest is an indication that a need is unmet in the soul. It also signals that the spirit is beginning an internal and external quest to meet this need. The need for the soul to evolve and change is rooted in how we see our relationships with those things that are important or amplified in our lives. Sometimes, we fail to look within and to the holy mystery for truth and what lies within our souls during these moments. During these times, we often miss opportunities to explore and absorb what we consider "natural" to our situation, being, or stories because we are used to the pragmatic or the customary. In change, we sometimes face choices that result in uncensored actions and emotions, and we make mistakes that we must learn from. Change is an opportunity to speak truth to power, provide beauty to brokenness, and become purposeful when examining accountability versus responsibility. Change also provides the opportunity to witness growth, examine boundaries, and see the role of grace, for there is always a question of the role of grace, especially when there is radical change.

As we begin this chapter, there is a guiding question of *Is there an argument to be made that the development of truth might be affected by the need for a personal sense of belonging, and how is belonging rooted in our soul?*

---

2. Kingsnorth, "Great Unsettling," §4.

## Bibliography

Brooks, Maegan Parker, et al., eds. "'Nobody's Free Until Everybody's Free': Speech Delivered at the Founding of the National Women's Political Caucus, Washington, DC, July 10, 1971." In *The Speeches of Fannie Lou Hamer: To Tell It Like It Is*, 134–39. https://doi.org/10.14325/mississippi/9781604738223.003.0017.

Kingsnorth, Paul. "The Great Unsettling: Simone Weil and the Need for Roots." Simone Weil Center for Political Philosophy, May 9, 2021. https://simoneweilcenter.org/publications/2021/5/9/the-great-unsettling-simone-weil-and-the-need-for-roots.

## Chapter 9

# Blessed Troubles

### Reading the Bible as Multivalent Voices

Sophia Park, SNJM, PhD

*Sophia Park is emerita associate professor in religious studies and philosophy at Holy Names University in Oakland. Her field of study is biblical spirituality, and she pursues it from a global and postcolonial feminist perspective. She published many books and articles in Korean and English, including* Conversation at the Well: Emerging Religious Life in the 21st Century Global World *and* An Asian Woman's Religious Journey with Thomas Merton *(forthcoming). She offers lectures, workshops, and spiritual directions to global sisters and brothers with joy.*

ONCE UPON A TIME, a boy wanted to grasp the concept of *tomorrow*. So, he asked his mother, *"Mother, what is tomorrow?"* His mother gently answered, *"Once you fully live today, go to bed. After a good night's sleep, when you open your eyes, then it will be tomorrow."* The boy went to bed in excitement, expecting to encounter tomorrow. When he opened his eyes in the morning, he ran to his mother, saying, *"Mother, this is tomorrow, right?"* His mother answered, *"Honey, it is today, not tomorrow."* Furthermore, she continued, *"Tomorrow will come when you go to bed tonight and wake up in the morning."* The boy was frustrated but was determined to try one more time. Finally, when he opened his eyes in the morning, he asked his mother if this moment was tomorrow, but she repeated her response. The boy sighed, saying, *"Oh, I see, there is no tomorrow!"* Even though it may sound funny, the boy's resigned cry signifies a moment of realizing that life is as it is. Never does tomorrow exist so that we cannot grasp it; tomorrow is just a construct of the mind. Tomorrow often symbolizes our hopes, dreams, and imagination, as well as our anxieties and fears. It may sound a bit sobering, but life stands on uncertainty, and we truly exist only in the present moment. Nevertheless, ignoring life's uncertainty, we pretend to grasp some certainty, often expressed as tomorrow.

We are currently living in an era of anxiety and uncertainty. With COVID-19, multiple wars, and the turmoil of discontent worldwide, we have experienced much emotional havoc, confusion, civil unrest, and human challenges. Many people have lost their jobs and are concerned about an unpredictable future caused by the virus, climate change, or any number of causes. We tend to believe that we control our world through social structure and, consequently, perceive the world as secure under a false sense of certainty. The myths that fame or material success guarantees happiness can rule our daily lives. The more we pursue these false convictions, the more people will express anxiety and panic as the mode of life.

With the pandemic, we have noticed that the facade that once covered life's uncertain reality has become thinner. What can we learn from this uncomfortable situation? Our current living conditions could invite us to face life as uncertain and remain in the present, neither running toward the future nor lingering in the past. We can only journey into the depths of life by embracing this uncertainty and embracing the world as a mystic who can see life as it is, beyond order or a framework dictated by the exterior world.

For some, religion and spiritual wisdom stand for the security of life. In this vein, some Christians believe that Christianity provides confidence in salvation, and the Bible is a fixed reference to the truth that will give them certainty. Often, the Bible is perceived as the anchor of life or the Law, which supposedly provides conviction and assurance of life. Ironically, the more we pursue certainty through reading the Bible, the more likely we will experience uncertainty and ambiguity. As such, it may be meaningful to examine the multivalent nature of the Bible and how it still functions as a text to guide us in the journey toward God.

## The Bible as the Locus of Multiple Voices

In my classes in biblical studies at Holy Names University, most millennial students claim that they either know little about the Bible or have no interest in it. Yet, these students who feel disconnected from the Bible can usually explore the meaning of the text with much freedom and ease. In contrast, the few students who claim familiarity with the Bible often experience trouble understanding the Bible as a revelatory wisdom text. Sometimes, they resist reading or interpreting passages critically out of their love or devotion to the Bible. They tend to repeat what they heard in the pews of their churches. I call their struggle blessed trouble. Their genuine feeling of disturbance and fear of losing faith can lead them to desire deeper, authentic faith and, more importantly, to true self-knowledge. At other times, Christians repetitively cite minimal passages, not looking into others, as a way to maintain the same voice of God.

Once, after class, one of my students told me he wanted to drop the course, boasting that he had confidence and certainty of salvation. I smiled at him and said, *"It is wonderful that you are certain of your salvation. But what is salvation?"* He was shocked and could not answer. I tried to comfort him, saying, *"It is great to have faith. But it would help if you searched for the meaning of salvation first. Then you can figure out whether or not you have confidence, not the other way around."* I truly wanted this young man to embrace his discomfort to grow in his faith journey. Instead, the student showed his love for the Bible, kissing the book before me. My heart was torn into two: I wanted him to remain confidently in faith as a young man; on the other hand, I wanted him to examine his faith critically.

Almost every religion has its sacred scripture, and in the Christian tradition, the holy scripture is called the Bible. The Bible remains the Christian scripture and includes many mysterious and unexplained things, like an ocean that holds many unexplained or unexplored things. As the sacred book, the Bible contains truths told through paradoxes, fragments, inconsistencies, and even violence, revealing very particular truths. Each story remains singular, negating uniformity and, more importantly, not losing universality or unity. The word Bible is derived from the Greek word *biblion*, which literally means "books." When we say "The Bible," it sounds like one book, but it is a compilation of texts, emphasizing its plurality of scope and thought. The Bible can vary according to traditions; the Roman Catholic Church, Orthodox Christian Church, and the Reformation Church have different Bible canon and completion dates. The varying traditions encourage the use of a particular canon as a method to support the interpretation of the Bible, creating alignment with the various tradition's theological underpinnings.

## The Old Testament as Multiple Voices

The Old Testament carries a polyvalence in terms of stories and interpretations. Even within a single book of the Bible, we experience various traditions, narratives, and explanations. For example, the Pentateuch, which holds a fundamental place in the Judeo-Christian tradition as the book of Law, shows multiple authorships.[1] The Documentary Hypothesis in modern biblical scholarship is a widely accepted model to explain the origins and composition of the first five books in the Hebrew scriptures. Scholars named the four documents Yahwist (J), Elohist (E), Deuteronomist (D), and Priestly (P) sources, each of which shows its unique perspective, thereby negating the single voice. For instance, each source calls God a different name: Yahweh in the J document, while Elohim in E. Their unique perspectives emerge through variations and differences within the same stories. We often find the same stories juxtaposed as a pair when reading the Pentateuch.[2] For example, there are two creation stories in Genesis. In the first chapter of Genesis, the Priestly source solemnly describes the creation of the world: *ex nihilo*, God created all things with his words. However, the second chapter, assumingly the Yahwist source, depicts the creation narrative in a very intimate and artistic way. In 2:7, "*the Lord* God formed man from the dust of the ground and breathed into his nostrils the breath of life; *and the man became a living being.*" Here, God resembles a gardener, and the first human seems like God's artwork, like pottery. Sometimes, evaluations or judgments of characters are dissonant in these multiple voices. For example, in the Hebrew scriptures, we find Moses an absolute authority

---

1. Collins, *Introduction to the Hebrew Bible*
2. Collins, *Introduction to the Hebrew Bible*

as the leader of Israel; Moses is the allocator of wisdom. He meets God face to face, unlike any other Israelite.

Along with Moses, we find Aaron and Miriam as leaders of Israel, and in Numbers, we read that the two criticize and challenge Moses's authority and wisdom. Miriam receives severe punishment because of their rebellious behavior, although the text does not explicate the punishment of Aaron. This story signifies that Moses maintains supreme power as a leader. Nevertheless, the Bible does not skip over Moses's faults: Moses bursts with anger by striking a rock forcefully against the people so that he cannot enter the Promised Land. Then, it is evident that none of the three leaders goes to the Promised Land. Then, we cannot consider that Moses had absolute authority, almost like God. Similarly, in Exodus, Aaron is a disobedient and rebellious leader, but he is a model leader and an honored priest in Psalms and other places. These acts indicate wisdom, and being an elder does not mean there are challenges to human character.

We hear more distinctive voices in the Wisdom literature. Unlike the Pentateuch, these books involve full human emotions and speculations in different times and spaces. The Qoheleth, as one of the most cited Wisdom literatures, conveys wisdom, describes the human condition as frail and vulnerable, and focuses on the absurdity of life. Literally, Qoheleth means "collector or congregator," and the sage, as the first-person narrator, brings his own experience and those of others, stressing the notion of vanity. He witnesses that seeking absolute knowledge, success, and wealth is meaningless because none is permanent. Buddha found the cause of human suffering as the *dukka* or impermanence. Similarly, for the Qoheleth, understanding the nature of the world as impermanent is the beginning of wisdom to know God.

The Qoheleth expresses the uncertainty of life in a distinct voice of wisdom, negating the conventional wisdom that the Torah carries. The Torah, especially Deuteronomy, commands Israel to *"choose life"* by following the Law to warrant success and health. For the author of Qoheleth, who lived in a particular time and space, every human condition can change quickly; staying in the present moment and enjoying the sun is the best wisdom. For the sage, it is impossible to cling to the certainty of life, although the author knew the Law well.

The Hebrew scriptures store diverse pearls of wisdom, even including an alternative version of God or theodicy. The book of Job offers a vivid description of Satan. The common myth that Satan, often called

Lucifer, is a fallen angel never appears in the Bible. Satan developed over the years in salvation theology as a personification of the adversary. In Job, Satan, amid an ambiguous nature, seems like a member of the courtly assembly; God is not the destroyer of Satan. Satan converses with God and accompanies his mission to test Job. In the story of Job, God is the agent, possessing even the power of darkness, the good and the bad together.[3] This understanding of God is quite different from the dualistic Augustinian theology of evil, which lacks good and, consequently, cannot reside in good, which is presumably God. The God in Job can have darkness, like the Tao, which includes Ying and Yang, as a constant flow of good and bad. After suffering from understanding God who exists beyond his knowledge, Job finally confesses, "*I had heard of you by the hearing of the ear, but now my eye sees you*" (Job 42:5). The whole narrative conveys the truth of God, which we cannot comprehend because God stands beyond our knowledge, often given by others.

## The New Testament as Multiple Voices

In the New Testament, four different Gospels manifest distinct perspectives of Jesus' life and teaching. The Gospels of Matthew, Mark, and Luke share similar structures and content, so we call them the Synoptic Gospels. Nevertheless, these three Gospels never fail to keep each one's literary characteristics and unique perspective. It is remarkable that the Bible is holy scripture, not because it brings a single voice of truth but multiple truths. Nevertheless, we do not lose the universal notion of truth in the Bible, keeping the singularity of each story. The various voices of the Bible reveal the open nature of the scripture, which remains in the present moment, rejecting any fossil-like knowledge and repetition of meaning. As the absolute Being, God exists beyond our understanding and stands on the impossibility of knowing. Thus, alternative views of God provide healthy resources to meditate on God's nature.

John's Gospel carries a unique voice and style. It was included in the canon later than the three Synoptic Gospels and is often called the spiritual Gospel. I believe all four Gospels are spiritual, but I particularly appreciate John's Gospel for its unique style. I love the story of the woman caught in adultery in 7:53—8:11. This famous story begins with an opening parenthesis and ends with a closing parenthesis, implying

---

3. Berrigan, *Job: And Death No Dominion*.

that this story might not belong to John's Gospel. Some ancient texts do not include this story, and the style of the story, meaning the story of a sinful woman, resembles Luke's Gospel.[4] I would liken this story to an immigrant who has moved into a new place—the narrative of John—and is considered less authentic within this hosting Gospel. This suspicious story itself manifests the unstable nature of the Bible, with its holes and cracks, through which readers can reach the Mystery of God, who is beyond the symbolic domain composed of language.

Reading the Epistles also becomes an exciting practice in appreciating differences and similarities. My students often say that the letters are quite different from their expectations. Sometimes, Paul is furious and busy defending his position as one of the apostles. Paul is a very gentle and joyful leader at other times, as a good friend. Reading the Epistles helps to understand the singularity of each faith community scattered throughout the Mediterranean in the first century. We will inevitably need clarification if we read the Pauline letters expecting a singular voice from a single author. In the letter to the community of Galatia, Paul proclaims: "*There is no longer Jew or Greek, there is no longer slave or free, there is no longer male or female; for all of you are one in Jesus Christ*" (Gal 3:28). This statement carries a strong vision of a Christian way of being, equality beyond social norms. However, the same Paul, but in the documents we call the First Letter to the Corinthians, teaches the women preachers and prophets of the congregation to cover their hair, using very misogynic rhetoric. One of my female students responded to Paul's admonition of women, "*I do not take strong offense to what Paul says about women. I know his letter is ancient, and misogynistic thinking was common. I'm not at all convinced that women should stay quiet and not speak out. I'm also not convinced that women should have to wear a veil. However, it depends on what the head covering symbolizes. I would not mind wearing one if I were taught to wear a veil early. If my church required me to wear a veil, I would do it. But I'm afraid I have to disagree with Paul's logic to explain why the women should wear a veil.*" I agree with the young student's well-made argument. Nevertheless, the nature of the letters is about particularity, negating repetition, and completion. We all carry different relationships with different people, and the letter's tone and statement cannot be uniform. In addition, we sense Paul's passion for being an emissary of Christ Jesus through

---

4. Park, *Hermeneutics of Dislocation as Experience*.

his dissonant tone and expressions throughout all the letters. Perhaps as a contemporary reader, we can enjoy the partial truth that Paul carried with his whole heart.

In the study of the Epistles, the Second Letter of the Corinthians causes much confusion because this letter does not follow a chronological order of events, and Paul's mood changes significantly throughout the letter. Today's scholars have reached a near consensus that this letter is a collage of fragments. Regarding logical order, it would be better if we skipped some lines. For example, in 6:13, Paul writes, "*In return—I speak as to children—open wide your hearts also.*" Then, he seems distracted in verse 14, saying, "*Do not be mismatched with unbelievers. For what partnership is there between righteousness and lawlessness? Or what fellowship is there between light and darkness?*" (2 Cor 6:14). These lines do not seem to flow smoothly. Instead, if we read 7:2, "Make room in your hearts for us; we have wronged no one, we have corrupted no one, we have taken advantage of no one," it makes much more sense. Paul seems to be teaching to accept him and his emissaries with an open heart. Also, in 7:13–16, Paul says that Titus returned to him joyfully. However, in the next chapter, Paul introduces Titus to the people in the church of Corinth, announcing that Titus would visit them. The narrative flows more clearly if we read chapter 8 first and then chapter 7 and the wisdom it offers.

It looks odd that the passages do not go chronologically. Also, the contents are structured in an eclectic way rather than logically. Even Paul could not have imagined that his letters would become canon in the Bible and that what he wrote in letters would be given chapters and verses. Paul's ideas and thoughts have influenced the theology of Christianity, but his letters were sporadic and not necessarily carrying the absolute truth, but rather sincere and heartfelt advice and admonitions. The way his letters present the truth of Christ does not explain the whole truth, and the very fact leads readers into the more profound mystery of Christ.

## The Bible as the Revelatory Text

Thus, the practice of reading the Bible invites us to encounter God, the Mystery, who stands beyond all culture, words, dogmas, and symbols. The French psychoanalyst Jacques Lacan explains that all human beings are formed by the concept of the "Other," as the location of total language. The laws, culture, and traditions force us to follow the meaning given by the Other.[5] Most people suffer from anxiety because it is impossible to grasp who the Other is and what the Other desires. In seeking God, God manifests perhaps as words, a symbolic system, while the true God exists beyond words.

As the revelatory text of God, the Bible expands our understanding of the world and God, emphasizing the virtue of diversity and dissonance. The biblical scholar Sandra Schneiders explains the nature of the Bible as revelatory, the locus of an encounter between humans and God. The Bible means a space for her, referring to the Tent of the Meeting between people and God (Lev 8:3). In this metaphor, Schneiders indicates that the Bible, as a living mystery, always stands as the present. In other words, the Bible as a Mystery remains an open text, keeping porosity and rejecting unison but offering opportunities to explore wisdom from various perspectives and in various situations.[6]

When we read the Bible from cover to cover, we encounter a grace that flows from page to page. Possible editors must have collected various sources, including the *Sitz im Leben*, roughly meaning "setting" or "place in life." Biblical criticism, particularly the source theory in biblical scholarship, explains the dissonance in the Bible narrative. In fully comprehending the complicated history of biblical authorship, we experience the Bible still as sacred scripture, which negates a closed meaning. The nature of the openness of the Bible clarifies the name of God as *I am who I am*, the everlasting present. When we give up speculation and look for the answers from the outside, the Bible becomes a set of words like fossils. The only reason the Bible is a source of wisdom is in the truth that God has multiple voices, and these voices do not always have to be in harmony.

In the twenty-first-century world, we encounter others who do not carry the same values, cultures, or racial backgrounds, yet we often attempt to force them to follow ours. Living our daily lives driven by anxiety, if we do not learn how to accept the uncertainty of life, anxiety could present as hatred or violence against others. The Bible leads us into deep wisdom through a gap or a lack, emphasizing its multivalent nature. For those who read the Bible as a set of books of wisdom, hearing the multiple voices with respect and openness, the Bible can be a

---

5. Lacan and Miller, *Anxiety*.
6. Schneiders, *Revelatory Text*.

space to meet one's deeper self, others, and God, gently guiding us to accept the uncertainty of life as it is.

## Deeper Conversation/Deeper Listening

1. The Bible is a locus of multiple voices. Which voice or voices do you identify with when examining the Bible? Why?
2. How does wisdom from the Bible and other sacred texts teach us to live within the margins of uncertainty?

## Spiritual Practice

To encounter God is to find God in liminal spaces (i.e., in spaces where we might subconsciously exclude God or in unexpected spaces). Observe a simple thing. It might be a bird, the glint of sunlight in a window, a running stream, or a baby's smile. Take time to visually and somatically cherish the moment. Ask yourself the question, *"Where do I see God in this moment?"* Take time to reflect. Follow up with the question, *"How does God see me in this moment?"* Remember to journal your thoughts and feelings as you ask yourself these two powerful questions.

## Bibliography

Barker, Kenneth L., et al., eds. *NIV Study Bible*. Grand Rapids, MI: Zondervan, 2011.
Berrigan, Daniel. *Job: And Death No Dominion*. Franklin, WI: Sheed and Ward, 2001.
Collins, John J. *Introduction to the Hebrew Bible*. Minneapolis: Fortress, 2018.
Lacan, Jacques, and Jacques-Alain Miller. *Anxiety: The Seminar of Jacques Lacan, Book X*. Cambridge: Polity, 2014.
Park Jung Eun, Sophia. *A Hermeneutics of Dislocation as Experience: A Resource for Asian American Spirituality*. Lausanne, Switzerland: Peter Lang, 2008.
Schneiders, Sandra Marie. *The Revelatory Text: Interpreting the New Testament as Sacred Scripture*. Collegeville, MN: Liturgical, 2016.

# Chapter 10

# Cleaning Out the Attic

CLAIRE COX-WOODLIEF, SPIRITUAL DIRECTOR

*Claire Cox-Woodlief is the founder and CEO of CCW Transformation Ministries, the co-founder of the North Carolina Institute for Spiritual Direction and Formation, and the retreat leader for the NC Academy for Spiritual Formation. She serves as a spiritual director, a certified facilitator of Sacred Conversations to End Racism (SC2ER), a Conflict Transformation Minister, and an administrator of the Intercultural Development Inventory (IDI) as she seeks ways to live into a call of being a disrupter of unjust systems. She graduated from Academy 41, a two-year academy for spiritual formation, and received her certification for completing a two-year formation program in the art and ministry of spiritual direction from The Listening Place, North Carolina. She also holds a business administration degree and currently serves as the director of operations for White Memorial Presbyterian Church, Raleigh, North Carolina.*

PHYLLIS TICKLE WAS ON to something when she wrote her book *The Great Emergence: How Christianity Is Changing and Why*. Tickle describes how every five hundred years, the Church goes through a *"rummage sale,"* where there is a re-formation, including a posture of *"out with the old and in with the new."* She reminded us of the *"rummage sale"* in the sixteenth century, around 1517, that we now call "The Great Reformation," and five hundred years before that was the "Great Schism" in 1054. Five hundred years before the Great Schism takes us to the sixth century and what was called "The Fall of the Roman Empire" or "The Coming of the Days," or some would say "Gregory the Great," as a tongue-in-cheek acknowledgment of Gregory's influence.[1]

Many factors contribute to these five-hundred-year re-formations that we have gone through and, I believe, are currently going through. Many contributing factors and events came into confluence, tripping every communal life and familiarity into chaos. These five-hundred-year cycles not only apply to Christianity, but they have upheaval in other faith traditions, communities, religious institutions, and in our wider social and political communities. These re-formations often take about one hundred years to be completed. Tickle and others have argued that we pull everything out of the attic in each of these re-formation periods and decide what to dust off and keep and what to get rid of, as if in a rummage sale.

In Tickle's book, she pointed to the reality that there is often one event or at least a series of events that will be remembered during the 100 years of upheaval and that will be marked as significant in the re-formation. She believed that a pivotal point during our current cycle of disruption was the terrorist attacks in the United States on September 11, 2001. That certainly marks a time we will never forget, but if Tickle was still physically with us, I wonder if she might add more recent events that have also been significant. The Church has been in a re-formation for several years. I believe the last few years have escalated a "pruning of the vine" already occurring in the Church.

Trump's presidency brought to the surface (what is hopefully) one of the final gasps of White supremacy in our country. In Europe, the Christian Church was further developed and promoted by people of European descent who became powerful and used their power for financial gains. They maintained that power with their knees on the necks of African, Indigenous, and other people of color, colonizing and pillaging the people and land to the brink of destruction. During Barack Obama's presidency, the fear of losing control began to surface. Based on current trends, many statisticians tell us that people of European descent (or "White" people) are going to become a minority in the USA. During the Trump presidency, Trump stoked a fire of fear that has been simmering in the underbelly of our country since the country's inception.

---

1. Tickle, *Great Emergence*.

Although those who supported Trump's presidency varied in their reasons, the fear of losing the grip on power became a focus. Among his supporters are blatant White supremacists who fear that there is not enough power or resources to go around sufficiently. White Nationalists erroneously believe they are losing ground and power because of ethnic minorities. Therefore, they see themselves as being deprived of resources and opportunities. They espouse the twisted belief that, for some to succeed, it must be at the expense of others, and the others in this way of thinking are White people. White Nationalism has gotten so intertwined with many churches that many have mistaken support for "USA" as an ordained gospel. I would be remiss not to point out that January 6, 2021, will go down in history as an event many of us cannot wrap our heads around, exhibiting just how dangerous Trump and his most enthusiastic followers are to our nation and the world.

Intertwined with all of the confusion is the pandemic of COVID-19. In early 2020, COVID-19 began to spread without clarity on how it started and how to address this deadly illness. The virus that began in 2019 became a global pandemic and affected every segment of society, including the Christian Church. The Christian Church had to rethink the way we do everything! The attitude of "we've always done things this way" had to be turned upside-down and examined. As complex and stressful as this has been on church leaders, being forced to get creative has been helpful in some respects. For a while, worshiping in person was out of the question in most instances, so faith leaders had to get creative and quickly! Many churches that had not done so before began to offer online worship services, Sunday School classes, and Bible studies. Parachurch expressions started to emerge with online spiritual retreats and various additional offerings. As the number of people affected by the pandemic continues to rise and fall and rise again, faith leaders remain on their toes, realizing that there is no such thing as "normal" and there is likely no going back to the pre-pandemic way things were.

If there wasn't enough going on, May 25, 2020, will go down in history as a significant event that many refer to as "George Floyd" without much explanation. A White police officer ended George Floyd's life with a smirk on his face. Floyd's pleas for mercy and help did not change the officers' response, several of whom stood by, ignoring the cries of bystanders who were witnessing his murder. For many Americans, particularly people of European descent, this was the first time they had witnessed police brutality against a Black man that could not be excused or explained away. For people of color, this event was one among countless others on their radar where lives were cut short at the hands of police officers. People of color, once again, could see how easily this could have been them, their spouse, child, friend, or neighbor. This was one more name to add to the growing list of those whose names are too often not even mentioned in the media. For some people of European descent, their heads began to pluck out of the sand with a recognition that there was no denying what took place in this senseless, heinous murder. An awakening began to occur, and a fraction of people of faith realized that racial justice issues needed to be addressed. In no way does today's Church reflect the upside-down kingdom that Jesus invites us to.

## Decline and Realizations

The Church has been in decline for quite some time. Realizing there are exceptions, most churches are on a trend of losing members and regular worshipers. For people interested in being a part of mainstream Christianity, church attendance for those who consider themselves active is not what it used to be. Fewer young adults are interested in being involved in the life of the Church.

In many instances, the Church has lost its relevance for some believers. For many engaged in the Church's life, it's more about community than deep faith or understanding of the tenets of their faith tradition and aspirations for its followers. According to Barna Group and their research released in *Faith and Christianity*, more than half of US churchgoers have yet to hear of the Great Commission.[2] Additionally, 37 percent need to recognize which well-known verses typically go by this name, even when presented with a list of passages. The likelihood is that one who can't remember or recognize the scripture would not likely have received any equipping or the gumption to go live into such a thing. For many, the Church is little more than a country club, where folks want to come and receive and hear a sermon preached that makes them feel good about themselves and go about their lives not doing anything differently. Giving to support the Church's mission is often done as an obligation or checking a box on their "get into heaven" or maybe even "stay out of hell" box rather than an opportunity to participate in God's kingdom work in the world. It would be easy to stray here, so we'll stop. The point is, for those not already embedded into the Church's life, with familial relationships and a clear understanding and buy-in to the

---

2. Barna Group, "51% of Churchgoers."

cultural norms of the particular worshiping community, there is nothing much offered to appeal to those not already inside.

The Church is already in a time of transition; a time for "pruning the vine" is already taking place. The global pandemic has accelerated what is already happening. The pruning of the vine, or the rummage sale, is a time to evaluate who we are as a people and, most importantly, spend time listening to God for direction. Moses went to Mount Sinai twice for forty days to listen to God. Jesus went into the wilderness for forty days, listening to God. In both cases, they emerged having received clear direction. They understood God and the need to focus on what was necessary, and they emerged with purpose. We've had way more than forty days of being in the wilderness. Hopefully, we will emerge with some understanding of how we are to move forward.

We entered the pandemic as a polarized nation, but we have become more polarized where racial inequities and disparities may have felt to many of us as if we were in the wilderness. We've been in liminality, neither here nor there. Our time during this pandemic has been a time of disorientation as well as a time of transition. Susan Beaumont's book *How to Lead When You Don't Know Where You're Going* explores aspects of how transitional experiences follow a predictable pattern involving separation, liminality, and reorientation.[3]

I believe in the last few years, we have spent much time in isolation, and we remain in liminality. Now is the time as we are moving into a time of reorientation. We must approach this reorientation with intentionality. We must raise questions such as *What did we lean throughout the pandemic? Did we consider everything we have discussed, including the needs of the Church, people, and growth? What should be saved or put into the rummage sale?* God made it clear to Moses that we are not "called to go back to Egypt." We are not called to be stagnant in the way we envision the Church of tomorrow. We must raise questions such as *What new ways of ministry have we experienced that we want to carry forward to our communities as we reorient? How is God calling us to emerge from this liminal season? What should this new season look like?* While only time will tell, I offer a few observations and predictions.

- Churches that have lost their "saltiness" and are dying are most likely on a shorter lifespan than before. How long such churches truly last depends on the resources of the founders and ancestors who

---

3. Beaumont, *How to Lead*.

endowed them combined with the resources of those who invest in "their" church today.

- Churches that only find value in doing "for" others in their community and are not interested in being "in ministry with" will also continue to decline. Charity is not going to get us to the promised land.

- Upholding traditions and rules and "the way we've always done things" without clearly understanding why we should do things a certain way is not enough.

So, what, then? Going back to Egypt is not going to happen, neither is doing things the way it has always been done. There are, for some, several uncomfortable realities that must be faced if we are to survive the rummage sale.

- The polarization in the United States divides people into broad categories, where the "us versus them" mentality with judgmentalism over human value and need must be reckoned and the realization that the Church has been and will become more so a place where intersectionality is a value.

- As the pandemic continues to move to a point where it no longer affects how we do ministry, it has already made its mark. There is a reality that some people will not come back to church. Those interested in remaining connected to the Church have grown accustomed to participating remotely and will want to have that option available to them. The question is, How do we become inclusive and serve when there are remote members of the Church?

- Systemic racism has been brought to the surface, and while there will be people who may want to fight to ignore it, there is a rising recognition that it is an accurate societal structure, that we must address to rid the Church of systemic racism from the pulpit to the pews.

- How race is perceived within the Church, and how we will make race a valued aspect of the community, will impact our view of Christianity.

- Nationalism and Nativism are anti-Christian, and we must expel these two movements from the Church if we are to become a more relevant movement again.

Finally, as with most change, I believe there is hope. We must not give up on hope and how it must be attached to the growth and change of the Church. Each time there is a re-formation, the Church has come out on the other end with a renewed purpose and better vision. God has not given up on the Church; we shouldn't either.

## Deeper Conversation/Deeper Listening

1. How has the COVID-19 pandemic, George Floyd's murder, or the Trump presidency affected your involvement in your faith community and other institutions?
2. What has been the impact of these events on your personal life?
3. What have you and your faith community learned that might guide how you will move forward with a renewed purpose and better sense of vision for the integration of faith and community?

## Spiritual Practice

Take some time evaluating the ways that you have come to understand the way things are and should be done in the church. Are there any traditions or practices that have been done a certain way for generations that may no longer be relevant in your current context? How might you lead, encourage, or participate in conversations to be held to evaluate the relevance of traditions and practices that may not be appropriate to continue moving forward?

## Bibliography

Barna Group. "51% of Churchgoers Don't Know of the Great Commission." Mar 27, 2018. https://www.barna.com/research/half-churchgoers-not-heard-great-commission/.

Beaumont, Susan. *How to Lead When You Don't Know Where You're Going: Leading in a Liminal Season*. Lanham: Rowman and Littlefield, 2019.

"Bishop Beard's Weekly Messages." Illinois Great Rivers Conference. Accessed December 23, 2023. https://www.igrc.org/bishop-messages.

"Trusting God's Process: Following the Path That Leads to Victory." *Some Inspired Thoughts*, Sep 12, 2022. https://www.someinspiredthoughts.com/trusting-gods-process-following-the-path-that-leads-to-victory/.

Tickle, Phyllis. *The Great Emergence: How Christianity Is Changing and Why*. Grand Rapids, MI: Baker, 2012.

## Chapter 11

# Out of Resistance Comes Revelation and Change

### Wilfredo Benitez, MS.Ed., M.Div.

*Wilfredo Benitez hails from the Bronx, New York. He is a priest, artist, poet, and activist. He was ordained to the priesthood in 1991 at the Episcopal Cathedral of Saint John the Divine in New York City. Wilfredo holds a Bachelor of Arts from La Universidad InterAmericana de Puerto Rico; a Master of Science in education from the Bank Street College of Education, New York; a Master of Divinity from the General Theological Seminary, New York; and a certificate in spiritual direction from the Haden Institute, North Carolina. He is retired and currently lives in Lisbon, Portugal.*

Wisdom is the essence of what makes us human and shapes community. I value human contact where care for "the other" is genuine, and a community spirit weaves society together. I value a sense of equality and inclusiveness, where people of mixed races, ethnicities, and different genders and sexual orientations treat each other as equals and a part of society. Likewise, I value a world where racism is kept in check through constant self-examination, in a world where there is growing awareness of White skin privilege. These are some things I consider meaningful and, if pondered, can open the door for the dance of wisdom to manifest in our hearts.

## The Dance of Wisdom: Making Meaning in the Post-Modern World

The postmodern world approaches wisdom with the shallowness of a restless mind out of touch with its inner muse, depth, or soul. Too many consider wisdom in terms of trivial insights and pithy statements, hardly asking the deeper and more profound questions. As people walking in Spirit, we are called to do the hard work of moving beyond our self-interests, egotistical yearnings, and the temptation to put ourselves first. To perpetuate a change in perspective, it is not enough to glance at ourselves superficially; we must take a deep, loving look at who we are individually and collectively.

Yet, we live in a world where the goal is to "have our cake and eat it too." Many verbalize clever phrases and rest upon them as a sign of wisdom. Clever phrases such as: *"Sorry, I don't listen to anti-gun lectures from people who think it's okay to kill babies"* or *"All Lives Matter!"* We live in an era—at least in the United States of America—where false statements are often presented as alternative facts, and a large segment of the population (perhaps half of the population) accepts these statements as gospel truth. Many who subscribe to "alternative facts" define themselves as religious and most typically Christian. Where have they "locked" away the wisdom contained in their religious traditions and placed it into action? Behind what doors have they "bolted" wisdom, replacing it with a veneer of sagacity masking a putrid corpse?

## Racism and Intolerance Are Not Supported by Wisdom

In recent history, we have seen the rise of the Black Lives Matter movement, a consciousness-raising movement exposing centuries of racism suffered by Black people and People of Color. To understand why Black Lives Matter as a movement became a reality, we need to understand the historical context where Black and Brown lives were not valued, and until we have clarity and change concerning the sordid racial struggles that have plagued this nation, we will always endure racism and the tenets of racism.

Racism and issues of "White skin privilege" are often heightened after the tragic deaths of too many Black and Brown people, especially at the hands of the police. Cases like George Floyd—being only one among many such cases—are finally coming out into the open like never before.

It seems we may have finally reached a tipping point in society, at least for those with enough wisdom and integrity to take a long, hard, honest look at how racism has shaped America. We who are Black, Brown, Indigenous, and People of Color have always had racism staring us in the face. When you are Black or Brown, you never escape discrimination, looks of suspicion, being followed, or White people turning their heads when you walk into a venue frequented by mostly Whites. It is as if we are being asked, "*How did you get in here?*" How did any of this become status quo in a land rich with religious wisdom traditions, a land where a majority of the religious still profess to be Christian? Racism is ingrained into the fabric of society and the status quo. The persistence of racism denotes an apparent disconnect from the wisdom traditions many of us profess in our creeds, in our beliefs and our houses of worship. Charles Strohmer, a prolific writer on wisdom traditions, states:

> *Wisdom has a vital interest in all peoples everywhere working together for more cooperatively peaceable arrangements. Understanding the agency of wisdom in the old-world Middle East [Ancient Near East] provides clues for this, even for today's cosmopolitan situations. Although this has become a lost way of engagement today, the sages lived, breathed, and taught it. Its recovery may be prophetic for a time such as ours—as a much-needed alternative to sectarian political, social, and religious programs and the vested interests behind the shrill rants of the blogosphere and talk radio. Learning wisdom together [with others] is essential for advancing cooperative and peaceable approaches to issues and initiatives where human diversity is normative, cooperation essential, and human flourishing desired.*[1]

It is indeed wisdom that is a much-needed alternative to sectarian political, social, and conservative religious TV and radio programs, as well as "the vested interests behind the shrill rants in the blogosphere and on social media." As a Person of Color, I would even go as far as saying that wisdom goes beyond being a *much-needed alternative* to be a much-needed component in society in general. The sense of urgency is more significant when one feels the weight and direct consequences of a status quo void of wisdom. Opening the door to wisdom is an invitation none should resist.

---

1. Strohmer, "Wisdom Traditions," §5.

## Linking Wisdom to Contemporary Society

So, where does that leave us, those of us who engage in soul work on multiple levels (spiritual companioning, preaching, pastoral care, leading liturgical worship); and those of us who attempt to embrace the wisdom presented in our faith traditions and beyond? How does wisdom fuel resistance to oppression and exploitation, as well as address racism and ethnocentrism? What is the link between wisdom and, ultimately, love?

The late Trappist monk Thomas Merton (whom I experienced as a student and a teacher in my life) wrote beautifully and poetically about *Sophia* in his many writings—*Sophia* being Greek for wisdom is explored as a gift that is reflected and Divine. The excerpt below states:

> *Sophia is Gift, is Spirit, Donum Dei.*
> *She is God given and God himself as a gift.*
> *God as all and God reduced to Nothing:*
> > *inexhaustible nothingness.*
> 
> *Exinnanivit semetipsum. Humility as the source*
> > *Of unfailing light.*
> 
> *Hagia Sophia in all things is the Divine Life reflected*
> > *In them,*
> 
> *considered as a spontaneous participation,*
> *as their invitation to the Wedding Feast.*
> 
> *Sophia is God's sharing of Himself with creatures.*
> *His outpouring and the Love by which He is given*
> > *and known, held and loved.*
> 
> *She is the union between them. She is the Love that unites*
> > *them.*
> 
> *She is life as communion, life as thanksgiving,*
> *Life as praise, life as festival, life as glory.*
> 
> *Because she receives perfectly, there is in her no stain.*
> *She is Love without blemish, and gratitude without*
> > *self-complacency.*[2]

---

2. Ecumenicus, "Hagia Sophia."

Loving the Eternal, Infinite Source of Mercy (that many refer to as God or the Creator) requires a steady growth in maturity and wisdom. It is the growth in wisdom that leads to a place of resistance in the face of unjust practices. When embraced by Hagia Sophia, or Holy Wisdom, one cannot assume a neutral stance.

Merton writes poetically about Sophia, with fervor and devotion. In reading Merton's words, one might consider an absence of anything resembling a prophetic call to resistance. Mystical language is very present in Merton's words and highlights the beauty of poem and rapture. These aspects of his writing seduce the reader and might mislead the reader into thinking that it's all about bliss, with no connection to justice, equality, action, and change. However, this could not be further from the truth.

It is not an uncommon belief that contemplatives such as Merton, or the Buddha for that matter (drawing from a tradition other than the Christian tradition I belong to), spend all their days in a state of blissful Nirvana, or mystical rapture, totally divorced from the woes and sufferings of the world. On the contrary, one of the central tenets of Buddhism is the practice of compassion and concern for humanity. Similarly, it is the teaching of the Christ to love God above all things, and neighbor as oneself, a lesson the historical Jesus championed anchored in his Middle Eastern Jewish religious heritage (see Mark 12:30–31; Deut 6:4–9). Therefore, those who believe in the power of change through spiritual direction or soul care should also pay attention and become advocates for the needs and issues of humanity within the modern society in which they live. Spiritual direction can and should be a tool for empowerment and a holy journey where Spirit leads the way (both for the directee and the spiritual director) toward becoming agents of resistance and transformation. Spiritual direction and soul care offer a safe place to explore topics such as systemic racism, economic exploitation, etc., and how these societal issues impact one's spiritual health, journey, and the call to be guided by Spirit.

In his book *A Way to God: Thomas Merton's Creation Spirituality Journey*, Matthew Fox quotes Merton as follows:

> The true vocation of the monks of the Benedictine family is not to fight for contemplation against action, but to restore the ancient, harmonious and organic balance between the two. Both are necessary.[3]

---

3. Zuercher, *Merton*, 190.

Fox, formally a Dominican monk and currently a priest in the Episcopal Church, further quotes Meister Eckhart, a German medieval spiritual master and Dominican monk, as follows:

> St. Thomas says that the active life is better than the contemplative, for, in it, one pours out the Love he has received in contemplation. Yet it is all one: For what we plant in the soil of contemplation, we shall reap in the harvest of action.[4]

This statement and position, I believe, is the wisdom of the elders, and it moves us toward action born of Love. I don't think this invalidates a monastic lifestyle, again, *"For what we plant in the soil of contemplation, we shall reap in the harvest of action."* Nevertheless, it does establish the essential role of action. I believe there is a symbiotic relationship between contemplation and action. The concern then becomes the type of action that should be taken, and this is something that is revealed through discernment and the intimacy and relationship with God.

## Seeing the Possibilities with New Eyes and a New Resolve

Historically, wisdom traditions have always been a respected part of our faith traditions, but where has it been hidden? Why is wisdom not moving our religious institutions forward? Institutions in the modern day have become complacent to the point of paralysis. How do we lend support in the care of the soul to those seeking wisdom in the service of humanity when so many find themselves stifled by the very religious institutions they belong to?

When we consider our modern-day prophets and martyrs of Color—individuals such as Martin Luther King Jr., Malcolm X, Óscar Arnulfo Romero y Galdámez, and Mahatma Gandhi (among others)—we meet individuals that possess the deepest experiences of spirituality, guided by wisdom, and each ascends without hesitation to a place most of us hope never to travel. This radical level of wisdom can seem frightening to most of us, and understandably so. In the end, it is an inner spirit nurtured by contemplative practices, prayer, meditation, and discernment, resting on a foundation of wisdom. When MLK preached his last sermon, sharing that he'd been to *"the mountaintop"* and had seen the promised land, that

---

4. Zuercher, *Merton*, 114.

was a moment of revelation; revelation born of the wisdom tradition he embraced as a follower of the Christ. Tragically, the next day, he was assassinated by a White supremacist. Gandhi offered in his many writings wisdom for going forward and inspiring change at the deepest levels of society. Both Malcolm X and Óscar Arnulfo Romero y Galdámez were assassinated for speaking against corruption, calling for change, and advocating for the poor. We can also see in these modern-day elders that wisdom assumes a prophetic dimension among the oppressed. All of these elders surfaced from the ranks of the oppressed, used their discernment and faith in making significant changes in society.

As I mentioned earlier, Merton has been sanitized by the institutional church, but his legacy is one of prophetic vision that too often is hidden from view. His early book *The Seven-Story Mountain* was written in the early stages of his monastic journey. As Merton matured, spiritual revelation guided him to new places, with wisdom taking hold of him with the recognition of each new experience as a gift. Merton died in Bangkok, Thailand, in 1968 in what is described as a freak accident. Quite a few admirers of Merton, Matthew Fox among them, are convinced that this too was an assassination. Whether it was an assassination or not remains in the realm of the nebulous. It is a fact that his prophetic voice had become increasingly quite disturbing to those in the Roman Catholic hierarchy at the time of his sudden death. Merton's world and upbringing were not one of the economic hardships as some people might experience, quite the contrary. But as he aged and matured, living into monastic poverty with enormous zeal, he morphed into a prophet. As his prophetic voice roared, Merton did not hold back when he spoke in the direction and discernment of prophecy that guided him throughout the rest of his life.

The war in Vietnam was one of the areas where Merton's prophetic voice resonated, much to the dismay of his superiors. Ironically, his body was returned to the US on a flight containing the bodies of US soldiers killed in the Vietnam War. Merton had a deep respect for MLK and resonated with King's prophetic message encompassing race, economic inequalities, and King's commitment to his life in service of Christ. His acknowledgment and denouncement of racism—even within the institution he served—touched the very core of his church. His words and legacy wounded the effect of racism, charging and reminding how racism diminishes the sense of self-worth through the treatment of individuals that don't really belong to the dominant White culture's viewpoints. Little did Merton know that he too would die in the same year as Dr. King was killed.

In his book *The Man in the Sycamore Tree: The Good Times and Hard Life of Thomas Merton*, Rice quotes Merton as follows:

> "When the Catholic Church gives the impression that it regards the South as a vast potential pool of 'Negro Converts' in which a zealous and ardent White apostolate can transform a few million 'Uncle Tom's' into reasonably respectable imitations of white Catholics, this actually does very little to make the Negro respect the truth of Christ, and practically nothing to help him understand the mystery of Christ." He warns that if the White man does not respond, the awakened Negro will forget his moment of Christian hope and Christian inspiration. "He will no longer be the gentle wide-eyed child singing hymns while the police dogs lunge at his throat. There will be no more hymns and no more prayer vigils. He will become a Samson whose African strength flows back into his arms. He will suddenly pull the pillars of White society crashing down upon himself and his oppressor. And perhaps somewhere out of the ruins, a new world (a Black world) will one day rise."[5]

The words of Merton are uncanny as if he were a witness to life in America today and the aftermath of the murder of George Floyd. The place and exploration of wisdom traditions among the marginalized are different from those who enjoy "White privilege," which is usually accompanied by a middle-class lifestyle and translates into economic stability.

There is plenty of debate around the issue of "White privilege" (i.e., whether it exists, how it is sustained, what it impacts, and how to eliminate it). Still, for the sake of simplicity, I will focus on the definition given by Kendall in her book *Understanding White Privilege: Creating Pathways to Authentic Relationships across Race*. According to Kendall, "White Privilege means *having greater access to power and resources than people of Color [in the same situation] do.*"[6] If this assessment is accurate, we cannot continue to have a society that believes in the "one size fits all" mentality. As a whole, society does not realize that "the one size" does not fit all, and we all bring our baggage, our history, and social beliefs for better or for worse, with us each day. Therefore, interpreting and applying traditions of wisdom and eternal truths to our lives is critical. We are at a time in this nation where we must turn

---

5. Rice, *Man in the Sycamore Tree*, 59.
6. Kendall, *Understanding White Privilege*, 62.

to eternal truths and wisdom to resolve our issues of the spirit that is reflected in our human actions. Time and again, compared to our White counterparts, the economic disparities among People of Color are often believed to be a fact of life, and such conditions are brought on and sustained without help from White Americans. How wisdom traditions are approached and interpreted in these same socio-economic areas do not coincide, nor are these beliefs compatible.

Those who enjoy privilege have the luxury of pondering wisdom traditions from a scholarly perspective—among other reasons because they have the resources and time to do this. Those living on the margins rarely have luxuries, and daily activity is reduced to pure survival. It is only through the examination and application of our spiritual practices that we can alter the dynamics of these actions and beliefs that have impacted society for generations. Nevertheless, when I think of the impact of wisdom traditions, and on my own Latine community, especially recent immigrants, I'm amazed at how receptive we are to Spirit. In this context, I am reminded of the "Magnificat," the Song of Mary in the Gospel of Luke, and how this young Middle Eastern woman of Color reacted to the message that she would birth the Christ:

> *My soul proclaims the greatness of the Lord,*
> *my Spirit rejoices in God my Savior;*
> > *for he has looked with favor on his lowly servant.*
> *From this day all generations will call me blessed:*
> > *the Almighty has done great things for me,*
> > *and holy is his Name.*
> *He has mercy on those who fear him*
> > *in every generation.*
> *He has shown the strength of his arm,*
> > *he has scattered the proud in their conceit.*
> *He has cast down the mighty from their thrones,*
> > *and has lifted up the lowly.*
> *He has filled the hungry with good things,*
> > *and the rich he has sent away empty.*
> *He has come to the help of his servant Israel,*
> > *for he has remembered his promise of mercy,*
> *The promise he made to our fathers,*
> > *to Abraham and his children forever.* (Luke 1:46–55)

This passage is the voice of a marginalized woman living the woes of Roman occupation. In reading her words, we cannot lose sight of how deep Holy Wisdom appears in her response, and the passage is drenched in Divine truth. Where did this young woman get such wisdom? It would appear that the mystical experience of her encounter with the Angel Gabriel provoked an outpouring of her innermost soul, the place where Hagia Sophia dwells unencumbered. Perhaps the fact that she was not a sophisticated woman enjoying rank and privilege gave her a greater receptivity to the angel's visitation. The words she spoke are the very words of Hagia Sophia; Holy Wisdom, and her reference to the proud in their conceit; the casting down of the mighty from their thrones; the lifting up of the lowly; and the rich being sent away empty are a direct identification with the plight of the marginalized and the hungry who have been *"filled with good things." "He has come to the help of his servant Israel"* is a politically charged declaration with dangerous consequences, yet it remains perilously the voice of Hagia Sophia. Mary stands in the tradition of the elders, a woman without means, a woman that does not speak like the rich and powerful, and she is a woman from whom we draw deep wisdom. This in itself is an example of intersectionality that most women of privilege do not experience.

With People of Color and the varied cultural backgrounds we bring to the table, sensitivity to our intersectionality and cultural ancestry deserves recognition and affirmation. Our unsung elders and unknown elders, who virtually had nothing written about them, remain alive in our DNA, our psyche, and in our soul. My background as a US-born Latine of Puerto Rican and Cuban heritage makes me aware of the importance of heritage in a land that has not traditionally welcomed people like me. This heritage makes me a descendant of Southern Europeans, Africans, and the Taino Native Americans that once populated the Caribbean islands. The spiritual DNA of my ancestry remains a part of who I am. As a Person of Color who has dealt with racism his entire life, it unfortunately comes with the territory of being a Person of Color in a world where White privilege continues to rule. When I observe my Haitian wife doing an Afro Haitian voodoo dance to the beat of Afro drumming, I sense the presence of the ancestors, the presence of Spirit coming through her and me. This awakens me to an unbroken connection to a past that has not been forgotten. At such times I am acutely aware that the Holy Wisdom comes to us in many ways. All of this points in the direction of deep soulful connections to the inner self and the sojourner who is making a way through the journey of life.

## Soulful Connections and the Need for Resistance

Holy Wisdom is an invitation to allow oneself to be guided and to embrace resistance as part of the integrated journey. A life void of resistance is a life void of revelation and the possibility of ultimate transformation. The historical Jesus was a model of resistance even when faced with the might of the Roman Empire coming down heavily upon his shoulders. For Christians, this is perfectly illustrated in chapter 22 of the Gospel according to Luke. We read the following in verses 39–44.

> *Jesus went out as usual to the Mount of Olives, and his disciples followed him. On reaching the place, he said to them, "Pray that you will not fall into temptation." He withdrew about a stone's throw beyond them, knelt down, and prayed, "Father, if you are willing, take this cup from me; yet not my will, but yours be done." An angel from heaven appeared to him and strengthened him. And being in anguish, he prayed more earnestly, and his sweat was like drops of blood falling to the ground.*

This scenario is not comforting, and it presents Jesus wrestling with emotions and about what he knows is to come. In the Christian narrative, Jesus is brutally crucified, and no, he does not use an esoteric yoga technique to keep him from feeling the agony and pain of his ordeal. Holy Wisdom cradled him to go forward. In the end, in the Christian narrative, he resurrects after dying on the cross, demonstrating all was not lost, the resistance was worth the challenge, and Hagia Sophia prevailed; she always does!

How can any one of us make that journey without a soulful connection to the spirit of Hagia Sophia? After all, wisdom manifests in many forms, from our recognized wisdom traditions that are lesser-known (especially in Eurocentric circles) to Indigenous traditions and what I call DNA-based knowing. Too often, religious and spiritual circles overemphasize "bliss" as a sign of enlightenment on the spiritual journey. Yet, even Jesus in the Gospels is the one we could call a manifestation of Holy Wisdom, a model of resistance. Enlightenment can be a very lonely place, and anyone on the spiritual journey seeking wisdom should be prepared for time in the "wilderness" and know resistance will occur and challenge the beliefs of their soul. Times in the wilderness will undoubtedly come to all of us as we venture forward in our spiritual journeys.

Resistance is born when our wilderness experience is linked to oppression, rejection, and exploitation, leading us to revelation and change. We can look at this in any order, as things born of Spirit are not tied to any particular order. When we come to places of revelation, epiphanies occur, resistance is birthed, and resistance leads to change. The belief that resistance leads to change is found in the murder of George Floyd, which morphed into a worldwide revelation that Black Lives Matter. Derek Chauvin, the police officer who killed him, was convicted of second-degree murder and sentenced to twenty-two years in prison. Resistance took the form of public outcry and initiated change, albeit too little, too late, for George Floyd, but change nonetheless. *Justice delayed is justice denied*, and this has been too long in coming. I pray that wisdom prevails in our legal systems, and wisdom with eternal truths becomes a focus for us as we begin the change to heal our wounds.

I will close this essay and perspective with my original poem "Sophia of My Soul." It is a kind of seductive energy one might find in the Song of Songs contained in the Hebrew Bible. Nevertheless, the beauty of Hagia Sophia permeates most profoundly regardless of the brokenness and plays a vibrant role in our spiritual maturity. Without her warmth and seductive embrace, we don't move forward. Wisdom beckons us; we would be lost without her. As persons tending to the care of the soul in a postmodern world with little appreciation for wisdom, we have our work cut out for us. Thankfully, Hagia Sophia is ever ready to carry us in her warm embrace.

> **Sophia of My Soul**
> *How beautiful to rest in wisdom,*
> *How beautiful the repose born of such sublime Eternity.*
> *What liberty when one is freed of ignorance,*
> *And the voluntary sentence of self-deception.*
> *Sophia of my soul,*
> *Beautiful lady of the light and night,*
> *Striking brightness that brings inner peace,*
> *Why deny your entry into my bed chamber?*
> *Why resist the caress of your knowing?*
> *Why refuse your seductive gaze calling me to freedom?*

*The door opens very slowly,*
*And little by little I see your nakedness;*
*Little by little, I embrace my nakedness,*
*Realizing the futility of trying to hide.*
*Sophia of my soul,*
*Lady wisdom,*
*I surrender to your seduction,*
*Break the resistance,*
*And dismantle the chains that keep me, prisoner.*
*Sophia of my soul,*
*Come rest in me,*
*Tear down my stubbornness,*
*And fill my being with the aroma of your light;*
*Your glow of knowing and understanding,*
*Your enveloping haze where neither falsehoods nor arrogance will enter.*
*Sophia of my soul,*
*Come and make your sanctuary in me,*
*Sophia of my soul.*

## Deeper Conversation/Deeper Listening

1. Wilfredo Benitez uses "resistance" as a spiritual concept that leads to spiritual liberation and change. Where in your life have you experienced "resistance" that has led to a spiritual change?

2. Have you witnessed "White privilege" in your life? How did it impact you? Did it make a change in you spiritually, socially, or both?

3. How would you respond if resistance became a topic in a spiritual direction or soul care exchange?

## Spiritual Practice

The term *presence* in the spiritual life has several meanings. There is the presence of being in attendance, supporting an action both physically and spiritually, as in a protest or service. There is the presence of the temporary or the here and now, where you might not be a physical witness but a spiritual witness of support. Stop and think about your presence at least three times for the next day or so. Using your journal, record what you were doing when you stopped. What are your thoughts? How did stopping to make time for presence remind you of something? Did noticing your ideas on presence make a difference in your outlook on life? How can you carry out this type of presence as an act of resistance?

## Bibliography

International Bible Society, ed. *New International Version*. Grand Rapids, MI: Zondervan, 1973.

Kendall, Frances. *Understanding White Privilege: Creating Pathways to Authentic Relationships across Race*. New York: Routledge, 2013.

Ecumenicus. "Hagia Sophia by Thomas Merton." Nov 8, 2016. http://ecumenicus.blogspot.com/2016/11/hagia-sophia-by-thomas-merton.html.

———. *The Seven-Storey Mountain*. New York: Harcourt, 1948.

Rice, Edward. *The Man in the Sycamore Tree: The Good Times and Hard Life of Thomas Merton*. New York: Doubleday, 1970.

Strohmer, Charles. "Wisdom Traditions—See with New Eyes." *Charles Stromer* (blog), n.d. http://www.charlesstrohmer.com/the-wisdom-project/wisdom-tradition-see-with-new-eyes/.

Zuercher, Suzanne. *Merton: An Enneagram Profile*. Notre Dame, IN: Ave Maria, 1996.

# PART 4

# *Introduction:* New Beginnings
## A Clarion Call

> *This section explores the transformative nature of spiritual practices and how practices are informed, defined, and redefined by the practitioner's experience and spiritual background. The writers explore the importance of holding space for wisdom and truth to develop over time and the essentials of honoring our various phases of life as spiritual gifts.*

ONE THING THAT IS certain in life is uncertainty. Generally speaking, Western cultures do not handle uncertainty well. Westerners deal with facts and need solid resolutions to most issues, and the expectation is that it will happen expeditiously. Many aspects of Western culture purport that we are "masters" of our destiny, and there is little that we cannot control. This stance is even more pronounced with the perception that we have choices in every aspect of life. Westerners also value the strong-arm approach of pushing through without considering anything except an issue's conclusion and the finality of any issue. However, Susan Jeffers, author of the bestseller *Feel the Fear and Do It Anyway*, believes embracing uncertainty is a wisdom path that makes perfect sense in insecure times. Living with questions and sorting through aspects of an issue has much value and is a sign of spiritual growth. When faced with unpredictability, we can find value in pausing, turning inward, and examining how to proceed rather than charging headlong into the issue. Pausing and reflecting can become the point of a new beginning and not the focus of a conclusion. This is why developing a spiritual practice is critical to aligning our desires and aligning with our purpose. I learned the value of taking the impregnated pause that allows for time, and the birthing of conclusions, and the opportunity to seek truth. It is during this impregnated pause when we come face to face with the uncertainty of our purpose, we reflect, we examine the necessary and unnecessary before we forge a new path. It becomes the beginning of a clarion call for renewal.

While the body is mortal, the soul is eternal, and how this connection is strengthened and revealed depends on the person's faith. This is another reason why establishing a spiritual practice becomes essential. Regardless of the faith or religion, the purpose of any spiritual practice is to focus on connecting the body, the individual, and collective experiences with the soul. Spiritual practices help "re-ground" by disconnecting us from the mechanisms of distractions within our minds and the outer world. It encourages us to realign with our souls by listening from within. A spiritual practice can cultivate and stimulate healthy living habits that strengthen our sense of belonging and purpose. This is why, especially in the age of social media, counterculture wars, and social influencers who deal mostly with the temporary, relying on the inner space and the truth that will emerge is critical. It allows us to never lose *wonder* as we discover what is sacred and fulfilling as well as what is in need of attention in our lives. We begin this chapter with the question, *Expectations are always about tomorrow. Regret is always about the past. What can we say or do about the here and now of our faith?*

## *Chapter 12*
## Living the Questions

### Lib Campbell, MDiv

*Lib Campbell is a retired elder in the North Carolina Conference of the United Methodist Church, named pastor emeritus of spiritual formation at Saint Mark's UMC in Raleigh, North Carolina. She and her husband, Tom, have been married for fifty-eight years. They are parents of two children and four adult grandchildren. Lib has a BA in religion from Meredith College and an MDiv from Duke Divinity School. Lib and Tom led the North Carolina Academy for Spiritual Formation for nine years.*

THE BINDING GLUE ON the spine of the small paperback book is dried out now. I have the pages held together by a binder clip. The book is too precious to throw away; I treat it tenderly. When Margaret handed the books out to our little circle of United Methodist Women, it was the beginning of Lent, March 1981. The book was the Christian Personhood Study for the year. Beth E. Rhude had written the book *Live the Questions Now* as an invitation to interior life and a new way to "live prayerfully." Little did I know that this study, its thesis set around a short poem by Rainer Maria Rilke, would capture my spiritual imagination and lead me into a deeper relationship with Christ and a ministry of spiritual formation as an elder in the United Methodist Church

The poem is from a work written to Rilke's young protégé. *Letters to a Young Poet* is filled with the wisdom of the elder poet. The poem brought wisdom to me also in the invitation to live the questions now. The poem states:

> *Be patient toward all that is unsolved in your heart . . .*
> *Try to love the questions themselves*
> *Like locked rooms and like books that are written in a very foreign tongue.*
> *Do not now seek the answers, which cannot be given you*
> *Because you would not be able to live them.*
> *And the point is, to live everything. Live the questions now.*
> *Perhaps you will then gradually, without noticing it,*
> *Live along some distant day into the answer.*[1]

In March of 1981, I was thirty-five years old, a young wife, and mother of two. Rilke's poem was not the beginning of my faith, nor was it the genesis of my call to ministry. It was a turning point, fueling the flame of my faith. From March of 1981 until now, I have been on an ever-deepening journey of knowing God. My ministry as a lay person increased to serving as a leader in United Methodist Women, teaching and leading retreats across our conference. As I grew in faith, I began to live into the call to ministry I experienced as a teenager. Divinity school and ordination were part of my answer. As an ordained elder in the United Methodist Church, teaching, preaching, and leading retreats allows me to live the fullness of God's presence through spiritual disciplines while inviting others into the depth and breadth of experiencing God. Christian spiritual formation has become the emphasis of the ministry I continue to live into.

Living the questions is being held in the Mystery that is God and living the dynamic of the *great unknowing*. For me, living the questions has been the beginning of wisdom that continues to be fed in the study of the mystics, of which Rilke is considered one, and reading the Scriptures with the eye and ear of the heart. Now, reading a line like *"for everything there is a season, a time to be born and a time to die"* brings interior assurance that relieves my need for control and invites me constantly into grace. I accept and find peace knowing that *"I see only in part."* Living the questions frees me for joy, frees me from fear, even fear of death.

Sometimes I think answers are overrated. They are static; they end the discussion. Too often, with answers, our seeking ends. Many of us

---

1. Rilke, *Letters to a Young Poet*, 35.

are satisfied with easy answers. Surely, we benefit from answers in medicine and science, especially when we recognize that the next question is born in the answer. The seeker who seeks in ongoing ways is always uncovering and looking beyond what is possible to what could be. It's like watching a child on Christmas morning. Gifts are torn into; paper and ribbons are strewn. Then what?

## Drawn to the Empty Box

For our three-year old daughter, the tricycle was pulled out of the box, and set aside. Lisa was drawn to the empty box. She played with it all Christmas morning. The box captured her creativity and her imagination. It became anything she could imagine. The questions, the enigma, are the box that holds possibility and potential. We are free to envision, imagine, dream, doubt, and test. We swim in the stream of a *great unknowing*; it is dynamic and brimming with notions of what could be. There grows a sense of being swept up in something beyond comprehension, yet there is trust that somewhere along the way we will know all things.

Western civilization is wrapped around rational thought and answers. We argue about who is right and who is wrong. Increasingly, we are a win/lose culture. Binary thinking is a way to name winners and losers. Such thought is antithetical to the call of Christ that we are one people. Even in the church, there is intentional division of who is in and who is out of God's favor. Herein lies the folly into which wisdom speaks. The human movement into answers has limitations, the limitation of human capacity. Answers follow the path of knowledge. That works well on a math quiz; we know the formulas and equations.

Answers put the onus on human capacity. But what happens when human capacity reaches its limit, as it surely will? Do we abandon the question? Do we rail against the one who poses the question? What happens if there is no answer? We get lulled into notions of self-madeness, with claims of being masters of our fate. For all the small steps we make, if/when we become deluded and disappointed, where do we turn? There is no back page with the puzzle answers.

A faithful people long ago were overcome and taken into exile by the Babylonians. They cry, "*Oh no! Were our prayers not effective? Were our offerings not enough? We have been as good as we could be. Why is this suffering happening to us?*" This question of why good people suffer is one place where wisdom is challenged. Dr. James Crenshaw was a professor at Duke Divinity School when I was a student. He was a scholar of the Wisdom Literature of the Hebrew scriptures. In his book *Old Testament Wisdom*, Dr. Crenshaw writes, "*The suffering of innocent individuals has posed a problem from time immemorial. For it has defied every effort of rational explanation.*"[2] We like knowledge and answers when the world seems out of control; they give us a sense of comfort and security. Such comfort and security are not enough when the storms come and the fires rage and everything seems completely beyond human capacity to control.

## God's Will in the World

Some may point to the will of God as an answer, as if our tiny selves can claim full knowledge of the will of God. Leslie Weatherhead, in his book *The Will of God*, speaks to the will of God in three experiences of the human condition: *the intentional will of God, the circumstantial will of God*, and *the ultimate will of God*.[3]

*The intentional will of God* was that we would live in a garden, one people in unity with one another and all creation. That did not last long. Human ego that wanted to be all knowing like God, ate of the tree of knowledge, and humans were dismissed from the garden. Ego: can't live with it; can't live without. The Ego Self unbridled is what drives us into recklessness, pride, and most of the poor choices we make. An attitude of "my way or the highway" drives us out of the garden every time.

*The circumstantial will of God* is where we find ourselves in the world today. There are circumstances of disease and poor choices; certain physical boundaries, which, stretched beyond their own limitation, lead to consequences we might find harsh. Like pouring carbon dioxide into the atmosphere and raising the temperature of the earth till the waters flood and we choke on the very air we breathe. Or smoking cigarettes until our lungs rot in our bodies. We might blame God and even walk away from God, murmuring, "*How could you do this to us, God?*"

God doesn't DO this to us. Our reckless choices often contribute to our human issues. The presence of disease in the world is something we have not necessarily brought on ourselves but rather something that

---

2. Crenshaw, *Old Testament Wisdom*, 14.
3. Weatherhead, *Will of God*.

exists in a broken world. We have learned a lot in the past couple of years about how viruses and microbes are a mighty foe. Laws of nature, like gravity and inertia, can bless us, or they can derail notions of self-control, leaving us adrift, lost, fearful, and angry. Growing in wisdom and trust of God can lift us out of the pain and heartache of the human condition and consequences born of a physical, material world.

*The ultimate will of God* is that, in the end, we will be with God in a place of wholeness and healing beyond the bounds of Earth. The victory has already been won in the life, death, and resurrection of Christ. Heaven is the value added for the life lived in love with God. It is not the goal, but the promise. Our relationship with God and our relationship with people and our care of creation are what we are called to; this is where the inward journey of wisdom intersects the outward journey of righteousness—love of God; love of neighbor.

This unsolved question of human suffering that is found in Crenshaw's Wisdom Literature of the Hebrew scriptures drives us to some pretty unhelpful responses, like "*God never puts more on you than you can handle,*" or "*You will be stronger in this; look for what this is teaching you.*" Not only are these responses unhelpful, they are infuriating and insulting to a woman who has just taken her husband to the hospital with a heart disease that will kill him if he does not get a transplant. Or to the mother who cares for her twenty-one-year-old daughter dying of cancer while a "friend" questions the efficacy of the mother's prayer life. Suffering is an untidy and unwelcome interruption, yet all of us sojourn with suffering.

Years ago, a small private plane went down in a bad storm on the Outer Banks of North Carolina. For days it could not be found. There were five people on the flight, a family of four, and a little girl who was a friend of the pilot's daughter. We were friends of the little girl's parents. We went to their house and the little girl's rain boots were on the back porch right where she had left them. We could have cut the shock and worry with a knife. The parents were being encouraged and consoled by another friend of theirs, "*Mac is a good pilot; he flew planes in Vietnam. He is likely in one of the marshes with no cell signal waiting for someone to spot him. He's likely got the children all cozied up and telling stories.*" She went on and on with what I thought was empty chatter until the day the sheriff called to say they had found the plane under one of the bridges. No survivors. Although well-meaning, her constant chatter ended in very painful false hope. False hope is avoidance of dealing with the reality that bad things happen to good people, to little children, to our babies and our husbands, and to ourselves. False hope becomes a stumbling block in acknowledging that suffering is the common denominator of life. Suffering and loss will come to all of us.

In the Old Testament Wisdom of Ecclesiastes, the Teacher named Qoheleth speaks about the issue of the meaning of life with its unanswered questions, paradoxes, and puzzles, claiming that it is the "unhappy business that God has given human beings to be busy with." The Teacher says that wisdom can be vexing. Unanswered questions are vexing until we learn to sit with them and let the questions themselves guide us. Socrates figured this out centuries ago; Jesus did, too.

### Liminality and Thresholds

In the somewhere between the question and the answer, there is God. And there is a spacious place where we can experience God. Liminality is a word I hear frequently these days. Liminality is defined as a "threshold," or as "a space between what is finished and what is yet to be." Questions themselves may be liminality. Questions may bring anxiety, wringing of hands and gnashing of teeth, but they can also bridge the in-betweens of life, the knowing within the unknowing.

Our little terrier, Lucky, has an issue with thresholds. When he looks down and sees a change in the path he is walking, he stops cold in his tracks. It's most humorous in the house when the floor changes from hardwood in the kitchen to tile in the laundry room. His food bowl is on the floor in the laundry room; therein lies his dilemma. After a little thought and a little drooling, he backs up and takes a running start to leap over his perceived threshold and eat his bits. Backing up and taking a running start may be what we all need to enter a new thing, whatever it is, and find what we are looking for somewhere on the other side.

We live life on the verge of something. The verge can be crippling, or the verge can be thrilling depending on our outlook, fear, and dread, or hopeful anticipation. But we also live with a level of trust that depends on our faith in God, utter trust, and a memory of God's presence with us through decisions past. We sing it, "*O God, our help in ages past, our hope for years to come.*" On the verge, at the threshold, living a question calls forth all God has been, all God is, and all God will be in the time to come.

Moments of connection with God come to us with a promise that God is with us and a call offered repeatedly in Scripture, "*Do not be afraid.*"

## Spacious Places

As the psalmist writes, there is a spacious place beyond loss, pain, anxiety, and disappointment. The Spacious Place is the place God brings us to as shelter, refuge, and safety in the face of trials, whatever they may be. God may be a Mystery, but God can be known in part as we seek with open hearts and attention to what is written and what creation is shouting to us. The Spacious Place is cleared of obstacles. The vista is open wide for an experience of God.

For a lot of my life now my most fruitful spiritual practice has been lectio divina. Elizabeth Canham[4] and Basil Pennington[5] have been great teachers of the way of lectio, listening to God *"with the ear of the heart."* The steps of *lectio, meditatio, oratio, contemplatio* reveal a living word from Scripture. The word comes as God speaking through the steps of holy reading—of Scripture, of the world around. Meditating, ruminating on what we read or see, praying—for me this step has been practiced through journaling, which I have done since 1972. The last step is contemplation, resting in, sitting with, breathing in and out the breath of God. Learning to live a lectio divina life is learning to pay attention, to marvel and delight in what God is doing amid and beyond the questions.

The idea of Spacious Places came to me through my practice of lectio divina. Over the years I have spent much time in Psalm 66:10–12. This psalm is a recognition of the human condition and an invitation to know and trust God beyond the trials, tests, and turmoil of life. There is wisdom in trusting God who acts on our behalf to shelter us in our troubles. "*For You, O God, have tested us. You have tried us as silver is tried. You brought us into the net; you laid burdens on our backs. You let people ride over our heads; we went through fire and through water, yet You have brought us out to a Spacious Place*" (NRSV). Human suffering is never the end; God leads God's beloved through the trials. God's grace and presence are known in the Spacious Place. So where is the Spacious Place?

I would say the Spacious Place is not necessarily a location on the map, although there are locales where we experience God. There are

---

4. Canham, *Heart Whispers*.
5. Pennington, *Lectio Divina*.

mountaintops. There are oceans and rivers and sunsets and sunrises that fill us with awe and awareness of God with us. Iona and LaVerna and Short Journey Center and Camp Don Lee are exterior, physical places, broad and big where wonder and delight set in. In these places, God is close; it feels like a thin place between where I am and where God is. God is as close as my next breath.

Then there are the interior and intangible Spacious Places where God can be known. These are everyday places and practices available as I pay attention and am intentional with my prayer. Much is written about the spiritual disciplines to help us discover ways of knowing God. The God who is everywhere and present, is in our "now" if we but open ourselves to hearing and seeing. The still small voice is speaking, and the heavens are declaring the glory of God. There are ways we can be present to God, the One who is ever-present to us. The Spacious Places offer the openness for questions to bubble up and answers to sing around us. I've experienced these Spacious Places. Places such as *silence and solitude* are chief among the Spacious Places. *Slowness* is another practice, to meander and smell the roses. *Stability* is one of the cornerstones of wisdom, and it too is a spacious place in which to know God. *Sacramentality* is a spacious place to acknowledge that all things created by God are sacred. *Study* is a spacious and ever-expanding place of knowing God. *Scripture*, especially when we read beyond the words to the intent and revelation of the new thing God does every day, is a spacious place. *Simplicity* is a spacious place, literally and figuratively. Simplicity is more than decluttering, is about detachment, letting go. Detachment is about being able to give a precious pearl cross necklace to someone simply because she admires it. Detachment is about being able to let something go. *Serendipity* is the spacious place of unexpected joy. We catch a glimpse, have a hunch, find a treasure, and recognize the God of grace is in it all. *Service*, *Sabbath*, and *Shalom* are spacious places. *Service* animates the life of Christ for the world. *Sabbath* is part of God's order for the world. It's the call of the seventh day of creation. *Shalom* is God's *hesed*, the lamb and the lion lying together, and plows turned into plowshares. Participation in these Spacious Places and making ourselves available to God's grace is answer enough to live a life of peace. We study to awaken curiosity and to formulate deeper and more faithful questions. Being in a Spacious Place allows us this connection to deeper meaning. In being held by the Mystery that is God with us, we rest assured and we are comforted. Wisdom has found us. We can resist God's presence and grace.

While God meets us and keeps us and blesses us, showering grace upon grace, human response can go in two opposite directions. We can bring our woundedness to God for God to heal, or we can sit in our suffering languishing, thinking this is a way out of it. Where is life that really is life found? Trusting God with our pain, our loss, our sadness, our bitterness, disappointment, resentment, anger, and grief can only happen as we love God more. Picking up a renewed relationship with God is like a great exhale when we at last know our personal agency is simply not enough to carry us through this life. We fight so for self-control; we cling tightly to notions that we are self-made. The wisdom of Qoheleth is still a good teacher who says, "*Folly. Vanity. All is vanity.*"

The wisdom of Hebrews in the New Testament teaches that "*faith is the assurance of things hoped for, the conviction of things not seen*" (Heb 11:1 NRSV). How could we not trust that God is with us in the questions if we grow our faith and tend the garden of our souls? How could we hear the wisdom of Jesus say, "*Why would you worry? Consider the lilies of the field; they neither toil nor spin, yet I tell you even Solomon in his glory [and in his reputation for wisdom] was not clothed like one of these*" (Matt 6:28–29 NRSV).

When I retired, I told my friends that I wanted to be the old frog sitting in the middle of the room . . . a Yoda frog, parsing out wisdom. It is wisdom and the place of living the questions that will get us through this life as whole people who love God and love one another. For we will trust the one who says, "*Do not be afraid, for I am with you even to the ends of the earth.*" Only in that promise can we thrive and live a life of joy that loves and serves and at the end of the day says, "*All is well.*"

## Deeper Conversation/Deeper Listening

1. What is the call on your own life? How are you living into this calling?
2. When have you been afraid to take a next step? What makes you afraid?
3. Name the Spacious Places God brings you to. How does Spacious Place make you feel?
4. What is the biggest question you are living into today?

# Bibliography

Canham, Elizabeth J. *Heart Whispers: Benedictine Wisdom for Today.* Nashville: Upper Room, 1999.

Crenshaw, James L. *Old Testament Wisdom: An Introduction.* Louisville: Westminster John Knox, 2010.

Pennington, M. Basil. *Lectio Divina: Renewing the Ancient Practice of Praying the Scriptures.* New York: Crossroad, 1998.

Rilke, Rainer Maria. *Letters to a Young Poet.* Novato, CA: New World Library, 2000.

Weatherhead, Leslie D. *The Will of God.* Nashville: Abingdon, 1999.

# Chapter 13
# *Pirkei Avot*
## Chapters of Wisdom

### Rabbi Sheila Peltz Weinberg

*Rabbi Sheila Peltz Weinberg served as a congregational rabbi for seventeen years. She has also worked in the fields of Jewish community relations, Jewish education, and Hillel. She has published widely on such topics as feminism, spiritual direction, parenting, social justice, and mindfulness from a Jewish perspective. She has contributed commentaries to Kol HaNeshama, the Reconstructionist prayer book. Rabbi Weinberg has taught mindfulness meditation and yoga to rabbis, Jewish professionals, and lay people in the Institute for Jewish Spirituality context. She serves as a spiritual director to various Jewish clergy, including students at Reconstructionist Rabbinical College in Philadelphia and faculty at Hebrew Union College-Jewish Institute of Religion in New York City. Her most recent book is* Let Us All Breathe Together: Prose, Poems, Practices.

MY INTENTION IN THIS chapter is to present several wisdom teachings from *Pirkei Avot*, a compilation of sayings attributed to Jewish sages ranging from Simon the Just in 200 BCE to Judah haNasi, the redactor of the Mishnah and the great legal compendium in 200 CE. The literal translation of *Pirkei Avot's* title is *Chapters of the Fathers*. Often it is called *Ethics of the Fathers*. Indeed, I like to call it *Chapters of Wisdom*. It is technically a tractate in the part of the Mishnah called *Nezikin*. However, it is the only tractate (treatise) of sixty-three that is not primarily a legal document. Rather, it is a Jewish teaching manual, a compilation of statements designed to inspire and orient the rabbis (all the rabbis at that time were men) who were creating a new paradigm of spiritual work based on teaching Torah.

I will seek to discern their intention, value, and applicability to our lives. I will also call upon contemporary spiritual teachers from a variety of traditions to comment on these sayings. During this time, the rabbis are particularly concerned about the integration of practice into their lives and relationships. For them, the study and teaching of Torah is understood as the highest human aspiration. It is a fulfillment of the Divine intention for humanity. Let us begin:

### What Is a Good Teacher?

Yehoshua ben Perachyah says: "Provide yourself with a teacher, acquire yourself a companion/friend [*chaver*] and judge all people favorably" (1:6). Here, we find three separate pieces of advice. First, ask yourself: *Who is my teacher? Where does my teaching come from?* Then ask: *Am I alone? Do I have colleagues? Do I love them—are they a true* chaver? *Can we teach in collaboration?* These are very powerful questions for reflection. In my experience, when I collaborate, the process is more about teaching and less about me. When a solo teacher is particularly charismatic or unduly self-centered, the teacher's personality can overtake and diminish the teaching. That is unfortunate because it takes away from the teaching and places the focus on the teacher. When I collaborate with someone I really love, I am less likely to be competitive. I am eager for my co-teacher to be well-received and eloquent and inspire me to greater depth. I get pleasure from just being together, which radiates to the students. The feeling of joy creates the best atmosphere for wisdom to enter.

The third piece of advice reflects on the qualities of heart we seek to incorporate into our teaching. It asks us to see the best in each student, to see their goodness. We may be tempted to make a broad statement: "*You are this type of person*"—perhaps even focusing on a negative trait. We are deeply conditioned to rush to judgment of ourselves and others.

When that occurs, it is wise to just note what is happening right now, to look for what is right and good, and ask about what is going well. This piece of advice is easy to forget; it is easy to focus on that which is not right rather than focus on what is going well. After all, we live in a very judgmental and competitive world filled with stereotypes and opinions of self and other.

## The Value of Silence

One of the most powerful tools in dealing with rushing judgment and cultivating wisdom is silence. Our ancient rabbis understood this. Shimon his son says: "All my life, I was brought up among the sages and I have not found anything better for the physical welfare of a person than silence. Study is not the most important thing, but practice is, and too much talk brings sin" (1:17).

This is hardly the way our world works. We are so constantly bombarded by noise, news, and opinions. How can we understand silence as a gift to others and as a gift to oneself? Silence is valuable especially when one does not have the answer, or when one wants to rush in and save and fix, or when the desire to figure out whatever is going on keeps arising. There is power in silence. In silence we can rest in the energy of the body in this moment. We can see impermanence, how everything arises, and everything passes. We can see non-separation, how nothing really stands alone but is a cause and condition of something else. We are indeed interconnected. We can make room for something that is truer than our immediate anxiety to know the answer. We can make room for wisdom to arise.

However, silence can also trigger discomfort, fear, a sense of punishment. "WAIT" is an acronym I really love. It stands for "Why Am I Talking?" It is a practice of attention and inquiry into habit. Talking can be a habit to cover anxiety and discomfort. When I notice that I seem to be going on and on, especially with someone I would like to help, I pause and ask this question of myself, "Why Am I Talking?" Often the answer will be because I am afraid. Because I am not comfortable. Because I want to please, or make myself or the other feel better in this moment. The practice, the action, is noticing where the mind is going and then allowing some space. Perhaps the balm of silence is what is the most healing. Silence may be inviting wisdom.

All traditions ask: "What is right or righteous speech?" Here, in *Pirkei Avot*, it is stated sharply: *"too much talk brings sin."* The Buddha's dharma invites us to ask questions before speaking: Is it truthful? Is it necessary to say? Is it the appropriate time? Can it be said in a kind way? If we were indeed to practice this form of speaking, there is no doubt there would be less said and less hurt induced. This surely is a practice to cultivate wisdom.

I especially notice this practice with loved ones and with students. With my most beloveds, I am so invested in their happiness that I have a tendency to jump into giving advice or trying to save them. I also know them so well that their preferences or habits might conflict with mine. I notice that it is usually not helpful to speak when I am annoyed. Rather, pause, observe the annoyance, and then see what the wise or helpful thing is to say.

With students, I have so much invested in their understanding what I communicate or teach that I might jump in before they have a chance to absorb what I am saying. It is wiser to pause and ask—*"How does this sit with you?" "How are you feeling?"*—than rushing right on.

## Practices of Intention, Restraint, and Humility

This next text deepens and develops the practice even further. Hillel said: "Do not set yourself apart from the community. Do not be sure of yourself until the day of your death. Do not judge your fellow person until you have been in his/her position; do not say of any word that it cannot possibly be heard, for in the end it will be heard. And do not say: 'When I have leisure I will study,' for you may never have leisure" (2:5). One cannot be sure of oneself because of the very fact of impermanence, and the absence of an unchanging self. There is nothing absolute to rely on. We see that it is all coming and going when we take the time to observe our minds, our bodies, the worlds we inhabit. Our strength and confidence come from our own practice and our own presence. This is a teaching about humility which is a core quality discussed in many traditions and sometimes misunderstood. According to the Jewish ethical tradition known as *Mussar*, humility is limiting oneself to an appropriate place while leaving room for others. It is a balanced understanding of oneself between the extremes of self-debasement and arrogance.[1] Humility is also one of the eight pillars

---

1. Morinis, *Everyday Holiness*, 49–50.

of joy as presented in *The Book of Joy*, that is a recording of the teachings of the Dalai Lama and Bishop Tutu in conversation.

Abram's understanding is reflective of the *Pirkei Avot* quote: "*The Dalai Lama and the Archbishop were both insistent that humility is essential to any possibility of joy. When we have a wider perspective, we have a natural understanding of our place in the greater sweep of all that was, is, and will be. This naturally leads to humility and the recognition that as human beings we cannot solve everything or control all aspects of life. We need others.*"[2] One way to show humility is to say: "*I don't know*" and be willing to investigate and return with a more complete answer. Showing and admitting limitations is powerful and it is not putting oneself down. There is a Jewish teaching that Mount Sinai, the holy mountain where the revelation occurred, is considered lowly. The teaching goes like this:

> *Therefore, the Holy Blessed One disregarded all of the mountains and hills and rested the Divine presence on the lowly Mount Sinai and did not choose to raise Mt Sinai up toward God's self. Rather the Divine chose to give the Torah on Mt Sinai, as it was a symbol of humility, due to its lack of height, and God lowered the Divine presence, as it were, to the mountain.* (Talmud Sotah 5a:8)

Another saying reenforces the sense of humility. Rabbi Yochanan ben Zakkai received the tradition from Hillel and Shammai. He used to say: "If you have learned a great deal of Torah, do not pride yourself in it, because you were created for this purpose" (2:9). We are encouraged to remember all the factors that we did not create that have blessed us in this life. That, too, is wisdom.

## Patience Yields Wisdom, but It Is Not Hard Wired

Hillel says: "A person without patience cannot teach" (2:6). The cultivation of patience is essential to practice, to wisdom, and to teaching. It comes right after humility in the *Mussar's* list of qualities. Alan Morinis writes that patience is a tool

> *we can call upon to help us endure when we find ourselves in difficult circumstances we did not choose and cannot avoid. The Hebrew word for patience is* savlanut, *which can also mean "tolerance." The same root gives rise to words that mean "suffer" and "endure" and also the noun for a porter who carries goods. We can*

---

2. Dalai Lama and Tutu, *Book of Joy*, 224.

*learn something fundamental from this pool of words that derive from the common source: patience means enduring and tolerating, and the experience may even have elements of suffering.*[3]

When we practice meditation, one of the early instructions is to be with what is arising without judgment, whether it is pleasant or unpleasant. I remember how incredibly hard this is when pain arises at a long meditation retreat. Every part of me wants to figure it out, move, worry about the future calamity I will face, or just do something. To sit without judgment is so much easier said than done. Patience is needed to be with the unpleasant. The more we can truly assimilate the idea of impermanence—this unpleasant sensation or thought will not last because nothing lasts—the more we can cultivate patience. Our tendency is to see everything as solid and everlasting which, of course, it is not. Patience might be most akin to the quality of acceptance when compared with the eight pillars of the Dalai Lama and Archbishop Tutu. "*So many of the causes of suffering come from our reacting to the people, places, things, and circumstances of our lives, rather than accepting them. When we react, we stay locked in judgment and criticism, anxiety, and despair, even denial and addiction. It is impossible to experience joy when we are stuck in this way. Acceptance is the sword that cuts through all of this resistance, allowing us to relax, to see clearly, and to respond appropriately.*"[4] Is this not wisdom?

## Loving God and Loving Ourselves

One of my favorite sayings in *Pirkei Avot* is attributed to Rabbi Akiba. He was an extraordinary teacher and leader and is known for insisting that the immortal love poem the Song of Songs be included in the Hebrew Bible canon. He believed it was of infinite value. We can see the connection between love and wisdom in this teaching. He used to say: "Beloved is the human being for he/she was created in the image of God. It was an act of special favor that it was disclosed to her/him that he/she was created in God's image, as it is said: 'For in the image of God did God create the human' (Gen 9:6)" (3:18). Akiba implores us to remember to honor and love ourselves as divine beings full of goodness. How do we do that? By staying connected to the infinite value that we each contain, beyond any measurements. How do we open to the power of the highest, the

---

3. Morinis, *Everyday Holiness*, 57–58.
4. Dalai Lama and Tutu, *Book of Joy*, 225.

eternal, field of care? This is the purpose of our study and our practice! Later in the text we read: "When love depends on achieving a certain goal, love vanishes when that goal is achieved; but a love which is not dependent on any goal, never vanishes" (5:18). How do we encourage ourselves and each other to tap into this deep sense of worthiness that is ever present? What experiences in our lives, what memories of places and people can we evoke to bring us into this reality?

In his book *Tattoos on the Heart: The Power of Boundless Compassion*, Father Gregory Boyle describes working with gangs in LA. He helps them establish a workplace, a community, and kinship. He writes that the main tool as a teacher is love: "*Everybody is just looking to be told that who they are is right and true and wholly acceptable. No need to tinker and tweak.*"[5] In *Listening to the Heart: A Contemplative Journey to Engaged Buddhism*, Thanissara and Kittisaro write: "*When our wounds are received with loving-kindness, the possibility of redemption and healing does indeed emerge.*"[6] In *The Book of Joy*, the Dalai Lama echoes Rabbi Akiba: "*On this planet, over the last three thousand years, different religious traditions developed. All these traditions carry the same message: the message of love.*" The archbishop chimes in: "*We are actually quite remarkable creatures. In our religion I am created in the image of God. I am a God carrier. It's fantastic. I have to be growing in godlikeness, in caring for the other. I know that each time I act compassionately, I have experienced a joy in me that I find in nothing else.*"[7] Again, and again, we are reminded that we are not alone in this life. We depend upon each other. We return to the first pieces of wisdom we began with—find a teacher, find a friend, do not separate yourself from the community.

## Karma and the End of Karma

Another teaching of Rabbi Akiba: "Everything is foreseen, yet freedom of choice is granted" (3:19). Our brains are set by our habits, and in every moment of awareness we can change the pattern. This suggests that wisdom emerges from awareness. By training our minds in awareness, we can see more and more of the patterns and habits. Sometimes these come from generations before us. They were established to protect us and our

---

5. Boyle, *Tattoos on the Heart*, 71.
6. Thanissara and Kittisaro, *Listening to the Heart*, 210.
7. Dalai Lama and Tutu, *Book of Joy*, 257.

ancestors. But we may come to recognize that they do not protect us now. Rather they separate us or lead us to foolishness. In Buddhism these patterns are called karma. The goal of cultivating attention and attaining inner freedom is to end the transmission of these patterns, to end karma.

As we become more aware, we can tell the truth. In Hebrew, the word for truth is *emet*. It is made up of three letters in the Hebrew alphabet—*aleph*, the first letter, *mem*, the middle letter, and *tav*, the final letter. We learn to see beginnings and endings truthfully. But awareness and truth can be harsh, upsetting, frightening. Because of this we also need to cultivate the quality of *chesed*, lovingkindness. When we bring loving awareness, truth and kindness merge. They support and enhance each other.

As previously mentioned, the authors of *Pirkei Avot* were teachers. They were especially concerned with transmitting wisdom to their students. They saw the world as made up of classrooms and learners. The learning they wished to transmit was inner wisdom. How they transmitted wisdom was more important to them than the content itself. This notion of the "how" above the "what" is pertinent today in our practice, our teaching and our understanding. We might have the holiest and highest ideals, but if they are presented with force, hate, anger, impatience, they are not going to be received and their form will deny their content. In our era, the questions surrounding "what's" are very easy to find. We Google, we search, we touch the screen .and infinite information pours forth. The "how's" might be more elusive.

## The Wisdom of Respect

Rabbi Elazar ben Shamua teaches: "The dignity of your student should be as precious to you as your own. The dignity of your colleague should be as precious to you as your reverence for your teacher. The reverence for your teacher should be as great as the reverence for God [*shamayim*]" (4:15). I see this as an expansion of the idea of each of us being created in the Divine image. How do we keep remembering this?

Rabbi Shimon ben Elazar teaches: "Do not pacify your colleague when his anger is raging. Do not comfort him when his dead lies before him. Do not challenge him at the time he makes his vow. Do not intrude upon him at the time of his disgrace" (4:23). How do we know when and how to intervene appropriately with our students or our colleagues when they are in emotionally difficult places? How do we develop the inner quiet to restrain our need to help, control, set straight, etc.? We have seen this before in the discussion of the value of silence. How do we speak what needs to be said so that it will be heard? This is wisdom. We meet our friend who has suddenly lost her partner. We blurt out: "*How are you feeling?*" We are trying to be kind and friendly, but in some ways this is a foolish question. In Jewish mourning practice, we are told to sit in silence until the mourner begins to speak. This actually offers more support and comfort than random babbling and questioning.

## Where Do We Stray?

Another teaching from Rabbi Elazar Ha-Kappar: "Envy, lust and pursuit of honor will ruin a person's life" (4:28). Ultimately these are outcomes of different kinds of desire gone astray. When we cultivate awareness, we see that the desire for the pleasant which we all possess can yield sometimes to envy, and lust and the pursuit of honor, wanting what we do not have.

These mind states come without intention or control. When we see them with kindness, we can become free of them. We can recognize them as unwholesome states of mind. Does this happen easily? No. "*How do we see the wholesome path?*" a student asked her teacher. "*Well, you also have to see the unwholesome path many times and recognize that you can make another choice.*" We are back to remembering, practicing, training the mind, and being part of a supportive, wisdom-seeking community. Working with these mind states is the practice. Here are two of the most popular and oft quoted lines in *Pirkei Avot*.

Hillel says: "If I am not for myself, who will be for me? And if I am for myself only, what am I? And if not now, when?" (1:14). This summarizes a wise life. We must take responsibility for our lives. We must take care of ourselves. However, we cannot lose sight of the contexts and structures in which we live. We cannot lose sight of others who have less or more, others whose wisdom and comfort we rely upon and who rely upon us. When is the time to act? When we are ready to act, we must act. Delay and doubt do not serve us in the cultivation of wisdom or in creating a life of value and joy. Now is the time to cultivate the qualities we seek. Now is the time for gratitude and discernment for freedom and connection for seeing the obstacles and allowing them to dissolve in the greater field of compassion.

And finally, Rabbi Tarphon says: "It is not up to you to complete the work, yet you are not free to desist from it" (2:21). This might be the wisest and most helpful teaching in *Pirkei Avot*. It reminds us that we are not able to finish the work of this lifetime. It is limited. We may have great aspirations and visions for transformations of personal and societal scope. That is great. We are encouraged to do our work. To get clear what our contribution is and make the efforts we can, giving the very real limitations of this life. There are limitations in time and energy and pure physicality. It is a paradox and a source of wisdom to know that we are empowered to act for the best and yet we will not see the end results. This need not be a cause of despair, but rather an expansion of perspective that is sustaining. In fact, the Dalai Lama and the archbishop see this as a crucial factor in creating a life of joy, which is also a life of value and connection. They call this *"the first attribute—perspective."* This is what Rabbi Tarphon is talking about as well.

Again, quoting *The Book of Joy*, as the Dalai Lama and the archbishop explained:

> The wider perspective leads to serenity and equanimity. It does not mean we don't have the strength to confront a problem, but we can confront it with creativity and compassion rather than rigidity and reactivity. When we take the perspective of others, we can empathize with them. One starts to see the interdependence that envelops us all, which reveals that how we treat others is ultimately how we treat ourselves. We are also able to recognize that we do not control all aspects of any situation. This leads us to a greater sense of humility, humor and acceptance.[8]

## A Summary, Perhaps?

Here is a final text which summarizes and enhances this exploration of ancient wisdom:

Ben Zoma said: "Who is strong? One who masters his impulse/inclination [*yetzar*] . . . Who is rich? One who rejoices in what s/he has" (4:1). The wisdom of these simple lines speaks to the relation and balance between aspiration and acceptance, effort and relaxation, compassion and mindfulness. The first phrase affirms that we value growth in character, in wholesome, connecting, and life-affirming qualities. These

---

8. Dalai Lama and Tutu, *Book of Joy*, 201.

are our aspirations. We engage in an active process of cultivating the qualities that soften the unwholesome parts of our nature like greed, hatred, and other forms of selfishness and reactivity. It takes strength to practice loving kindness, generosity, and compassion. It takes courage to be responsive and not reactive.

In the second phrase, rejoicing in one's lot is the practice of gratitude or acceptance of what we have received. This is akin to mindfulness. We see what is true in our lives without pushing it away, tuning it out, or clamoring for something else. We are curious and open, soft, and receptive. This stance is conducive to happiness. We have what we need. This is being rich. It frees us from tension, excessive ambition, and conflict, major causes of unhappiness. Both aspiration and acceptance depend on seeing clearly as we claim our freedom and our power. They are the foundation of training the mind and heart. This is the center of spiritual practice.

There are many more beautiful teachings in *Pirkei Avot*, but what I find most enduring and meaningful is the encouragement that we really can shift our perspective, we can learn to love more deeply, we can be liberated from our destructive habits, and we can change our minds to be more whole and ultimately more fully human. This is the pathway to a world of peace and justice. May we have the strength and courage to follow this ancient wisdom. Our world cries out for it.

## Deeper Conversation/Deeper Listening

1. The *Pirkei Avot* provides directives on how to develop wisdom through our interactions and practices. How do the directives align with your personal beliefs about wisdom?
2. What spiritual practice could be developed and used as spiritual directors from this knowledge?
3. Reflect on the power, potential, and risks of silence in your life as you cultivate wisdom.
4. How do you see humility as connected to wisdom cultivation?
5. Who are your important wisdom teachers and how do they operate in your life?

# Bibliography

Boyle, Gregory. *Tattoos on the Heart: The Power of Boundless Compassion.* New York: Free Press, 2010.

The Dalai Lama, and Desmond Tutu, with Douglas Abrams. *The Book of Joy.* New York: Avery, 2016.

Morinis, Alan. *Everyday Holiness.* New York: Trumpeter, 2007.

Sefaria. "Pirkei Avot." https://www.sefaria.org/Pirkei_Avot?tab=contents.

Thanissara and Kittisaro. *Listening to the Heart: A Contemplative Journey to Engaged Buddhism.* New York: North Atlantic Books, 2014.

## *Chapter 14*
# Expanding on Spiritual Eldering
## A Quaker-Hindu Dialogue

PREETA M. BANERJEE, PHD

*Preeta Banerjee is a spiritual companion who draws on a broad and deep range of experience, having spent over twenty years in academia, coaching, and consulting as an advocate, educator, researcher, and author. She is a strong voice for combining spirituality, creativity, innovation, entrepreneurship, and social change. Her passion lies in creating brave spaces at the intersection of contemplation, activism, and healing and deepening in interreligious manyness from a lens rooted in bhakti, gyan, karma, and raj yoga, including her work as the first Hindu chaplain at Tufts University and as a founding board member of the North American Hindu Chaplains Association. She has a PhD in strategic management from the Wharton School, a BS in computational biology and business from Carnegie Mellon, and a graduate certificate in interreligious studies from Hartford International University for Religion and Peace.*

IT WAS ONE OF our first formal meetings as 2019–20 Hebrew College Miller Center Boston Bridges Fellows. I had the opportunity to be led in silence by a fellow who did not attend the program afterward for reasons I know not. Yet it was a meeting that will remain with me for a long time; it was my first encounter with the spiritual eldering with a Quaker. I was intrigued by the similarity to sitting in meditation within my practices as a Hindu. I immediately became drawn to Quaker teachings as I hoped to learn more about the role of spiritual eldering in listening to one's inner light.

In this chapter, I explore an understanding of spiritual eldering gained through interviews with Quaker colleagues, readings of Quaker writings, and experiences with Quaker meetings. While I hold myself to practice "the platinum rule" of treating Quakers as they would like to be treated, I understand my limitations as a practitioner-scholar of the Hindu worldview. As eloquently described by my mentor, Dr. Lucinda Mosher, in her description of *"religious manyness and pluralism," "we can't help but view, hear, and understand the religious other from our religious perspective. We always stand somewhere when we meet; we always start at a location when we move. No matter how open-minded we are, we assess the truth and beauty of another religion according to our, rather than its criteria."* That said, there is much to learn from this Quaker-Hindu dialogue that expands the concept of spiritual eldering. In today's world, examining comparative faiths, including the ability to engage in spiritual eldering of ancestors and nature, is necessary.

## What Is Spiritual Eldering?

The term *spiritual eldering* can be found very closely linked to the practices of the Quaker tradition, also known as the Religious Society of Friends. Before delving into the specifics of spiritual eldering, I found it essential to understand more about Quakers' theological doctrine. I found this quote to be most representative of what I heard in interviews and experienced with Quaker doctrine:

> *The primary theological doctrine and spiritual experience of Friends is that the living Christ is present to teach us Himself. No priestly intermediary is necessary for Divine access, for "there is One, Christ Jesus, who can speak to thy condition."*[1]

Rooted in such texts as John's prologue, Quakers believe that the Light of Christ is given in some measure to all people. This experience of the immediate presence of Christ, both personally and corporately, implies

---

1. Grace, "Eden Grace on Quaker Business Practice," §3.

that the Inward Teacher may lead us. Since Christ is not divided, the nearer we come to him, the closer we will be to one another. Thus, the sense of being led into Unity with one another becomes a fundamental mark of the Divine work in the world.

I resonated deeply with the direct experience of inner knowing that is accessible to all people—the Inner Guru. And by knowing this Divinity within us, we come to see the Divinity within each other and to Unity. Like drops of water that flow in tributaries to the seas, we are all one with the vastness.

## How Is Spiritual Eldering Practiced in Quakerism?

In Quakerism, the expectation is that everyone equally participates in ministry. As people gather in the presence of God for service in worship, all barriers of inequality must be brought down.[2] While there are different branches of Quakerism, and not all gather in silence (as I first experienced in 2019) where one can meet the Mystery without the trappings of words and where Quakers listen for the still, small voice that comes from God.[3]

As Greg Woods described to me about "*waiting for worship*," Quakers wait for a time when they feel called to give/hear messages from God. Anyone—adult or child—may feel inspired to give vocal ministry (speak out of the silence). After the person speaks the message, the silence resumes. Such messages may be offered several times during a meeting for worship, or the whole period of worship may be silent. Someone will signal the close of worship by shaking hands with another person, and then everyone shakes hands with those seated nearby.

In this light, elders have a fundamental role. Eldering is a gift that is often informally witnessed, cultivated, and uplifted. Elders are responsible for the growth of the religious life of the meeting, encouraging and initiating opportunities for learning more about the life of the Spirit, growing in wisdom, and carefully listening and sharing insights. Eldership is not defined by age, though elders are typically Friends who are well-versed in the Quaker process and possess ministry gifts. As one member describes it, elders are reminders of personal accountability; when a Friend calls a clearness committee (a discernment committee),

2. Malande, "Concept of Hierarchy."
3. Anderson, "Meeting for Worship."

and elders show up, it reminds one to persevere. Quakers use queries for personal reflection, self-examination, or spirited discussion. Thus, this account harkens to the word *integrity*, and it is described as *"the need to deal honestly with all others and with oneself has long been a foundational belief among Friends."*[4] I recently had such a transforming experience of persevering in discernment through a clearness committee on vocation and appreciated the depth that such inquiries can lend to difficult moments of discernment.

## Expanding on Spiritual Eldering through Dialogue

Dialogue is defined as a relationship of openness and trust that is clear, unambiguous, and has no other purpose than itself.[5] Dialogue is my method of being in the world and achieving spiritual growth and understanding. In particular, this dialogue on spiritual eldering in the form of a publication is an "internal dialogue,"[6] within a practitioner-scholar of the Hindu worldview who has experienced and studied the practices mentioned above from the Quaker tradition and has the desire to deepen existing roots and expand the concept and usefulness of spiritual eldering in practice toward religious manyness and pluralism.[7]

Let us move toward understanding the Hindu lens in this dialogue. As Dr. Anant Rambachan describes: "What is spoken of today as 'Hinduism' is an astonishingly diverse phenomenon . . . the term has been used at different times, and even at the same time, to signify geographical, religious, culture and, in recent times, national realities . . . It is helpful to think of Hinduism as a family name, recognizable through shared features, but preserving also the uniqueness of its individual members."[8]

As Dr. Rambachan goes on to describe, the Hindu tradition does not require membership in a congregation or denomination, does not offer a creedal statement (Quakerism also does not have creeds) to which one must subscribe in order to be admitted, does not have a single ritual, does not excommunicate. Instead, the word *dharma* encompasses the way of life, the sacred spaces and rituals, the food and

---

4. Annapolis Friends Meeting, "Our Values," §6.
5. Lochhead, *Dialogical Imperative*.
6. Pitman, "Quaker Symbolism and Ritual."
7. Mosher, "Episcopal Church Religious Manyness."
8. Rambachan, "Worship, Public Good," 108.

eating practices, dress, arts, occupation, beliefs, values, and practices that promote our human flourishing.

There is a role for the ancestors and nature; it is our personal responsibility and integrity during self-inquiry in silence, as well as highlighting the role of spiritual eldering in the Hindu practices of silence called meditation. Spiritual discernment for Quakers is heightened in many ways by the role of spiritual eldering, just as meditating is heightened with the role of ancestors and nature.

## Spiritual Eldering Through Ancestors

When speaking of ancestors, we might immediately jump to genetic predecessors, our biological mothers and fathers, their biological mothers and fathers, and so on. Our body, therefore, creates a physical tie to prior wisdom. There is an additional element of spiritual eldering with ancestors to explore, precisely that of reincarnation. By reincarnation, I refer to the concept that the everlasting energetic essence of a living being can begin a new life in a different physical form after physical death.

The association between Hinduism and ancestor worship (special ceremonies paying homage to the deceased) can be traced back to one of the oldest scriptures, the *Vedas*. *Veda* means "knowledge," and there are four Vedas, each with their respective area of discourse: Rg Veda (the oldest collection of the four, includes the Vedic sciences—like the practice of yoga, meditation, mantra, and Ayurveda), Sama Veda (includes approaches to music and ways of singing), Yajur Veda (includes approaches to different rituals and customs), and Atharva Veda (the most recent of the four, includes practical issues of daily life of the Vedic society like protecting crops from lightning and drought). Matthew Sayers studies the development of ancestor worship. He finds mention in the Rg Veda about the *pitr-yajna* or Sacrifice to Ancestors (RV 10.16.10–11), where the moment of culmination in the cremation of the deceased is a first offering as an Ancestor.[9] Siobhan Banwari finds that though these early texts of the Vedas anticipate the doctrine of reincarnation, the idea is not fully developed until the Upanishads.[10] Also known as Vedanta ("the end of the Vedas"), the Upanishads are a collection of philosophical texts that form a theoretical basis for the Hindu worldview and reincarnation. In

---

9. Sayers, "Śrāddha."
10. Banwari, "Theory of Reincarnation."

this light, we hold the scientific genes of genetic ancestors, spiritual ties to former lives, and genetic ancestry.

In terms of the spiritual eldering of ancestors, many Hindus attribute their devotion and the accompanying actions to faith in ancestors. Also, most families, believing in reincarnation, maintain connections to their ancestors who are physically dead, believing that the Spirit of the ancestor remains alive, watching over, protecting, and guiding them. Thus, meditation is an opportunity to connect with that wisdom and guidance. For example, a beautiful closing ritual of our 2019 Mystic Soul Project annual conference was led by Sojourner Zenobia. We were meditating and then asked to pick an item from the altar. I saw an ancestor in my meditation and was drawn to pick tobacco from the altar, not knowing why. Later that day, my father sent me an article about our ancestor who had a temple for the only Krishna holding a hookah to which you bring tobacco as a gift, unknowingly confirming the presence of that ancestor in my earlier meditation that day.

## Spiritual Eldering through Nature

We might immediately think of the scenic view outside our window when speaking of nature. The colors and rhythm of life outside our own might calm and connect us. There is an additional element of spiritual eldering with nature to explore, specifically that of animism. By animism, I refer to the concept that all things have a spiritual essence—animated and alive.

The association between Hinduism and nature worship can also be traced back to the Vedas. The Rg Veda (described above) speaks to the *Pancha-Bhuta* (Sanskrit: पञ्चभूत: five elements) and material reality as manifested through *Prithvi* (Sanskrit: पृथ्वी: earth), *aap* (Sanskrit: अप: water), *Agni* (Sanskrit: अग्नि: fire), *Vayu* (Sanskrit: वायु: air), and *aakaashaa* (Sanskrit: आकाश: space). Not seen as abstractions or metaphors, there is the relationship between body, Divinity, and relationships with nature.

As Christopher Key Chapple writes:

> The Mokshadharmaparvan, one of the books of the Mahabharata epic, summarizes the relationship between body and cosmos first articulated in the Rg Veda and the Brhadaranyaka Upanishad: The Lord, the sustainer of all beings, revealed the

sky. From space came water and from water fire and the winds. From the mixture of the essence of fire and wind arose the earth. Mountains are his bones, earth his flesh, the ocean his blood. The sky is his abdomen, air his breath, fire his heart, rivers his nerves. The sun and moon, which are called Agni and Soma, are the eyes of Brahman. The upper part of the sky is his head. The earth is his feet, and the directions are his hands.[11]

Amita Sinha elaborates that this representation of the cosmos (plant, animal, minerals, sun, moon, and planets) in a human form is duplicated in art, architecture, and landscape, expanding to the Gods and Goddesses and the animal vehicles by their side: *"Every Hindu God and Goddess has an animal as his or her vehicle. This means that the animal is associated with that God's Divinity and symbolizes the chief virtue for which he or she is renowned."*[12] Across distinctions and divisions, Hinduism's relationship with nature is a vehicle or conduit for divine manifestation. It is regarded as sacred, venerated rather than controlled, deified, and invoked instead of bent to human will.[13] I have sat in front of a campfire and tended its peaceful burn as an inner meditation to my fire, not letting too much wind and wood, such as ideas and thoughts, swirl into a wildfire and not letting lack of wind and wood put the fire out.

## Silence, Meditation, Spiritual Discernment, and Spiritual Eldering with Ancestors and Nature

Throughout the Quaker tradition is an ethos of spiritual discernment. In dialogue with spiritual discernment, I refer to the Sanskrit word *Viveka* (Sanskrit: विवेक), right judgment or wisdom on the spiritual path, allowing us to discover what is real or unreal, illusions, *Maya* (Sanskrit: माया). This is the light in which I turn to meditation as the Hindu version of silent worship. In my studies of the Yoga Instructors Course (YIC) with Swami Vivekananda Yoga Anusandhana Samsthana (S-VYASA), as studied under Mr. Sudhir Parikh, I explored the experiencing and embodying of the Divine in meditation.[14] As mentioned before, Quakers also talk about that of God in everyone. In this exploration, through dialogue

---

11. Chapple and Tucker, *Hinduism and Ecology*, 271.
12. Das, "Vehicles of the Hindu Gods," §1.
13. King, "Religion as Practice."
14. Banerjee, "Experiencing and Embodying the Divine."

between Hindu and Quaker traditions, I expand on how we sit in silence and what we do in meditation.

What meditators do when they meditate is precisely the study undertaken by Karin Matko, Ulrich Ott, and Peter Sedlmeier. They find exciting distinctions between the two main categories of meditators (Hindus and Buddhists):

> Both top-10 lists have only three meditation techniques in common: observing the respiratory flow, observing the abdomen while breathing, and scanning the body. All other techniques differ and reflect tradition-specific preferences for techniques. Buddhist meditators prefer observing thoughts or emotions, walking meditation, and cultivating compassion or lovingkindness. Hindu meditators, on the other hand, practice singing or reciting mantras, concentrating on locations in the body or "energy centers," and manipulating the breath.[15]

What a rich intersection for dialogue is suggested that practices while meditating for Hindus could create more space for listening to the Divine voice within.

How can our Hindu, Quaker, or spiritually fluid practices integrate these learnings? First, we need to acknowledge the importance of spiritual eldering in our lives. As Greg Woods writes: "We need Friends who are willing to be eldered when needed."[16] Second, whether a Quaker meeting or a Hindu meditation, let us make a deliberate effort to connect to the natural world around us consciously. Whether in the city, country, the mountains, or the coast, we find a sacred place and feel a connection using our senses. By allowing our senses to heighten our awareness, we can thus receive guidance and wisdom (a type of spiritual eldering) from nature. Let us listen beyond the veil with spiritual openness to ask for guidance from our ancestors. Listening has different dimensions, and we can receive messages with our hearts and heads. Fourth, let us embrace the mysticism—the direct experience of the Divine—present in many traditions, including Quaker and Hindu practices and beyond.

In conclusion, this dialogue lends insights in all directions; as our overseers and elders, we can connect with our ancestors as spiritual elders help us remember the wisdom from past lives and similarly listen to nature's wisdom. And sitting in silent worship, we can tend to our

---

15. Matko, Ott, and Sedlmeier, "What Do Meditators Do," 1800.
16. Woods, "Need for Eldering," §1.

spiritual discernment with the accountability and integrity modeled by the Quaker tradition. Friends turn to each other in community, Scripture, and inward, leading to tune into the belief that God works through our intellects. We must expand our discernment to gain a fuller perspective of what is within us and before us. Expanding our sources of discernment raises our vibration and opens our senses to new hues, tones, and vibrations—while Dr. Lucinda Mosher is accurate in naming that we will continually assess through ourselves what we stand to gain from dialogue and the respectful connection is potentially a larger self, a more appreciative and colorful self—equipped for more profound understanding, and deeper connections.

## Deeper Conversation/Deeper Listening

1. What opportunities have you experienced to dialogue with someone from a different faith?
2. How did the dialogue change or enlighten you about your own spirituality?
3. How can such opportunities for dialogue be used to expand your spiritual practice?

## Spiritual Practice

1. First, find a comfortable position. Perhaps sit upright in a chair with your feet flat on the floor or sit cross-legged and straight-backed on a meditation cushion.
2. Second, let your gaze soften or your eyes close, and begin to notice your breath. You can count to four on your exhale, pause for four, count to four on your inhale, and pause for four. When doing this, picture the four sides of a square and repeat.
3. Third, take note of any thoughts and feelings that arise. Whenever you notice that a thought or feeling has taken your attention away from the breath, with compassion and care, name it and return to following the breath.
4. Fourth, when you feel your body, mind, and spirit at ease, you can ask for any guidance that is helpful to arise. After a comfortable

amount of time receiving, you can begin to end your meditation practice. Slowly return to normal breath, wiggle your fingers and toes, and open your eyes. You can write down any guidance you received and consciously allow the sense of calm and ease to remain present through the rest of your day.

## Bibliography

American Friends Service Committee. "An Introduction to Quaker Testimonies." Sep 2011. https://www.afsc.org/sites/default/files/documents/AFSC-Quaker-Testimonies.pdf.

Anderson, Paul. "The Meeting for Worship in Which Business Is Conducted—Quaker Decision-Making Process as a Factor of Spiritual Discernment." *Quaker Religious Thought* 106.1 (2006) 4. https://digitalcommons.georgefox.edu/cgi/viewcontent.cgi?article=1106&context=qrt.

Annapolis Friends Meeting. "Our Values." https://annapolisfriends.org/beliefs/spices/.

Banerjee, Preeta. "Experiencing and Embodying the Divine with Om and Cyclic Meditation" Yoga Instructors Course, 2019.

Banwari, Siobhan. "The Theory of Reincarnation and the Journey of the Soul: A Comparison between Ancient Greek and Indian Belief." Diss., University of KwaZulu-Natal, Howard College Campus, South Africa, 2015. https://ukzn-dspace.ukzn.ac.za/bitstream/handle/10413/12707/Banwari_Siobhan_2015.pdf?sequence=1&isAllowed=y.

Cairns, Rebecca. "Dharmic Environmentalism: Hindu Traditions and Ecological Care." Diss., Memorial University of Newfoundland, 2020. https://research.library.mun.ca/14660/1/thesis.pdf.

Chapple, Christopher Key, and Mary Evelyn Tucker. *Hinduism and Ecology: The Intersection of Earth, Sky, and Water*. Cambridge: International Society for Science and Religion, 2007.

Das, Subhamoy. "Vehicles of the Hindu Gods: The Vahanas." Learn Religions, Feb 8, 2021. learnreligions.com/vehicles-of-the-gods-1770297.

Friends General Conference. https://www.fgcquaker.org/resources/defining-eldership.

Grace, Eden. "Eden Grace on Quaker Business Practice." World Council of Churches, Mar 8, 2000. https://www.oikoumene.org/resources/documents/eden-grace-on-quaker-business-practice.

King, Sallie B. "Religion as Practice: A Zen-Quaker Internal Dialogue." *Buddhist-Christian Studies* 14 (1994) 157–62. https://www.jstor.org/stable/1389832.

Lochhead, David. *The Dialogical Imperative: A Christian Reflection on Interfaith Encounter*. Maryknoll, NY: Orbis, 1988.

Longkumer, Arkotong. "Is Hinduism the World's Largest Indigenous Religion?" In *Handbook of Indigenous Religion(s)*, 263–78. Brill Handbooks on Contemporary Religion 15. Brill, 2017. https://doi.org/10.1163/9789004346710_017.

Malande, Oscar Lugusa. "The Concept of Hierarchy and Doing Ministry in the Church: Evaluating the Roles of Leaders and the Use of Authority in Quakerism." *Quaker Religious Thought* 133.1 (2019) 32–41. https://digitalcommons.georgefox.edu/cgi/viewcontent.cgi?article=2403&context=qrt.

Matko, Karin, Ulrich Ott, and Peter Sedlmeier. "What Do Meditators Do When They Meditate? Proposing a Novel Basis for Future Meditation Research." *Mindfulness* 12 (2021) 1791–811. https://link.springer.com/content/pdf/10.1007/s12671-021-01641-5.pdf.

Mosher, Lucinda Allen. "The Episcopal Church Religious Manyness: Steps toward a Theology." *Anglican Theological Review* 96.1 (2014) 57–72. http://www.anglicantheologicalreview.org/wp-content/uploads/2020/02/mosher_96.1.pdf.

———. "Public Theology: Characteristics from the Multireligious Neighborhood." *Anglican Theological Review* 102.2 (2020) 251–62.

Pitman, Ruth M. "Quaker Symbolism and Ritual: Communication of Meaning in Quaker Practices." *Quaker Religious Thought* 50.1 (1980) 20–36. https://digitalcommons.georgefox.edu/cgi/viewcontent.cgi?article=2024&context=qrt.

Rambachan, Anantanand. "Worship, the Public Good and Self-Fulfillment: Hindu Perspectives on Calling." *Calling in Today's World: Voices from Eight Faith Perspectives* (2016) 107–32.

Sayers, Matthew R. "The Śrāddha: The Development of Ancestor Worship in Classical Hinduism." *Religion Compass* 9.6 (2015) 182–97. https://doi.org/10.1111/rec3.12155.

Sinha, Amita. "Nature in Hindu Art, Architecture and Landscape." *Landscape Research* 20.1 (1995) 3–10. https://doi.org/10.1080/01426399508706449.

Woods, Greg. "The Need for Eldering." *Friends Journal*, Mar 27, 2013. https://www.friendsjournal.org/the-need-for-eldering/.

## Chapter 15

# Take Me into a Suffering World

MARY GLAZER, MSFL, SPIRITUAL DIRECTOR

*Mary Kay Glazer is a spiritual director, retreat leader, Life-Cycle Celebrant, and writer. Having been raised in the Roman Catholic tradition, she has been a Quaker since 1989. Her background includes a master's degree in spiritual formation and leadership from Spring Arbor University, Shalem Institute's Spiritual Guidance Program, and School of the Spirit's Spiritual Nurture Program. She once was a television news producer, then worked in public relations for various places, including the Susan B. Anthony House in Rochester, New York. She lives in Greenville, North Carolina, with her husband.*

*Jesus, please take me with you into the suffering of the world.
Help me to love the world as you love the world.*
—Mary Kay Glazer

I BELIEVE GOD LAID this prayer on my heart. It was sometime around February 2016. I don't remember exactly how it came to me, but it was not easy to accept. I typically try to avoid the overwhelming, ubiquitous suffering of the world. I resisted this prayer, sensing that it was a dangerous prayer, as it seemed to open the way for a season of suffering in my life. Of course, there has been suffering in my life before this prayer and certainly since. In this instance, though, the painful challenges were especially intense and seemed to be a direct result of the prayer. My experience has led me to wrestle in new ways with the burden of suffering and the question of why God allows suffering in the world.

I am certainly not the first person to try to come to terms with why God allows suffering. Take the biblical book of Job, for example. This book begins with Job being called "blameless and upright, one who feared God and turned away from evil." His life sounds lovely. Until the Adversary and God start talking about him.

> One day the [beings] of God came to stand in attendance before the Lord, and the Adversary, too, came among them. And the Lord said to the Adversary, "From where do you come?" And the Adversary answered the Lord and said, "From roaming the earth and walking about in it." And the Lord said to the Adversary, "Have you paid heed to my servant Job, for there is none like him on earth, a blameless and upright man, who fears God and shuns evil?" And the Adversary answered the Lord, "Does Job fear God for nothing? Have You not hedged him about and his household and all that he has all around? The work of his hands You have blessed, and his flocks have spread over the land. And yet, reach out Your hand, pray, and strike all that he has. Will he not curse You to Your face?" And the Lord said to the Adversary, "Look, all that he has is in your hand. Only against him do not reach out your hand." And the Adversary went out from before the Lord's presence.[1]

Thus begins for Job and his wife suffering upon suffering. The book of Job attempts to address the randomness and meaninglessness of suffering in the world. Job *"is a radical challenge to the doctrine of reward for the righteous and punishment for the wicked."*[2] While the book of Job addresses unfair suffering, according to Alter, it *"is not exactly an answer to the problem because for those who believe that life should not be arbitrary there can be no real answer concerning the good person who loses a child . . . or the blameless dear one who dies in an accident or is stricken with a terrible wasting disease."*[3]

---

1. Alter, *Wisdom Books*, Job 1:6–12.
2. Alter, *Wisdom Books*, 3.
3. Alter, *Wisdom Books*, 10.

## Help Me to Love the World as You Love the World

I don't remember ever thinking of prayer in terms of safety or danger, until I prayed this prayer asking Jesus to take me with him into the suffering of the world. I think God may have led me to this prayer to teach me how to engage with suffering, to help me wrestle with suffering as a reality in our world and in my relationship with God. Wanting to be faithful, I began regularly praying this prayer, somewhat reluctantly and most definitely unaware of what it would bring to me. I have no idea if the prayer itself opened the way for the events that occurred; I only noticed the events that came after I began praying this prayer.

Ash Wednesday was a part of my rhythm of faith. As a Quaker since the late 1980s, I continue to be aware of this day, but it has not been a major part of my faith life for decades. On this particular Ash Wednesday, I had an acupuncture appointment where the acupuncturist was surprised at my low energy readings. He used the needles to give my body a boost. The next day, I felt fatigued and achy and I assumed I was getting the flu.

In the following days and weeks, I suffered from a severe migraine and a potentially life-threatening health issue that required a hospital stay and surgeries. I tried in the midst of the pain to connect with those suffering unbearable pain and to pray for others who were also in pain. I don't think I did a very good job. My pain and suffering were too intense and demanded my attention.

During the following weeks, I continued to experience physical pain. I began fasting followed by food restrictions, I had a heightened awareness of how my privileged life provided me access to amazing healthcare. My personal suffering brought me to a deep encounter with my own vulnerability and frailty. There was more suffering to come in following months, including an unfair job loss and a difficult encounter with law enforcement.

During these days, I often tried praying into the pain, praying into an awareness of the pain of so many others in this world—often a pain without the hope of relief. Too often, I wanted to curse the pain and my vulnerable body. And, I felt afraid of what I had asked for in my prayer—to go with Jesus into the suffering of the world. I felt I couldn't do it! I've spent *a lot* of my life trying to avoid physical and emotional pain, but who hasn't? And yet, looking back on those days, there was a sense that I was walking with Jesus toward the cross and unbearable suffering. Reluctant as I was, I knew that I needed to continue to ask Jesus to take me with him into the world's suffering. I prayed this prayer, even though

I had no idea what I was asking. I prayed, even though I was not sure I had the capacity for how God would answer that prayer. I felt like the sons of Zebedee saying to Jesus that of course they could drink the cup he must drink—yet they had no clue (Matt 20:20–23; Mark 10:35–40). Inasmuch as I can say yes to that cup, it is only because of grace and a God-given desire to be faithful to the call of the Divine.

"Pain is inevitable. Suffering is optional." (I don't even understand this statement. It seems that in our culture and some Christian teachings, there is a false belief that there is a way to live a life without suffering.) The hard truth that I need to face is that suffering is part of the human condition. We see the reality of suffering in Job as well as throughout the Hebrew and Christian scriptures. We see that when our eyes are open to the reality of life in our communities and around the world. We see that in the accounts of those who report from the places where suffering abounds. While this realization could, and sometimes does, lead to despair, there is, surprisingly, a flicker of hope.

Artist Bob Schmitt, a painter and teacher, reflects on hope in his exploration of hope that hope is *"not some Pollyanna . . . [or] cockeyed optimism. But a deep belief that whatever I am experiencing, whatever we are experiencing, it is not the first time this level of adversity has been experienced. And it won't be the last. But as others have done before, we need to find a way through."*[4] He says hope is about possibility. *"It is about the trust that there will be a reality after this one that might be true."*[5]

> Jesus, please take me with you into the suffering of the world.
> Help me to love the world as you love the world.

## Deeper Conversation/Deeper Listening

1. What is your experience with suffering and how has it affected your relationship with God?
2. When you have suffered, what responses from others have been helpful? What has been unhelpful?
3. Who or what has helped you reconcile the reality of suffering with your faith?

---

4. Schmitt, *Art of Hope*, 7.
5. Schmitt, *Art of Hope*, 7.

## Spiritual Practice

Consider a period of suffering in your life.

Reflect on that time of suffering.

Reflect on and pray with these queries:

- What do you most remember about that time of suffering?
- How did you feel at the time?
- How do you feel now?
- Is there a place in your body that carries the imprint of that time of suffering?
- Bring all of this to God, holding it tenderly in light and love and prayer.
- What has arisen for you in this time of reflection?

## Bibliography

Alter, Robert. *The Wisdom Books: Job, Proverbs, and Ecclesiastes*. New York: Norton, 2011.

Schmitt, Bob. *The Art of Hope, The Hope of Art*. Laughing Waters Studio, 2020.

Stafford, William. "Spirit of Place: Great Blue Heron." *Even in Quiet Places: Poems*. Idaho: Confluence, 2010.

# PART 5

# *Introduction:* **Reaching for Higher Ground**

## Humans, Earth, and Spiritual Connections

*This section examines the need for critical internal examination and acceptance of self for spiritual growth. The chapters reflect Celtic and Christian expressions of life, the need for imagination in healing, and the usefulness of somatic manifestations, essential for deepening wisdom as a critical component of life.*

REACHING FOR HIGHER GROUNDS and spiritual consciousness is an inside job. Most spiritual directors or persons in faith formation know that God does the most significant work on the inside before it is manifested and made apparent on the outside. On the inside, we often discover our foresight, and when we do, it is like a resume with three parts—Who are you? What is your purpose? And what are you prepared to do? This is why finding joy from within is a fundamental truth and a necessity. Joy is different from happiness; happiness is circumstantial. Happiness is built around a happenstance, which is often temporary and circumstantial. Happiness is stimulation from the outside that most often affects internal perceptions and reactions. Joy is richer in texture and more profound. Joy is developed over time from a spiritual consciousness that is extended through our actions, manifested by experiences, and challenged by our perspective. Joy makes for renewal on every level of consciousness and can make us reach for higher ground, rejoicing about the good or bad experiences. As a result of joy, we can actualize our truth.

This section opens with a chapter by Mary Earle on Celtic spirituality and how intergenerational experiences can teach us values that, as we age, can turn into eternal truths to sustain us as a community. This section has reminders of our obligation to the earth as custodians and the responsibility to attend to ourselves, our connections to each other, and, most of all, our connections to the earth as we age. It is followed by Donna Coltrane Battle's views on the importance of seeing possibilities and re-visioning ourselves on who we can become using the power of prayer, faith, role modeling, and the role of imagination in creating the future. The section closes with Jessica Felix Romero's views on using somatics. Felix Romero highlights the history of age-old practices that encourage us to connect to our inner wisdom to support our well-being. The chapter encourages tapping into entheogenic wisdom, knowledge, and the traditions of somatic practices as an impetus to explore our personal beliefs about individual and collective community healing.

These three very different perspectives address the need for reaching human consciousness through our attention to the natural earth, imagining the future with faith, and the importance of increased spiritual connections to internal wisdom that can be used for healing. In doing so, we call for stronger spiritual connections. The intentions of these chapters encourage us to explore the necessity of space within ourselves while making space within society that cannot be contingent upon exalting accomplishments and goals as the deciding factor to our spiritual development. It must be how we increase and sustain our collective self as communities. This chapter allows us to expand on the question: *If we trust our internal truth as a guide, are we leading with optimism or a type of inert wisdom? Can we trust our internal guides to lead us to different outcomes than expected?*

## *Chapter 16*

# Bless to Me, O God, the Earth Beneath My Feet

MARY C. EARLE, MDIV, MAR, MA

*Mary C. Earle is an Episcopal priest, author, poet, retreat leader, and spiritual director. Until her retirement, she taught classes in spirituality for the Seminary of the Southwest in Austin, Texas. Mary has authored ten books; the subjects include the spirituality of living with illness, the rule of life, Celtic Christian spirituality, the Desert Mothers, and Julian of Norwich. Her latest is a book of her poetry,* Did You Sing Your Song?

> *Bless to me, O God,*
> *The earth beneath my foot.*
> *Bless to me, O God,*
> *The path whereon I go.*[1]

GROWING UP IN SAN ANTONIO, TEXAS, I spent a lot of time with my maternal grandparents. They lived close by and had land in the Texas hill country north of the city. They called it "the ranch." This idea was sort of a joke since there was no running water, no central heat or air, and only an outhouse for a toilet. Nevertheless, that place on a tributary of the Guadalupe River was magical. We grandkids were allowed phenomenal freedom, partly because both grandparents had been raised in rural settings. As grandkids, our basic instructions included not getting

---

1. Carmichael, *Carmina Gadelica* (Scottish Academic Press), 244.

in the creek without an adult, being on the lookout for snakes of the venomous variety, and always going at least two by two to explore. We grew up with a vivid sense of the land being alive with presence, even when we were baking in 100-degree heat. The sound of cicadas was so loud it was deafening. We learned to listen to bird calls. We could identify the birds by their songs. We dug up milky quartz from a vein of it in one cliff. We watched out for scorpions and centipedes, having received instruction about their stings.

We also fished with cane poles in the creek. I am convinced that that practice of standing still, waiting for a cork to bob, gave me a rudimentary awareness of contemplative prayer. Having gotten a catch, we were gathered together by my physician grandfather to watch him teach us how to humanely clean a fish. He would always start by severing the nerve that ran from the brain. "*This*," he explained, "*keeps the fish from hurting.*" In other words, the fish is a gift for us to eat, and we are invited to do no more harm. Being present to the gutting and the scaling with a kind of pragmatic reverence. We got anatomy lessons. We learned about care for the finned creatures. Pawpaw would hold up a sun perch and turn it upside down, squeezing gently to see if yellow eggs were brought forth. If they were, that mama fish went back into the creek. He was always aware of what we often call "the circle of life."

My grandmother was from Scots-Irish stock. My grandfather was the son of Czech immigrants who had come to live in the Czech colony outside of LaGrange. Grandma Golda was a registered nurse. Pawpaw Joe was a physician who later specialized in cardiology when it was in its early stages. They both had grown up close to the land. Each had the DNA of generations of healers. While they were not inclined to make big spiritual declarations, they lived with a kind of awareness of Presence that was passed on to their grandchildren. A story to make this clear: The wood building (which we called "the shack") was the center of activity. It was close to the edge of a limestone cliff above the creek. Grandma occasionally would trek down to the stream by following deer tracks down through the cedar trees and underbrush. She would come back by the same path. On a summer day, while we kids were playing, she appeared at the edge of the cliff, red-faced from the climb up. She saw us grandkids and exclaimed, "*I have received such a gift! I saw two king snakes mating!*" This is not the average child's formation. We were surprised and somewhat bewildered. Snakes? Snakes mating? Snakes doing a dance? Grandma Golda's way of being in nature was grounded, pragmatic, and finely attuned to the mystery.

Grandma Golda gave us a model for how to be with the creation. She showed no fear of the snakes. She knew that king snakes were "good snakes." They took care of mice and rats. She also perceived an exquisite beauty in their mating dance. We saw her exuberance and delight. We heard her sense of kinship with those creatures. She handed on the tradition she knew from her ancestors without any didactic moments. Her way of being was to be in reverent delight in the midst of a land she did not create. From this beloved elder and grandmother, I was tutored from an early age in a kind of kinship with all that is created. Though Golda never said this out loud, she lived the truth that everything comes from the Spirit, and everything returns to the Spirit.

Her gardens at their home in San Antonio were sacred spaces. Flowers of all kinds grew there. She loved the lily of the valley—not easy to grow in central Texas. She had lovely patches of violets underneath mountain laurel trees. One garden bed was full of narcissus bulbs. We all kept watch in early spring, waiting to see the tips of the leaves breaking through the soil. Once the buds appeared, my grandfather would take a daily tally of how many narcissus buds had opened and report the daily count to us. Golda's gardens were a place to learn to pay attention and to be grateful. She glowed with delight when the ferns began to unfurl, and when the roses started to bud. This was contagious in the best way!

In my studies, I've learned about "schools of spirituality." These "schools" could be from any monastic tradition. Once, I had a professor in spirituality who remarked, "*When you become a spiritual director, you will form your own 'school of spirituality.' Your directees will begin repeating your counsel, and then those who hear that repeated wisdom will repeat it anew.*" In my case, I grew up in the Grandma Golda school of spirituality. Following a premise from the Celtic tradition, the main "text" was the entire creation. She taught me to be still, to watch, and to notice changes in plants and animals as the seasons changed. She led me to marvel at the shifting iridescence in the sun perch. She helped me listen for the snuffling in the dark that was an armadillo seeking grubs under the cedar tree. She pointed out turkey buzzards circling high above, signaling that some creature had died and would soon become their dinner.

I am now in my seventies. Every day that goes by, I realize that much of whatever wisdom I might have comes from Grandma Golda. Though she was an active member of a Methodist congregation and had a Bible that she read regularly, she did not sense a need to preach to us (in contrast to my other grandmother). Instead, she let us see and hear on our own. We followed her example. We practiced being still, being quiet, and letting the creation speak to us. We learned to be on the lookout for four-legged and feathered relatives and friends. One of my fondest memories is going out to the garden with her in the morning light, watching the water from the hose sparkle with sunshine as we faced east. We did not speak hardly at all. It was a silent communing with light, water, plants, birds, bugs, and one another.

## The Book of Creation

In the mid-1980s, when I first became acquainted with the Celtic Christian tradition, I felt like I was coming home. As I began to read the poems and prayers that were being translated into English for the first time, something deep within me began to stir and quicken. These received prayers were initially spoken and written in Irish, Scots, Breton, Welsh, Cornish, and Manx. They were often part of oral tradition, handed down from generation to generation, and treasured as the oral prayer book of an entire lineage. Some were from poets who served royalty; the medieval Welsh poets sang exquisitely of the glories of the creation. Others were recent offerings from more modern poets like Ruth Bidgood, R. S. Thomas, Euros Bowen, Evan Boland, Seamus Heaney, and so many others. I felt I was opening a treasure chest, a chest overflowing with wisdom and beauty, insight and grace.

In the traditions we have received from Celtic Christianity, we encounter a vision of the whole universe shot through with glory. The tradition emphasizes God indwelling all that is made. In this way of being on this Earth, every particle is eternally created, redeemed, and sanctified by divine life. In the poems and songs that we inherit and that are being written today, we hear praise (from the Welsh tradition) for our Beloved, whose "*presence makes the world.*" A morning prayer offered by an older woman from the Hebrides taught me how to begin the day:

*Glory to thee, thou glorious sun,*
*Glory to thee, thou sun, Face of the God of life.*[2]

This way of being Christian is very grounded. The matter of the universe is perceived as inherently sacred because its Source is holy. By extension, humans are also inherently religious, for our physical being is sustained at every moment by the breath and delight of the One in whom we live, move, and have our being. To put it in a nutshell: The Celtic way is profoundly incarnational and sacramental. From the Celtic perspective, our relationship with the Beloved is intimate, immediate, and delightful. The creation is a gift, and we are called to treat it as such. As Saint Columbanus put it, we are *"hospites mundi,"*[3] guests in a world not of our making. As guests, we receive a moral imperative: to behave with each other and with the natural world in such a way that this planet and its inhabitants are treated with utmost respect and kindness. This vision of the world as the dwelling place of the Beloved is transformative. Our awareness of our deviations from the way of love becomes radically apparent, and the desire for amendment of life takes hold. It may be something as simple as wanting to plant native plants in your yard so that the species that live around you may feast and the pollinators may find plenty to sip. It may be more complex: recognizing regional policies that do not offer beautiful natural environments to whole communities of people and creatures. These moments—like Golda's—when the inherent beauty and complexity of nature astound us are a means of deliverance. The Spirit speaks to us in the language of the heart and soul. We are stirred by complacency. Small beginnings may lead to deep changes. That has been my experience and the experience of others I have known.

I needed to be fully aware of it to find an anchoring in this Celtic way. I had been looking for a spirituality that did not regard humans as separate from the creation. I had been hoping that somewhere in our tradition, there was a way in which the taste of the sacred that I had had in Golda's gardens held true for the whole wide Earth. I had had a bellyful of the kinds of theology and spirituality that start with denigrating women, seeing the natural world as something to be dominated, and supplying awful, punitive images of God that clearly were not God. I started my search with those early collections of prayers. A dear friend, Dr. Nelle Bellamy, brought me a collection of Celtic prayers edited by Esther de

2. De Waal, *Celtic Way of Prayer*, 58–59.
3. Swan, "St Columbanus."

Waal and A. M. Allchin. Many of these prayers had never before been read in English. *Threshold of Light: Prayers and Praises from the Celtic Tradition* became my new prayer book. I voiced these words:

> *Let the birds and the honeybees praise you,*
> *Let the shorn stems and the shoots praise you,*
> *Both Aaron and Moses praised you:*
> *Let the male and the female praise you,*
> *Let the seven days and the stars praise you,*
> *Let the air and the ether praise you,*
> *Let the books and the letters praise you,*
> *Let the fish in the swift streams praise you,*
> *Let the thought and the action praise you,*
> *Let the sand grains and the earth clods praise you,*
> *Let all the good that's performed praise you.*
> *And I shall praise you, Lord of glory:*
> *Glorious Lord, I give you greeting!*[4]

From sand grains and earth clods to stars and air, everything is called forth to offer praise and thanksgiving. There are echoes here of Hebrew scriptures, in particular of the psalms. For example, consider these lines from Psalm 19:

> *The heavens are telling the glory of God;*
> *and the firmament proclaims his handiwork.*
> *Day to day pours forth speech,*
> *and night to night declares knowledge.*
> *There is no speech, nor are there words;*
> *their voice is not heard;*
> *yet their voice goes out through all the earth,*
> *and their words to the end of the world.* (Ps 19:1–4 NRSV)

The whole creation speaks, sings, and offers praise in voices that we no longer remember how to hear. We need to remember the deep connection to the creation. We have allowed our ability to notice this phenomenal speech to atrophy. We cannot speak it. We can become attuned to it. The psalmist abided in an awareness of the divine speaking in and through the rocks and the dirt, the sea, and the sky. That awareness suffuses the

---

4. Allchin and de Waal, *Threshold of Light*, 3.

Celtic tradition. When we pray these prayers and allow these elders to urge us toward a deep remembering and reconnection, the barnacles of a wrong-headed formation begin to fall away. We muster the strength to take off our shoes and stand on the holy ground that is this planet, your landscape, your backyard. Golda's Scot-Irish DNA led her to put herself outside, in the growing, greening, changing microcosm of her yard every day. She watered. She weeded. She planted. She pruned. In those regular, daily activities, she taught me to be in regular "conversation" with nature. She listened to the birds and watched for the fox that dwelled in the ravine close to her house. She had an Advent spirit, for she understood that being attentive to the natural world reminded us of several basic truths. First, we are not God, and we did not create the world. Second, the world is alive with divine presence, and we have a sacred responsibility to revere this outward and visible sign of God's handiwork. Third, we are mortal. Our days are numbered. We have a moral responsibility to leave things here on Earth better than we found them so that future generations might enjoy and delight in all that is a gift. In this time of climate change, we have a sacred responsibility to attend to the health of the Earth, thereby attending to the health of all peoples.

From Welsh Anglican poet R. S. Thomas, we are given this insight, received as he was savoring a place in Wales:

> *I will simply say that I realized there was really no such thing as time, no beginning and no end, but that everything is a fountain welling up endlessly from immortal God. There was certainly something in the place that gave me this feeling. The chapel stood in the fields amidst the waving grass, its roof covered with a layer of yellow lichen. Tall nettles were growing around, and at its side, there swayed a big old tree like someone leaning forward to listen to the sermon. It was, therefore, easy to believe that I was living centuries ago. It might have been the first day of Creation, and myself one of the first men. Might have been? No, it was the first day. The world was recreated before my eyes. The dew of its creation was on everything, and I fell to my knees and praised God—a young man worshipping a young God, for surely that is what our God is.*[5]

Thomas leads us to see anew. This capacity is God-given. As he is awakened to God's presence in the grass, in the lichen, in the tree, in the dew, he shows us the capacity we have to receive this kind of encounter. He wasn't searching for it. He was out walking. Then, unexpectedly, this

---

5. Allchin and de Waal, *Threshold of Light*, 15.

landscape around the old chapel became a "thin space." In the Celtic tradition, a thin space is a place *"where earth and heaven meet, and the veil is very thin"* (the traditional way of describing it). The encounter given to Thomas leads him to adoration and thanksgiving, his whole being praising along with the creation. He is delivered from our plague of self-concern and self-pity, self-focus and self-denigration. He is participating in the glory for which all is made. He is discovering that he is a beautiful part of an intricate, phenomenally beautiful whole, and that he is part of an entire chorus giving glory to God. In that moment, he is made new and "young." He knows that God is ever-young and ever-with-him. He is a being of divine making amid a creation of divine making—through holy breath, holy speaking, holy song.

The Irish tradition holds that creation is brought forth by the *oran mor*, a deep, eternal song. The Divine Source sings everything into being, at every moment, in every breath. We are invited to listen to that Song, and to join that great Song, our voices along with all the others, offering praise and glory. It seems that our true identity as humans is revealed in the singing. We each have a part to sing in this grand chorale of creation, and we—as with any choir—find our way in the music by attending to the voices all around us. Paying kind and gracious attention to the magnificent throbbing, hooting, snorting, bellowing, whistling, calling world around us leads us to hear that Melody that we have forgotten. This literally changes and transforms our way of being with others and with the creatures. My mother often made up goofy little songs for our dogs and cats. She would hold Jay the beagle on her lap, gently pat his velvety ears, and sing to him of his canine beauty. The songs were silly, and they were dear. I have no doubt that they warmed Jay's dear beagle heart. Golda had a habit of bowing toward her plants. The tradition has taught me to bless seeds as they are planted in the name of the "Three of my Love" (the Trinity).

Do you see? Do you sense how this care and intentional regard for the natural world shifts everything? Do you have the quickening that comes when what we have forgotten stirs to life and leads us to see with love for all? This exuberant tradition teaches us to behold with eyes and hearts of love and compassion. We are strongly moved away from complacency toward embodied kindness. We begin to be on the watch, with contemplative patience, noticing glimmers of Presence where we never hoped to see them.

At the same time, one of the best gifts of this tradition is its practicality. The prayers walk with us throughout the whole day and into the night. We aren't so much asked to set aside hours for a new technique or to be overly concerned with how we sit. Instead, these prayers accompany us through the day, hallowing the time we have been given, directing us to shift our gaze, to receive the good gifts being offered at every moment, to find creative ways to love our neighbors, love the creation, love God, love ourselves.

## Traveling on the Currents of Divine Love

Lastly, because we are ever abiding in this sacred text of the creation, encountering the living Presence in every particle and creature, our lives unfold in constant, ever-present Love. Within this context, in the Celtic tradition, pilgrimage is made in a unique way. No other tradition offers this model and metaphor for journeying. As Esther de Waal remarks, "*The Celtic understanding of peregrination, a word, and a concept, is found nowhere else in Christendom.*"[6] What did this look like? The pilgrim or seeker first got into a small round boat called a coracle or a curragh. The boat had no oars. Once the pilgrim got in the boat, she cast off on the "currents of divine love," allowing the boat to float on the sea or a river, going where the current led. In practice, this was a radical act of trust, a way of moving through life following the lead of the Spirit. Once the coracle was deposited on a shore, that land was known as "the place of my resurrection." Many of the Celtic saints founded monastic settlements once their coracle journeys had arrived at this place. The stories we receive are full of narratives of men and women entrusting their lives to divine love and going not where they chose but where they were led. Saint David's mother, Saint Non, sailed away to Brittany after she had raised her son in Wales. Once there, Saint Non, apparently led a fruitful life, founding new communities. Place names throughout Brittany bear witness to her presence. Her place of resurrection was the place of fruitful work and of her dying to eternal life.

How does this practice and metaphor offer elder wisdom? As we age, we become ever more aware of the fact that our lives have not unfolded as we expected. We look back at life scripts that we created for younger selves; we notice how differently our lives have turned out. In

---

6. De Waal, *Celtic Way of Prayer*, 2.

other words, sometimes life makes us get in a coracle. Sometimes, circumstances lead us in ways we would never have chosen or expected. Those ways may have been hard or dark. They may have caused us great pain or great joy. What is for sure, we did not put them in the original script. We may also become aware of the guidance we have experienced and of the ways in which even painful and difficult events have formed us for the good. We learn to allow our wounds to teach us compassion. We choose to be open-hearted. We look back, and we discover that the gracious presence of God has been with us in all places and at all times. "The place of resurrection" is both an ending and a beginning. We arrive in an unforeseen place (sometimes literally), and we begin anew. We encounter the Beloved in renewing life, and the divine Presence frees us from all imprisoning and demeaning interpretations of our lives.

In my own case, acute and chronic illness led me to begin appropriating the reality and metaphor of the coracle when I was in my forties. As one ages, the sheer fact that one never knows how a day will turn out becomes less startling and more of a lived reality. We don't like to live from this truth. We don't like knowing that as we age, we are more likely to have a definitive diagnosis that alters our regular rhythms. We don't like having friends drop dead. We don't like seeing the world rife with so much violence, war, and hatred. The coracle, as metaphor and reality, reminds us of this: Even when things are dark, the Holy One is ever with us, and we travel on currents of divine love. Even when those currents are rough and the water is turbulent, we are not alone. We will end up in the place of our resurrection; we will return to the Home that we have never left. We pray with our brothers and sisters from the Outer Hebrides:

> *Bless the pathway on which I go,*
> *God, bless the earth that is beneath my sole;*
> *Bless, O God, and give to me thy love.*
> *O God of gods, bless my rest and my repose;*
> *Bless, O God, and give to me thy love,*
> *And bless, O God of gods, my repose.*[7]

---

7. Carmichael, *Carmina Gadelica* (Lindisfarne), 244.

## Deeper Conversation/Deeper Listening

1. The Celtic tradition believes men and women are equally able to inspire, lead, and participate in all aspects of community and spiritual practice. How can this ancient practice become more infused into the practices of today's Christian church?
2. In Celtic tradition, the *anam cara* was not merely a metaphor or ideal. It was a soul bond that existed, was recognized, and admired as a social construct. It altered the meaning of identity and perception. How can this practice be a part of today's wisdom development?

## Spiritual Practice

Using these lines from the last Celtic prayer in this chapter, take a regular, slow, steady walk daily for a week. Allow yourself to notice the earth beneath the soles of your feet; give thanks for the land and all who dwell therein.

> *Bless the pathway on which I go,*
> *God, bless the earth that is beneath my sole.*

## Bibliography

Allchin, A. M., and Esther de Waal. *Threshold of Light: Prayers and Praises from the Celtic Tradition*. London: Darton, Longman and Todd, 1986.

Carmichael, Alexander. *Carmina Gadelica: Hymns and Incantations: With Illustrative Notes on Words, Rites, and Customs, Dying and Obsolete*. Edinburgh: Scottish Academic Press, 1972.

———. *Carmina Gadelica*. Edinburgh: Lindisfarne Press, 1971.

de Waal, Esther. *The Celtic Way of Prayer: The Recovery of the Religious Imagination*. London: Canterbury, 2010.

Swan, Billy. "St Columbanus—Lessons from an Extra-Ordinary Life of Mission." *The Hook of Faith*, Nov 18, 2021. https://www.thehookoffaith.com/single-post/st-columbanus-lessons-from-an-extra-ordinary-life-of-mission.

# Chapter 17

# We Cannot Create What We Cannot Imagine

## Creation and Imagination

Donna Coletrane Battle, PhD, MDiv

Donna Coletrane Battle is a spiritual practitioner, soul coach, and educator focused on justice as it relates specifically to the intersection of race, gender, and spirituality. Donna is a mother, wife, sister, and friend who also coaches leaders, pastors those without a pastor, partners to cultivate healing in relationships, and commits every day to a life of being present, though not always successfully! She holds a BA in public relations from North Carolina A&T State University, an MDiv from Duke University, and a PhD in marriage and family therapy from Eastern University.

*We cannot create what we cannot imagine.* —Lucille Clifton

In *Jesus and the Disinherited*, Howard Thurman explains how those "with their backs up against the wall" often struggle against real transformative solutions to their problems because their ongoing experience creates confusion between when they should fear versus simply being cautious.[1] In our humanity, we continuously seek ways to avoid the pain we have experienced in the past. This is particularly true in cases of trauma. Ongoing collective trauma can yield a defensive practice of always responding to situations of change and difference with fear. When fear is the default, there is little room for genuine hopeful change options to be cautiously tested. In short, hope flees with fear.

The elder poet Lucille Clifton taps into the reality of what happens when there is no hope for change or change for the better. If we fail to imagine change, or if we do not imagine something better, then we will not work to create something new, something different, something better. The good news for me is that my elders knew this, and they, in their own way, gifted me and many others with a far more robust interpretation of imagination. It is an interpretation steeped in an understanding of hope that challenges the beautiful, warm feeling and definitions the world likes to offer. While sitting with a group of colleagues several years ago, discussing a current event and how it would most likely play out, I began sharing a few statistics I was privy to. In response to the dismal outlook, one of my colleagues said, "*Wow, that makes this all sound so hopeless.*" I replied, "*On the contrary, hope can only begin at the point we have the courage to stare at the truth of reality head-on. If what we call hope is based upon misinformation and illusions, then that is false hope. True hope means seeing reality and still believing there is a way out.*"

## Imagination Hones Visions out of Dreams: Visions versus Dreams

Have you ever noticed how one word, despite definitions, develops meaning far beyond those definitions? Interpretation creates nuances that muddy the waters, sometimes for the good and other times not. This is true for most things in life, from law to sacred texts, because interpretation is steeped in a multitude of varying experiences, knowledge, and the bias of socialization. How often do we wade past our initial interpretation of how a thing is presented in a moment? Take fairy tales, for example. The wonderful world of make-believe given to us early in life nurtures the wonder of our minds in a beautiful and innocent way. Fairy tales are straightforward and uncomplicated in terms of good and evil, but what happens when the rules of make-believe get applied to real life?

---

1. Thurman, *Jesus and the Disinherited*, 12.

What happens when generation after generation of children learn the very polarized nature of fairy tales and then encounter that same narrative in life? The narrative that says some people are bad and others are good? The narrative says that some people are more qualified to judge, and others are not simply because of who they are? The shift goes from a wondrous world of fairy godmothers who always right the wrongs in the world to a real-life nightmare for those portrayed as villains because, unlike the make-believe nature of fairy tales, real life is far more complex and riddled with dynamics of power and hierarchy.

For example, have you ever stopped to ask why the roadrunner always seems to outrun the coyote? Does the coyote have a right to eat? We often watch and interpret the story as it is given, within its context, without question. We do not apply further imagination when we interpret a thing as being as we think it should be. We do not pause to ask questions about the coyote and the roadrunner because the roadrunner is "good" and the coyote is "bad." However, perhaps more importantly, we do not pause to imagine beyond the story given because we believe to the point of knowing that the story will not change. The roadrunner will always outsmart the coyote. What is the point of imagining anything differently? Depending on where your experience aligns in the story, this can make it much easier for the conscience to fall back on the original narrative. The coyote is bad and deserves this treatment, and the roadrunner is innocent and deserves to win—EVERY SINGLE TIME. For others whose experience has rarely been on the winning side, they may become trapped, like the coyote, continuing to do the same thing over and over, hoping to survive, even though it isn't working.

Hope does not always see the way out. It is always believing there is a way out. Understanding hope requires accepting what is currently true and possible for change. It becomes a catalyst for recognizing when our imaginings will lead to creativity or the actual production of reality and when it simply remains in the make-believe. The imaginations of dreamers only live in the definition of the image as merely the forming of a mental image or concept. This does serve a great purpose. We do not want or need to ever let go of dreams, but the invitation here is to move a bit deeper. Our closest connection to dreams on a daily basis happens while we are sleep—unconscious.

Moreover, even in the cases of daydreaming, we also often do so while not conscious of the realities that are or would be at play if the things we dream about were to come true. A young person dreams of being famous in the realm of make-believe for years, and when the moment comes for them to go for it, they are faced with rejection. They are told to do more work to get better. They need to study the craft more, and, perhaps most disheartening, they are told how they look is not good enough. They are shattered because, in the world of make-believe, they remain asleep to the true realities of the world of fame. At this point, they must now decide whether to walk away from the shattered dream and defer it or whether they are willing to press past the odds to envision something that is past the harsh realities they face.

As with most things in life, this is much easier said than done. There are very real mountains to climb in moving from dreams to visions. As a matter of context, these words are being written in the midst of a time that will be remembered for generations to come. The global pandemic that began in 2020, not surprisingly, has applied pressure to the suppressed and repressed emotions of entire communities of people. For example, one reality revealed the underdeveloped state of emotions for many. There are many reasons and causes for the underdevelopment of our emotional selves, which range from privilege and entitlement to the fatigue of extreme trauma. In either event, it is revealed in our inability to face the facts. The rising fear and anxiety take over and participate in the press for us to remain in the make-believe. This has given rise to the strange arrival of "fake news."

It is the weaving of narratives by those in a particular place of dominant power to maintain such power. Womanist scholar Dr. Emilie Townes presents an example of this as she describes the work of the late elder Toni Morrison. "*Morrison observes that slave narratives do not mention the interior lives of the enslaved because the writers shaped their narratives to be acceptable.*"[2] The denial of the inward struggle of the enslaved by omitting it from the narrative further dehumanizes the enslaved to the reader who wishes to justify dominant society's treatment of actual living people. The key here is the power that lies not only in the story but in who is telling the narrative. To discredit the narrator, no matter how accurate their telling, is to render obsolete everything they say. If I am perceived as worthy of holding the mic, and I know people want to deny the truth, then I can maintain dominant power because, true or not, everything I say will be received as such. I can manipulate the emotional immaturity of a people by only giving them what they wish

---

2. Townes, *Womanist Ethics*, 11.

to hear and maintaining my oppressive power. More can be said here, but the point is made. Moving from make-believe to envisioning is not a matter of simply knowing that it must be done. It is hard and challenging emotional work. It cannot be done in a vacuum alone, but it must be a converging of community, faith, and the facing of fears.

So then, we must all begin with dreams, but we cannot stay there if the creativity that produces tangible change—tangible wins—is to materialize. We must meet hope in the despair of reality and dare to allow new visions to emerge from the shattered pieces of our dreams. It is not what happens while sleeping but fully awake to the truth, no matter how dismal. Another way to define vision is to describe it as an act or power of imagination as a direct mystical awareness of the supernatural. This is a different meaning of imagination than make-believe. Here, imagination is to believe to exist or be true. As the mystics would say, hope through faith becomes its own self-fulfilling prophecy.

My mother has defied the odds of her life in ways most will never know. The daughter of sharecroppers in rural North Carolina, she was the eighth born of nine children. Determined to access life, not only for herself but for those she loved beyond the suffocating confines of poverty, she was the only one of her siblings to attend college. Working to pay her way through school, she graduated from North Carolina A&T State University in 1972 and returned home to work, marry, and eventually raise my sister and me. My maternal grandmother came to live with us the year I was born, and when she developed a sore on her leg decades later, my mom became her primary caretaker. Trips back and forth to a specialized wound center became a routine. My grandmother had poor circulation, making even the smallest abrasions on her body a big ordeal. This was the second time my mother had been through the process of caring for a wound on my grandmother's leg, and she was well accustomed through research, detailed questions and notes during doctor's visits, and experience to what the process looked like. The sore had become especially painful over one weekend, rendering my grandmother immobile. Two days until the wound center opened, the only option was the emergency room. After being admitted, the surgeons immediately sought to amputate my grandmother's leg, citing gangrene as the reason. My mother calmly and assertively said no. Mom explained that they saw evidence that her wound needed to be cleaned, and if they brought her dressings, she could do so. They mentioned the smell, and Mom explained that the medicine used on the wound always smells that way. The doctors were insistent, and Mom refused. She asked about a treatment of antibiotics first, and the answer was no. She called Grandma's wound doctor on Monday and was told by the receptionist that he did not make hospital calls. The nurse assigned to my grandmother scolded my mother for thinking she knew better than the doctor. So, we prayed, and Mom held her ground despite rising doubt. At that moment, she was the guardian of my grandmother's quality of life. She knew the necessity of getting this right. There was no reversal of amputation, and she also saw signs of healthy tissue in the wound. She believed there was another way. We prayed and prayed. Moreover, the answer to that prayer walked through the hospital door. My grandmother's wound doctor, who did not make hospital visits, walked in. He examined the wound and confirmed that what they saw was not gangrene. He turned to the nurse and instructed her to provide the appropriate dressings for my mom to clean and dress the wound because she was trained to do so by his staff. He ordered antibiotics as my mother requested, and my grandmother's leg healed completely before her death several years later.

An often-missed piece of testimonies like this is the embodied experience of necessity. This is another pivotal part of whether we tip toward vision. As we watch the cracks creeping up the porcelain wall of our precious and fragile dreams, there is a feeling that we need to find a way despite the odds. We must find a way, even if we must change our previous plans, shift the timeline, or even adjust expectations. This is even more important in such moments when giving up is not an option. This is the moment a portal to the plane of vision peels open. My elders and ancestors were and continue to face more than their fair share of pivotal moments. There were and are plenty of moments where choosing not to press only reflected the exhaustion of living in a world that has declared what feels like, at times, an unending war on Black bodies. And as humans, there were and are moments in our lives when we wallow in the pieces of shattered dreams. However, an ever-present access to necessity because of the world's oppression meant there developed somewhat of a skill in learning when we step through the portal of renewed possibility and let faith lead fear.

## Imagination and Creativity Made Reality in Necessity

The adage "necessity is the mother of invention" is not new to most. However, naming what necessity does is. While visiting Haiti many years ago, I met an elderly Haitian woman who shared words of wisdom with me. During our conversation, she asked me, "*Why do Americans say life is good? Life is hard.*" I replied, "*Yes, many Americans do say life is good, but there are those who also say from experience that life is very hard.*" She nodded contemplatively and said, "*I've heard Philippians 4:13 quoted as 'I can do all things through Christ who strengthens me,' but the Haitian Bible says, 'I can make do with all things through Christ who strengthens me.' No matter how little we may have, God can make that thing stretch. No matter how little we have, we can share and make a way.*" This is more powerful than one might initially realize because it is the difference between thinking there "might" be a way and believing there is a way. This is hope making space for faith—hope passing the baton in the middle of the relay race. If I believe, no matter what, there is a way, then all my energy can shift to discovering that way. My energy and thoughts are not split between imagining and the anxiety of wondering if there is a way. There is a focus, a determination, and an act of will that continues to expand the area for imagination and creativity to be nurtured and to grow. Necessity lowers the risk of taking a chance because the greater risk is in doing nothing.

I often heard my parents recount the gas shortage of 1974. The long lines and the uncertainty of being able to get to work created a necessary shift to ensure the security of jobs and provision. My dad appeared in a newspaper article in May 1974, along with nine of his friends and coworkers at Goodyear Tire and Rubber Company of Danville, Virginia. Mr. Sylvester Madden, a man I knew from family cookouts and his visits to our home every Christmas Eve to pick up a tin of crunchy drop cookies, had a dream that became a vision during that gas shortage. He had for some time imagined how hearses, used to carry caskets and the remains of loved ones, could be used creatively in other ways. When the gas shortage hit, necessity was the push to act on faith. He found an old hearse that he could afford, added seating in the back, and transformed a vehicle made to carry the dead into one that not only carried the living but also gave access to the sustainability of life. My daddy and eight others joined him in a 1974 carpool from Caswell County, North Carolina, to Danville, Virginia, every day in a ride filled with laughter, camaraderie, and the shared cost of gas. There are times when necessity presses us to imagine and create. Still, there are other times when imagination has already been stirring, and necessity becomes the catalyst for moving imagination to creation—dreams to visions that manifest. In this example, we also see another common element of this gift from the elders. It's the ability to rely on each other as a communal need.

Madam C. J. Walker, born Sarah Breedlove, created her hair care line in response to her own hair loss.[3] Her personal necessity forged a creation that met the necessity of many other women and made Walker the first Black woman millionaire in America. Dr. Patricia Bath, a graduate of Howard Medical School, studied ophthalmology at Columbia University, where she discovered you were twice as likely to experience blindness and eight times more likely to develop glaucoma if you were Black. In 1986, she completed her invention of the laser probe (one of many inventions), a device using laser technology to create "a less painful and more precise treatment of cataracts."[4] Further, her research led to a system to increase the amount of eye care given to those unable to afford it. In Madam Walker's case, it was her experience of necessity; in Dr. Bath's, it was her proximity to knowledge of an unknown necessity. In both cases, as with my father's friend Mr. Madden, it was a shared imagination and creation. Whether the opportunity to make a living from the process comes or not, the motivation in these cases was not money or transaction but need. There are countless examples of aunties, uncles, and Ms. so and so's down the street who create and share with others right from their kitchens, back rooms, or sheds. Necessity is about need, and need is about what is necessary to access life. The work of imagination and creation is steeped in the essence of life.

## A Reflection of the Divine

In the Christian context, we believe that humanity is created in the image of God the Creator. Further, all of creation is formed by the intention and intellectual design of the Divine. Insofar as we can comprehend it, life is born through the process of creation. Regardless of a person's belief about the origin of creation, there are quite a few wonders that sustain life on our planet. Our bodies alone are remarkable. Pause to consider how we

3. Bundles, "Madam C.J. Walker."
4. Biography.com Editors and Piccotti, "Patricia Bath Biography."

breathe constantly, but we do not consciously will ourselves to breathe. Alternatively, according to National Geographic Kids, an adult's blood vessels could circle the earth's equator four times if laid end to end.[5] I can recall the elders in my life discussing how the earth was made. It was the kind of wonder that motivated imagination and made one believe that the impossible is, in fact, possible. In a Sunday school class as a young girl, one of the kids asked the teacher what the purpose of a rhinoceros was. The teacher was visibly caught off guard, but then she smiled and said, "*I do not know, but no one who looks at rhinoceroses cannot say God does not have a vivid imagination.*"

From this perspective, life as we know it springs from the creative imagination of the Divine. Moreover, if we are created in the image of God, then our capacity to imagine and create is a reflection of God. It is the Divine at work in us and through us to sustain and bring forth life, even amid what appears to be impossible realities. This is at play in most faith-based community organizing strategies. The active imagination of something completely different from the overbearing oppressive systems is necessary to create a just world. As a descendant of the formerly enslaved of this country, I recognize that every enslaved person who took the risk to run away had imagined something beyond the despair of the moment. We are the answered prayers of our ancestors. We are the products of their imagination for freedom. The visions we dare to form in the face of necessity and pursue will be the tangible prayers we offer for our descendants. What we create has the capacity, like our prayers, to outlive us, as the creations and prayers of our ancestors have proven. This means this work of imagination and creation also crosses time through relationships. Though we are bound by time, in this way, we also transcend time in our ability to benefit from the past and impact the future. At the very least, the work of our imaginations and creation that brings forth life kisses the realm of timelessness where God dwells. Have you ever felt that though you have human limitations, it seems like an essential part of you was designed to be limitless? There is a yearning to span all of time at once. This is not the same as living mentally in the past or future as a form of emotional escape. However, instead, pulling from within says the possibility for transcendence is not only there but intended. It is a "we were made for this" feeling.

---

5. National Geographic Kids, "15 Facts about the Human Body!"

If this does not resonate, take some time and be attentive in imagining. How does it feel? Just sit in it, and that is, in part, the experience I seek to describe. It is enthusiasm. Howard Thurman explained that enthusiasm means *"god-possessed."*[6] The act of creating emerges from this place of enthusiasm. It is intimate, pleasurable, and a reminder of the moments in which children are conceived—the creation of life. This is the work of life that reflects the God in whose image we are created, and it is an invitation to explore humanity's capacity across time. However, too often, we imagine, even amid necessity, and at times struggle to still move to creation.

## Blocks, Bridles, and Bullhorns

There may be many reasons why we struggle to move from dreams to visions and from imagination to creation, but grief, fear, and shame are big ones to be aware of. All change comes with some form of grief. Grief is experienced with loss, and with change, there may be many losses. At the least, there is a loss of the familiarity of a norm. When it comes to change for the better, we may not name what we experience as grief because we are conflicted. Why would I grieve what I had when what I could have is better? A patient who chooses to have gastric bypass surgery may do all of the required psychological work to have the surgery and still discover grief afterward. When they are no longer physically capable of eating more at a meal, the reality that they have lost a coping mechanism brings sorrow. This is true even though the very catalyst for the sorrow is also the same catalyst designed to create what they desire. Unattended grief can block the pathways of imagination and creativity. In these types of situations, expect grief to rise. It is essential to explore practices and seek community support to help honor the grief rather than letting grief hinder living a fulfilled life.

Then, there are other times in the space between imagination and creation when we glimpse a bit of how much a new creation will change things. We glimpse changed relationships, a different way of life, and a new set of challenges. Strangely, our imagination then shifts from the creation that brings life to the imagination (often make-believe) of all things we may have to give up or deal with, and we decide, sometimes unconsciously, that it was just a nice thought. Fear can be helpful if it reminds us

---

6. Thurman, *Jesus and the Disinherited*, 24.

to lean on our faith. Fears can also help us ask questions that help us weigh the risk. It is true that not all things we imagine will become creations. However, if there is no wrestling with our fears before giving up, we have decided based solely on fear. We bridle faith before it has a chance to make a counter argument. At such times, we may learn new and curious ways of engaging fear and ways to engage faith.

Finally, the most difficult of the three is shame. In psychology, we describe shame as "*I am bad.*" This is different from "*I did a bad thing*" or "*a bad thing happened to me.*" Shame is never, I repeat never, helpful. It often enters our lives through trauma and pain, often through acts beyond our control. Shame takes from us our sense of worth and sometimes our will to fight for what we deserve. It must be said that there are many truths and few absolutes in life. The enslaved ancestors who fawned or froze in the face of trauma and necessity rather than fighting or fleeing were not wrong or bad for surviving in the best way they knew how. We must be careful not to shame ourselves or others simply because we follow what feels, in the moment of pain, like the easiest path. Nor should we use the presence of shame to escalate the feelings of shame. Accessing imagination and creativity is an invitation, and the presence of shame is simply one possible reason why we might not believe we deserve to be offered access to what we need to thrive in life. The voice of shame is amplified as a voice is through a bullhorn, and it can be very hard for us to hear anything above it. Shame shrinks with exposure. It makes us feel like we will not be able to survive the revealing, but that is precisely what is needed to overcome it. Commit to a few sessions with a trained professional in spiritual care or therapy. Who is the person that loves you most in this world? Spend time sitting in the feeling of being loved by them. As it goes, Elder Lucille Clifton spoke and wrote the truth. And the power of her words is found in what they imply. We cannot create what we cannot imagine, but we can create what we do.

## Deeper Conversation/Deeper Listening

1. How can we promote the use of imagination as a spiritual practice?
2. Can we find eternal truths through the use of imagination?
3. What is the most powerful discovery you have ever made about yourself regarding creativity and imagination?

## Spiritual Practice

One of the greatest blocks to our imagination is exhaustion. This week find an extra fifteen minutes each day for rest. Breathe and give yourself permission to lay down all your burdens. Then, near the end of the week, carve out time to consider a situation or a desire from a new perspective. Grab your journal, get a cup of tea, and go to an inspirational location. What is your desired outcome for the situation or new creation? How would you approach the situation or new creation if there were no limitations? What curiosities do you have about what is possible? What resources are available to you (strengths, skills, people, etc.)? What fears come up? What most excites you? Consider creating space for regular imagination sessions.

## Bibliography

Biography.com Editors, and Tyler Piccotti. "Patricia Bath Biography." n.d. https://www.biography.com/scientists/patricia-bath.

Bundles, A'Lelia. "Madam C.J. Walker." *Encyclopædia Britannica*, Oct 16, 2023. https://www.britannica.com/biography/Madam-C-J-Walker.

Clifton, Lucille, Kevin Young, and Michael S. Glaser. *The Collected Poems of Lucille Clifton 1965–2010*. Rochester, NY: BOA Editions, 2012.

National Geographic Kids. "15 Facts about the Human Body!" Jun 29, 2023. https://www.natgeokids.com/uk/discover/science/general-science/15-facts-about-the-human-body/.

Thurman, Howard. *Jesus and the Disinherited*. Boston: Beacon, 2022.

Townes, Emilie Maureen. *Womanist Ethics and the Cultural Production of Evil*. Basingstoke: Palgrave Macmillan, 2007.

# Chapter 18

# God's Wisdom Implanted in All Things

JESSICA FELIX ROMERO, PHD

*Jessica Felix Romero has over fifteen years of experience in social justice advocacy, organizing, and communications. She has served as a communications expert on various issues, including labor rights, health, the environment, corporate social responsibility, peacebuilding, and agriculture. With a doctorate in conflict analysis and resolution, she integrates holistic system analysis and transformative design to help nonprofits advance social change. She is the chief strategy and impact officer at Sojourners, a faith-inspired nonprofit that works with Christians to put their faith into action in the passionate pursuit of social justice, peace, and environmental stewardship.*

IN THIS CHAPTER, I will explore the wisdom of God implanted in the materials of all organic matter, including the human body, by expanding on John 1:3: *"Through him, all things were made; without him, nothing was made that has been made."* By combining current research, Indigenous entheogenic plant wisdom, Christian mystical traditions, and embodied theology, this chapter will share a new perspective on wisdom located within us and how we can cultivate an emergent wisdom practice in our lives.

## Ancient Traditions

The ancient practices of ingesting psychoactive plants go back millennia. The archeological record suggests humans have been engaged with plant life to nourish our bodies and engage our consciousness for over ten thousand years.[1] Prehistoric cave art depicts shamanic/religious rituals involving plants, and Indigenous communities across the globe have deep spiritual histories with these plants—often called entheogens. Entheogens are typically of plant origin and are ingested to produce a non-ordinary state of consciousness for religious or spiritual purposes. The term was formally defined by Carl A. P. Ruck, Jeremy Bigwood, Danny Staples, Jonathan Ott, and R. Gordon Wasson in 1979.[2] The Greek etymology of the term translates to "becoming divine within" and reflects the sacred nature of these plants.

Non-ordinary consciousness or altered states have long been associated with spiritual practices across various traditions, incorporating practices of meditation, fasting, sensory deprivation, chanting, drumming, ecstatic dance, and prayer. Spanning the asceticism of early Desert Fathers and Mothers through the vision-seeing mystics of the European Middle Ages, eighteenth-century Shakers, and modern-day Pentecostalism, Christianity has had a relationship with "non-ordinary consciousness" in various worship expressions.

So, how do we begin to explore intersections between entheogens and Christianity? Are there guiding theologies and lived experiences that provide touch points? Can an entheogenic Christianity contribute to a growing wisdom tradition within contemplative traditions? Since entheogens are of plant origin and ingested into our bodies, exploring theologies of ecology and embodiment may be useful. Theologian Sallie McFague proposed an ecological and embodied model of the universe or world as God's body.[3] In the model, divine embodiment makes all embodiment sacred. McFague's work deepens our understanding of God's relationship to the natural world and how all bodies, organisms, environments, and universes are interrelated. "*Whatever more or other we may be, we are bodies, made of the same stuff as all other life forms on our planet.*"[4] She goes on to say that we must love and honor the

---

1. Furst, *Hallucinogens and Culture*, 9.
2. Mellinger, "Tripping with the Gods."
3. McFague, *Body of God*.
4. McFague, *Body of God*, 16.

universal body, our own bodies, and the bodies of all other life forms on this planet—these life forms include entheogens.[5] This correlates to the biblical verse 1 Timothy 4:4–5 that points us in the direction of goodness in all of God's creation: "*For everything God created is good, and nothing is to be rejected if it is received with thanksgiving, because it is consecrated by the word of God and prayer.*"

Theologian Elisabeth Moltmann-Wendel writes, "*A theological return to embodiment recalls the distinctive feature of Christianity, that God became a body and in doing so has confirmed and healed all our bodily nature.*"[6] Our brains have receptors that connect with the substances within entheogens. "*The human potential for entheogenic experiences and visionary encounters appears to reflect innate properties of our nervous system.*"[7] Theology that centers on the goodness of the body provides frameworks to appreciate the ability of our bodies to enter non-ordinary consciousness.

Others seek to find historical evidence of the role of entheogens in the foundations of Judeo-Christianity. Danny Nemu presents evidence of the use of entheogenic substances in ancient Judaic traditions. He compiles proof from scripture, historical sources, and archeology to identify the plants likely found in the Old Testament. In particular, his research on the preparation of the holy ointment and the tabernacle incense suggests that the priestly caste's herbal preparations contained various psychoactive components to facilitate a direct experience of the Israelite God. "*The preparations indicate that the ancient Israelites had a profound understanding of synergism, and the way they are consumed and the taboos around them are highly suggestive of their use as psychoactive agents.*"[8] Brian Muraresku traces the ritualized use of consciousness-altering plants and fungi in ancient Greece and how those practices influenced emerging Christianity.[9] The work of Brown and Brown explores the presence of entheogens in early Christian art.[10]

---

5. McFague, *Body of God*, 17.
6. Moltmann-Wendel, *I Am My Body*, 103.
7. Winkelman, "Introduction: Evidence for Entheogen Use," 44.
8. Nemu, "Getting High with the Most High," 114.
9. Muraresku, *Immortality Key*.
10. Brown and Brown, *Psychedelic Gospels*.

## How Do Entheogens and Christianity Fit Together?

Moving beyond the question of "can" entheogens and Christianity intersect toward "how" they do, we can begin to place entheogens into a broader pattern of non-ordinary consciousness experiences called extraordinary spiritual experiences (ESEs).

According to Hufford, ESEs are a particular type of spiritual experience that involves direct perception or contact with spiritual realities. ESEs often occur in liminal spaces and may occur spontaneously or be facilitated. Spontaneous ESEs can include experiences of lost time, vivid dreaming, sleep paralysis, near-death experiences, encounters with spirits, auditory and visual experiences, and unexplainable synchronicities. Facilitated ESEs can occur with sensory deprivation or repetitive movement, extended meditative states, and ingestion of entheogens. ESEs cognitively reframe one's life and, according to Hufford, have transformative healing potential for those who experience them.[11]

Rev. Dr. Seth D. Jones has created a framework for understanding the meaning-making process of ESEs within the Christian context. He argues that ESEs are at the very core of every religious movement and describes how many religions are founded based upon a telling of an ESE—from Muhammad receiving the Qur'an in a cave, Buddha receiving enlightenment under the Bodhi tree, Moses conversing with God as the burning bush, Mary's visitation by an angel, to the central Christian ESE of Jesus' resurrection.[12]

According to Jones, ESEs in the Bible help us to prepare for our ESEs and help us understand past ESEs. His work outlines a variety of ESEs in Scripture—angelic visitations, prophetic dreams, visionary events, interventions into the natural world, possessions, and resurrections.[13] *"The ESEs in Scripture is a model for our ESEs, a way to frame and help make sense of these deep spiritual experiences that happen over and over again in the lives of faith of those in the Bible and also in the world."*[14] Jones also notes that many of the high holidays of the church revolve around the occurrence of ESEs. He urges the Christian church to be at the forefront, becoming a safe place to share spontaneous and facilitated ESEs.[15] Applying an ESE lens to

---

11. Hufford, "Sleep Paralysis as Spiritual Experience."
12. Jones, "Extraordinary Spiritual Experiences."
13. Jones, "Extraordinary Spiritual Experiences."
14. Jones, "Extraordinary Spiritual Experiences."
15. Jones, "Extraordinary Spiritual Experiences."

Scripture allows the recognition of a foundational pattern of non-ordinary consciousness within Christianity and provides an intersection between the actual entheogenic experience and faith.

Descriptions of entheogenic experiences are often similar to the described non-ordinary states of consciousness of mystical experiences. Scientific and medical experts at the Johns Hopkins Center for Psychedelic and Consciousness Research have been conducting clinical research to understand the effects of psilocybin, an entheogenic fungi, on the brain and mind as a potential therapeutic for mental illnesses and overall wellness.[16] Research by Griffiths et al. concluded that, when administered under supportive conditions, psilocybin occasioned experiences similar to spontaneously occurring mystical experiences. Griffiths et al. conducted a fourteen-month follow-up to determine the long-term effects of the substantial personal meaning and spiritual significance recorded by participants in their earlier study.[17]

Although the critical research by Griffiths et al. and others is advancing the empirical analysis of mystical experiences through entheogenic research and provides yet another intersection for us to consider, Christianity has a long, experiential history of mysticism that embeds the experiences into a larger wisdom tradition. However, for mystics, the only way to know God is to experience God. Mysticism describes the explorations and conclusions of extraordinary states of awareness and consciousness that an individual experiences when they relate to the beyond or eternal. Although mysticism occurs within most religious traditions, Christian mysticism draws upon both scripture and wisdom teachings from the early desert hermits of the Middle East, cloistered individuals throughout the Middle Ages, to a variety of saints, visionaries, and spiritual teachers.[18] By studying the experiences of the mystics, we can learn how others oriented their extraordinary experiences within the Christian tradition.

Julian of Norwich, a thirty-year-old anchorite nun during the 1300s, received a series of intense visions of Jesus and his Passion during a severe illness.[19] At the time, she believed she was on her deathbed, and the experience lasted over twelve hours. After her recovery, she immediately

---

16. Johns Hopkins Medicine, "Johns Hopkins Center for Psychedelic and Consciousness Research."

17. Griffiths et al., "Psilocybin Can Occasion."

18. McColman, "Putting the 'Christian' into 'Christian Mysticism.'"

19. Grange, "Julian of Norwich."

recorded the visions as the *Revelations of Divine Love* and continued expanding upon them throughout her life. *Revelations of Divine Love* is the earliest surviving book in the English language written by a woman and clearly documents her life-altering extraordinary spiritual experience. Her written account serves as a continual foundation of wisdom for those who engage with her writings and the meeting with Jesus she describes.

The experiences of Christian mystics weave into the larger perennial or wisdom tradition. The wisdom tradition, which situates mysticism as core to all spiritual traditions, provides a conceptual framework for developing the inner self, living a spiritual life, and discovering union with God. By looking at the commonalities between Christianity as a wisdom tradition and entheogens as a wisdom tradition, we set a larger container for both traditions to interact and influence each other.

Rev. Dr. Cynthia Bourgeault, modern-day mystic, Episcopal priest, and writer, positions Jesus first and foremost as a wisdom teacher who emerged out of and worked within the ancient tradition called *sophia perrennis* or *wisdom*.[20] She describes Jesus as a "teacher of the path of inner transformation flowing from the stream of living wisdom that has been flowing through the human condition for at least five thousand years."[21] Bourgeault describes Jesus' use of parables—a wisdom genre—and his focus on the transformation of human consciousness concerned more with timeless questions of the human heart than religious reform as evidence that Jesus was indeed a wisdom teacher transmitting a wisdom lineage to those he met.

Bourgeault describes her own foundational mystical experience at the age of twelve when she raged at God, trying to make sense of her childhood playmate's impending death. Soon after, she asked God why prayer wasn't working and how the situation could be happening. She felt herself being suffused in golden light and heard a voice saying Dan would die, but all would be well. "*While I certainly couldn't understand the message itself, I understood that warm, golden light and somehow relaxed and rested. I discovered in that moment that there was something in me that knew. It didn't know what it knew, exactly, but it knew that it knew.*"[22] Bourgeault also calls this *recognition energy*—the capacity to ground truth a spiritual experience in your own being. "The gospels are built on it—and so was the early church—as the powerful liberation energy of

20. Bourgeault, *Wisdom Way of Knowing*, 4–8.
21. Bourgeault, *Wisdom Way of Knowing*, 6.
22. Bourgeault, *Wisdom Way of Knowing*, 7.

the Christ event spills over and travels forward, moving from recognition to recognition." She reminds the reader of Jesus' repeated question documented in the Gospels, "Who do you say I am?" and reframes Jesus' question as "Who or what in you recognizes me ?"[23]

This recognition energy is at the heart of exploring entheogenic Christianity. Just as Julian of Norwich has spiritual assurance that all revealed to her was done to glorify God, Bourgeault's recognition energy provides a faith-secured anchor for those who love Christ and are experiencing a facilitated ESE. Bourgeault writes, "*Wisdom is an ancient tradition, not limited to one particular religious expression but at the headwaters of all the great sacred paths . . . . One of the greatest losses in our Christian West has been the loss of memory (in fact, almost a collective amnesia) about our own Wisdom heritage.*"[24] She goes on to say:

> *The real Source of Wisdom lies in a higher or more vivid realm of divine consciousness that is neither behind us nor ahead of us but always surrounding us . . . . [Wisdom] seems to go underground for a while; one loses the thread. Then, in ways inexplicable to linear causality, it pops up again. It re-creates itself over and over, so it seems, in the minds and hearts of those who have been taught (or discovered on their own) how to listen and see. It never really goes away, and it always comes back in a fresh new form, customized to the conditions of the world.*[25]

## Connections to Entheogenic and Indigenous Spiritualities

Entheogenic spiritualities also have deep wisdom heritages that have been lost to memory. Institutional Christianity must accept its role in destroying indigenous entheogenic wisdom traditions through colonization, genocide, and violent conversions.

As Medina and Gonzales write in their book *Voices from the Ancestors: Xicanx and Latinx Spiritual Expressions and Healing Practices*, "The banishment and criminalization of our ancestral ethical and ceremonial practices that ensued with colonization disrupted and silenced Latin American, Caribbean Indigenous, and African knowledge systems that centered our relationship to the sacred cosmic forces, the natural world, the

---

23. Bourgeault, *Wisdom Way of Knowing*, 8.
24. Bourgeault, *Wisdom Way of Knowing*, 4.
25. Bourgeault, *Wisdom Way of Knowing*, 25–26.

*ancestors, the land, and one another as well as the knowledge embedded within ritual practices and ways of acting in the world.*"[26]

Sallie McFague's theology of the body further explains the consequences of embedded distrust of the body within Christianity and its intertwined relationship with colonization.

> *Christianity is a religion of the incarnation par excellence. Its earliest and most persistent doctrines focus on embodiment: from the incarnation (the Word made flesh) and Christology (Christ was fully human) to the eucharist (this is my body, this is my blood), the resurrection of the body, and the church (the body of Christ who is the head), Christianity has been a religion of the body. . . . And yet, the earliest Christian texts and doctrines contain seeds that, throughout history, have germinated into a full-blown distrust of the body and deprecation of nature and abhorrence and loathing of female bodies.*[27]

And I would add a loathing of Black and Brown bodies that remains today as a result of such colonization beliefs. During conquest and colonization, the "*profound understandings of the human body holding spiritual energies correlating to the spiritual powers in the universe were deemed irrelevant. Our ancestors' knowledge and ways were deemed ignorant or demonic.*"[28]

Thankfully, not all entheogenic wisdom knowledge and traditions were lost, and entheogenic practices have been continuously used across various cultures, including Mexico, South America, West Africa, and Siberia. Some entheogenic cultures have integrated aspects of cultural Christianity into their modern practices, while others have remained within the container of their indigenous spiritual lineages.

## Envisioning a New Perspective

An intentional, entheogenic Christianity must seize the opportunity to decolonize and decenter Whiteness within current expressions. There should be efforts to develop interspiritual relationships with indigenous spiritualities that place alternate consciousness wisdom within the shared context of the perennial wisdom tradition. So, how do we begin

---

26. Medina and Gonzalez, *Voices from the Ancestors*, 7.
27. McFague, *Body of God*, 14.
28. Medina and Gonzalez, *Voices from the Ancestors*, 11.

to understand an entheogenic-driven decolonizing of Christianity? Are there lived experiences that provide us a glimpse into what part of this path could look like?

The first place to look would be to those who have been directly or historically impacted by colonization and the pathways that support them in healing and liberation. Citing medical doctor Lewis Mehl-Madrona, Medina and Gonzalez connect the power of ritual ceremony to transform, "*the healing power of spirit and the spiritual dimension in our lives, including the role of ritual and ceremony in catalyzing change, in connecting us to nonphysical energies, in giving us a view of ourselves as capable of more than we had previously thought, and by enfolding us in the comfort of the Divine.*"[29]

## A Personal Need for Healing

I didn't realize how much I needed ceremony until I participated in an embodied leadership program where I was introduced to the power of entheogens as healing and transformation tools. I had no prior exposure or experience with entheogens, but after several months of preparation, I decided I was ready to participate in a facilitated ceremony. My first experience was truly life-changing. I was shown my sacred vocation and experienced what abundance felt like in my body. As each cell of my body seemed to swell with aliveness and satisfaction, I distinctly remember connecting the sensation in real-time to Jesus' words, "*I am come that they might have life and that they might have it more abundantly*" from John.[30] The experience radically changed my relationship with that verse, and I can still tap into that feeling years later. As I continued participating in entheogenic ceremonies, my Christian faith deepened profoundly. Although most people associate entheogenic experiences with expansive, non-ordinary states of consciousness that take you more up and out, some entheogens bring you into a deeper relationship with your body. These body-oriented entheogens brought the incarnational aspect of the Christian faith alive in ways I could have never imagined. I have had a variety of entheogenic ceremonies and have experienced some of the classic hallmarks of unity consciousness, divine union, and all-encompassing love. I realized early on that I could surrender and navigate the entheogenic

---

29. Medina and Gonzalez, *Voices from the Ancestors*, 15.
30. Barker and Kohlenberger, *Zondervan NIV Bible Commentary*, "John 10:10."

experience because of my faith upbringing. In my Christian tradition, we are encouraged to learn to discern and follow prompts of the Holy Spirit, and navigating entheogenic non-ordinary consciousness feels very similar to me. The awe in the entheogenic space resonates with open-hearted, raised hands singing during communal worship. The spark of divine fire can feel as activating as a spirit-filled revival or as soft as the glow of a candlelight Christmas service. My church experiences have been anchors for my entheogenic experiences, and, increasingly, my entheogenic experiences are becoming anchors for my church engagement. But as these two parts of my spiritual life began interacting more and more, I started having questions about how each modality might reflect my spiritual heritage. I am a granddaughter of El Salvador. My parents immigrated to the United States in the 1960s, and I was born in Chicago in the 1970s. We only visited El Salvador once during my childhood, so I didn't grow up with a relationship with the land or its people beyond my immediate family. My mother was orphaned at the tender age of three, and my father was the only member of his small family to immigrate, so I had a minimal ability to connect with my ancestors. In fact, it was very much a tender topic for me. I was envious of stories of people tracing their genealogy back hundreds of years while I only knew the names of my great-grandparents and no further. Any archives that did exist were destroyed during the Civil War. I knew that both sides of my family had indigenous roots and varying degrees of Spanish heritage, but I felt that part of who I was and where I came from would always be a mystery.

Although I may have hit a wall in my family history and lived experiences, I had the opportunity to dive into learning more about the works and records of the contemplative Christian tradition. I began to learn about Christian mystics and found it exciting. It was so enriching to read the accounts of their experiences and to find resonance with what I was experiencing in the entheogenic ceremony. The Christian mystics started to become spiritual ancestors for me. Different mystics reminded me of different entheogens, and their faithfulness encouraged me to develop my own practices of devotion. Then, during a lecture where the teacher reviewed the history of Christian mystics, it became clear to me that we would be predominantly studying the development of Western, White Christianity for several months. As I read the timeline of people and dates, I thought, "There were other people on the planet," and not just other people—my people. Something deep inside me knew that my people knew how to connect to the divine, which was good. This visceral reaction was wholly unexpected but opened the gate to a series of explorations central to my healing.

For the first time, I began to wrestle with what it meant to be a Christian. I know that my soul's delight is in the Christ path, yet I had come to a crossroads with what that possibly meant for the long story of who I was and where I was from. I began to wonder who among my ancestors might have been the first to encounter formalized Christianity. I had to face that it was probably not voluntary in all reality. The conquest of the New World was violent and ruthlessly targeted indigenous spiritualities. I had to sit with the knowledge that the Spanish heritage running through my veins and looking back at me in the mirror could be that of the colonizer. This was no academic exercise; this was a radical perspective shift where my beloved faith was at the center of very challenging complexity.

As I sat with these new faith questions and pondered them in my heart, I also knew that, deep down inside, these complexities coexisted in harmony. The old hymn "It Is Well with My Soul" kept coming to mind, and I found myself humming it quite often. It is one of my favorite hymns because it reminds me of my childhood church days of playing in the handbell choir. I spent many hours learning that hymn, and to this day, my muscle memory kicks in, and I move my hands to the notes whenever I hear it. One day, I caught myself doing the hand motions while humming, and something clicked inside me. My soul and body knew how to hold these tensions together and could be a resource in my spiritual inquiry.

I knew the best way to access my soul and body was in ceremony with the support of entheogens. I wasn't sure how the insight I sought would appear, but I had true faith that it was possible to receive it because it was in my heart. I sat in a circle with twenty other individuals and a trusted facilitator, shared my heart's desire, and surrendered myself to God and the direction of the Holy Spirit. About three hours into the experience, I was sitting up with my eyes closed and singing in deep devotion, and I felt the prompting of the spirit to open my eyes and look down at my hands. I looked down and saw that my left hand had a rosary wrapped around it, and in my right hand, I was holding a slight egg-shaped rattle. Although I had brought them with me to the circle, I did not remember picking them up from the spot where I had placed them beside me. I felt a strong loop of energy going between my two hands. An endless circle of energy flowed from my left hand, up my arm, across my chest, down my other arm, and across to the other hand in continual flow. I focused on my rosary-wrapped left hand first. Having a rosary was pretty edgy for me as a lifelong Protestant. Still, when I began to explore the possible Christian roots of my ancestors, I decided to start a practice to examine that connection. I had found a way of rewilding my perspective on the rosary. I liked the concepts within praying the rosary and the fifteen mysteries, but the practice had not fully taken root in my heart that was described by Strand and Finn.[31] As I looked down at the blue-green beads, I realized that I associated the rosary with colonization, so I was not resonating with the practice. I looked to my right hand and the rattle perfectly tucked into my palm. I gave it a shake and felt the beads inside and the energy between my hands swirls. It was very clear that it represented my ancestors. Both of these tools, the rosary and the rattle, were the tools of my spiritual heritage. I moved both hands in front of me and looked at them simultaneously. I felt the prompting of the spirit to sit quietly and feel the energy circling between them and the rest of my body. The loop of energy was smooth—giving me the impression that they existed seamlessly together through the bridge of my body. The spirit prompted me to think deeply about my associations with the rosary, and I realized I mostly associated the rosary with priests. The word in Spanish for priest is *cura*. The rattle accompanies the prayers and work of the *curandera*, the word for medicine woman or healer. At that moment, it was clear that entheogens were a part of both traditions, and entheogens were the throughlines to the longer story of how my individual constellation of heritages accessed the divine and many others, too. The word *cura* in Spanish also means to *heal*—and I experienced a multi-layered healing that night. For the first time, I felt like I got to experience all parts of my spiritual heritage working together. I might not know their names, but I know something about how my ancestors encountered God, which has given me a peace that surpasses understanding. Following the same pathways to knowing God has restored a missing part of me, and I know it also has for others.

Medina and Gonzales, discussing the importance of reclaiming spiritual and cultural traditions for Latinx and African communities, write, "*In our collective willingness to share, we acknowledge the importance these spiritual expressions and practices play in pointing the way to healing possibilities. . . . We receive the stories, the medicine, and the danza (dance) they carry; we participate in ceremony in communal ritual; we share oral tradition; we research, read, paint, dance, drum, and sing. We*

---

31. Strand, *Way of the Rose*.

*learn about the knowledge that our bodies carry, the medicine of the plants that help us heal."*[32] And that collective willingness to share the wisdom of ceremony and wisdom of entheogens must be honored.

We cannot extract the wisdom of entheogens to benefit a majority and not prioritize the healing of those historically harmed by Christianity and racism, nor exclude their in-ceremony experiences from our collective meaning-making. Theologian Sallie McFague reminds us, "*We do not use nature or other people as a means to an end—our union with God—but see each and every creature, everybody, as intrinsically valuable in itself, in its specialness, its distinctiveness, its difference from ourselves.*"[33] This highlights the way we can have an intentional process of shared meaning-making, which is central to decentering Whiteness and decolonizing Christianity. Centering the meaning-making and experiences of Black and Brown perspectives is the only way to sustain a healthy, entheogenic-informed Christianity. Seth D. Jones prompts us to be intentional in our sharing of ESEs. "*How shall we make meaning of what we have brought back from that mystical awareness, from the ESE we have experienced or heard about? I believe that, whatever our faith commitment may be, we need to begin to share what those forms of mind and spiritual realms are like for one another. I think this is what we are up to on Sunday mornings. Making meaning together of the deeper things of this universe.*"[34]

An entheogenic Christianity already exists—because I exist. And others exist. We exist. Requiring people to prove their Christianity replicates the toxic patterns of the past. Still, by prioritizing the entheogenic experiences of Black and Brown people and supporting them to lead the development of today's entheogenic-informed faith, we can better align with the future of the global church.

The Christian faith is undergoing a dramatic transition from being a predominantly Western to a non-Western religion. The center of the Christian church body is no longer encapsulated within Western, White culture. Today, the church is almost exclusively growing in non-Western cultures or among immigrant communities.[35] Granberg-Michaelson writes that a re-orienting will need to take place among US congregations as a result of this shift and that they will need to learn "*to*

---

32. Medina and Gonzalez, *Voices from the Ancestors*, 15–16.

33. McFague, *Body of God*, 211.

34. Jones, "Extraordinary Spiritual Experiences," "Set and Setting: The Where and the When of ESEs."

35. Granberg-Michaelson, "Not a 'White' Christmas."

de-Americanize the gospel, reject the heresy of individualism, embrace the color of the future, affirm Spirit-filled communities, perceive the world as sacred, and overcome divisive culture wars."[36] If we seriously consider the role of entheogens in Christianity, we must do so in the context of the new church reality. The church is changing and deconstructing the foci of the power and centering needs of those the church serves now, and their realities are central to the future of faith.

## Conclusion

Entheogens are an emergent wisdom practice within the larger contemplative tradition that provides a way to understand and recenter Christianity to the lived experiences of the current and future church. They also offer new avenues for interfaith and interspiritual dialogue and relationship building around our mutual experiences of the sacred and integration within religious frameworks.

The questions we ask about entheogens and religious practices will determine our perspectives—just as Jesus' question, "*Who do you say I am?*" determines theological orientation toward his presence. If we choose to ask "if" this works, we will go down the road of dualistic inquiries that seek to polarize and prove a singular approach that will silence meaningful lived experiences. However, should we ask "how" entheogens work within Christian traditions, we position ourselves to learn and follow the leadership of various wisdom perspectives and sources.

We have the opportunity to gather threads and weave a new tapestry that tells the story of becoming one in Christ through all lived experiences. The experiences of each of us matter to God and the church. Indeed, through him, all things are made. May we make the church according to that goodness and consider how God has revealed through all creation and many modalities. Just as the garden of Eden was filled with lush diversity, may we honor the variety of needs to experience union with the divine. Let us grow a new church intertwined and blooming with entheogenic wisdom, revelations, and insight.

---

36. Granberg-Michaelson, "Not a 'White' Christmas," $10.

## Deeper Conversation/Deeper Listening

1. How can the suggestions of honoring the diversity of cultures within the context of modern Christianity become a norm and not an exception?
2. How do we better preserve the ancient wisdom traditions and make them a part of the context of today's worship?
3. In what ways can somatic practices be used to make common grounds as an interfaith practice?

## Spiritual Practice

Somatic spirituality is a wisdom spirituality that mindfully includes the body and is not new. Walking a labyrinth, singing, dancing, chanting a hymn, striking a rhythm in a drum circle or bell choir, as well as kneeling to pray or using dance are all somatic practices. Select a time and space to engage in a somatic practice. Record in your journal how it felt. Refer to reputable websites on somatics to expand your practices.

## Bibliography

Barker, Kenneth L., and John R. Kohlenberger. *Zondervan NIV Bible Commentary*. Grand Rapids, MI: Zondervan, 1994.

Bourgeault, Cynthia. *The Wisdom Jesus: Transforming Heart and Mind: A New Perspective on Christ and His Message*. Boston: New Seeds, 2008.

———. *The Wisdom Way of Knowing: Reclaiming an Ancient Tradition to Awaken the Heart*. San Francisco: Jossey-Bass, 2003.

Brown, Jerry B., and Julie M. Brown. *The Psychedelic Gospels: The Secret History of Hallucinogens in Christianity*. Rochester, VT: Park Street, 2016.

McColman, Carl. "Putting the 'Christian' into 'Christian Mysticism.'" *Anam Chara: Carl McColman*, Nov 4, 2021. https://anamchara.com/putting-the-christian-into-christian-mysticism/.

Furst, Peter T. *Hallucinogens and Culture*. San Francisco: Chandler and Sharp, 1976.

Granberg-Michaelson, Wesley. "Not a 'White' Christmas." *Sojourners*, Mar 10, 2020. https://sojo.net/articles/not-white-christmas.

Grange, John M. "Julian of Norwich—Her Relevance To Healing Today." *Spirituality and Health International* 4.4 (2003) 7–12. https://onlinelibrary.wiley.com/doi/abs/10.1002/shi.188.

Griffiths, R. R., et al. "Psilocybin Can Occasion Mystical-Type Experiences Having Substantial and Sustained Personal Meaning and Spiritual Significance." *Psychopharmacology* 187.3 (2006) 268–83. https://doi.org/10.1007/s00213-006-0457-5.

Hufford, David J. "Sleep Paralysis as Spiritual Experience." *Transcultural Psychiatry* 42.1 (2005) 11–45. https://doi.org/10.1177/1363461505050709.

Johns Hopkins Medicine. "Johns Hopkins Center for Psychedelic and Consciousness Research." Accessed March 15, 2022. https://www.hopkinsmedicine.org/psychiatry/research/psychedelics-research.

Julian of Norwich. *The Showings: Uncovering the Face of the Feminine in Revelations of Divine Love*. Translated by Mirabai Starr. Newburyport, MA: Hampton Roads, 2013.

McFague, Sallie. *The Body of God: An Ecological Theology*. Cambridge: International Society for Science and Religion, 2007.

Medina, Lara, and Martha R. Gonzalez. *Voices from the Ancestors: Xicanx and Latinx Spiritual Expressions and Healing*. Tucson: University of Arizona Press, 2019.

Mellinger, Wayne Martin. "Tripping with the Gods: On Entheogenic Spirituality." *Doing Modernity* (blog), Aug 24, 2020. http://doingmodernity.blogspot.com/.

Moltmann-Wendel, Elisabeth. *I Am My Body: A Theology of Embodiment*. New York: Continuum, 1995.

Muraresku, Brian. *The Immortality Key: The Secret History of the Religion with No Name*. New York: St. Martin's Griffin, 2023.

Nemu, Danny. "Getting High with the Most High: Entheogens in the Old Testament." *Journal of Psychedelic Studies* 3.2 (2019) 117–32. https://doi.org/10.1556/2054.2019.004.

Rockland Congregational Church. "Extraordinary Spiritual Experiences." Sermon series, Nov 7–Nov 28, 2021. https://rocklandcongregationalchurch.weebly.com/extraordinary-spiritual-experiences-series-nov-7---nov-28-2021.html.

Strand, Clark. *The Way of the Rose: The Radical Path of the Divine Feminine Hidden in the Rosary*. New York: Spiegel and Grau, 2019.

Winkelman, Michael. "Introduction: Evidence for Entheogen Use in Prehistory and World Religions." *Journal of Psychedelic Studies* 3.2 (2019) 43–62. https://doi.org/10.1556/2054.2019.024.

# PART 6

# *Introduction:* Love, Hope, and Beauty in All Things

> This section explores the experience of life within the natural world and the shifts that bring on new realities. These chapters use examples from the Qur'an and the Quaker, Christian, and Catholic traditions.

WHEN I WAS A teacher at a local university, I used to keep a poster in my office that read:

> *The body heals with play.*
> *The mind heals with laughter.*
> *The spirit heals with joy. (author unknown)*

It reminded me and my students that life has more than one component, and our ultimate goal is to keep a spirit that reminds us that life is always in a healing process. This simple reminder also taught me that sometimes life will take you behind "enemy lines," where all you can say is, "*I did not sign up for this.*" These are the times when you find yourself in your own "Garden of Gethsemane," where you may be alone, behind enemy lines, with people you cannot communicate with, identify with, or find a common interest, let alone common ground. You realize that one of the gifts of God is always prayer and seeing the joy within that occurs with prayer. Connecting to the power source we call God is essential during these times. Howard Thurman calls prayer your "*centering moment.*"

To be centered, there is also a form of interior isolation that must occur and a realization and confidence in faith that all is within God's will, no matter what. After all, the sovereignty of love is God.

Change always begins on the inside. We are the first to know something new happens in our inner lives. When it is noticed, and we are committed to making a difference, the change we have experienced shows up on the outside. This is the emotional resonance that, for some, is a lifelong goal. For most, we find within our lived experience that we tell ourselves many stories, which, for the most part, is a reflection of a reflection. Essentially, our story is true. However, along the way, our story may become part myth, part fairy tale, and a healthy portion of fantasy. At times, it is hard to share the unvarnished truth about ourselves. After all, we have a right to the private corners of our lives, and the absolute decision of what we need to share lies within us. However, ensuring the reason for our sharing is highly important. This is when we must check our alignment with what we believe we know versus what we have experienced. When we can share with a clear purpose, this brings us one step closer to a spiritual, emotional resonance.

Sharing our experiences takes fortitude. The comparison I like to use is one of a ship. When a ship goes through a hurricane, it is the only time the boat and the captain will receive hurricane certification. This is because the captain learns valuable lessons that can only be taught in the experience of a hurricane. These lessons include the swells being more prominent the farther your journey goes into the storm. Or, the vessel's strength is relentlessly tested at the height of the storm, and skills the captain has been reading about are used. But the most important lesson is that there is peace in the center of each hurricane as the boat passes through the eye, and the captain can sense when the vessel is nearing the center or the eye of the storm and can pass safely through to the other side.

Personal hurricanes are transformational. They demonstrate the critical importance of taking your happiness and reaching for joy seriously. We develop a divine, unshakable confidence and reminder that deep within, if we honor our fears, we learn more about ourselves and what we truly value. It is an honest way of assessing our beliefs and learning if our values align with Divine truths. When in the midst of our personal hurricane, if we remind ourselves of the beauty that can be found within God and that beauty can be reached through prayer, we will come out with our own transformational certification. It is a certification that demonstrates love transforms, God's word is sacred insight, and even in the most broken moments of our existence, there is a higher connection with the divine that will bring you through. In today's world we are wrapped up in the process of becoming or the process of being. We are striving to reinvent, change, or promote to the next level. All of these steps are built on the benefit of hope, fear, or failure. We must not see hope with a posture of dependence or fear and failure as the ultimate downfall with no recovery. All of this is the expectation and experimentation that is a part of life; the hardest part of life can often be the courage to persevere.

The last section combines several ways to look at beauty, love, joy, and the importance of dreams. In closing with these chapters, we come to the question, *Can we find beauty in all things as a way of reforming, changing, and seeing a new community?*

## Chapter 19

## I Am a Dreamer

### Marsha Holmes, Spiritual Director

*Marsha is a vocational deacon in the Episcopal Diocese of Florida and a graduate of the Spiritual Direction Intensive at the Haden Institute. She currently mentors spiritual direction students at the Haden Institute and has an active spiritual direction practice—Your Sacred Guide.*

*Marsha spent almost thirty years in corporate America, retiring as a vice president at a major telecommunications company. Since her retirement, much of her focus has been in the area of pastoral care. Her outreach focus has been on Black and Brown children, including ministering to orphanages in Bolivia and Uganda. She currently serves as deacon and clergy-in-charge at St. Philips Episcopal Church in Jacksonville, Florida. Dreams have always been a part of her life. Understanding them and considering them as a part of her life's work has been a later in life work and experience.*

I AM A DREAMER and have always been. I believe my dreams mean much more to my life now as I have moved into the spaciousness of my later years. I am more open to listening to them and hearing what they offer than at any other time in my life. As "a woman of a certain age," I choose to identify in archetypal terms such as a "crone." In general, our modern society considers this term a hostile assault on women. I, however, am proud to be a crone. I start here because I believe it helps to understand why and how dreams are more important than ever at this stage of my life.

I love the personal ideation of the crone at this point in my life. Let's first talk about what a crone is and why it is vital to my journeys in the world of my dreams. The visualization of the crone archetype is a haggard, witch-like, ugly woman with the expression of a harsh laugh. Hence, we imagine a woman with distasteful habits and a woman past her prime. While this may be one representation of a crone, the crone archetype actually pre-exists in our collective unconscious. She guides us through the changes in life, channeling wisdom and intuition. I often think of her as the driver in the process of metamorphosis as the butterfly moves from egg to larva to chrysalis to butterfly. The crone has guided me through all these stages, but I hear her more clearly in my fully formed butterfly stage. It includes the ability of a woman to accept the process of aging and to embrace death—all death, not just physical death—and, most importantly, renewal. The crone embraces the new starts in life. With each death and each renewal comes new experience and wisdom. She teaches me from the experiences of her youth. Her maturity allows her to live the life she wants. The crone can live in the today because she has let go of the past—let go of what others want her to be.

Sometimes, I am the crone in my dreams, but mostly someone else or even something else represents the crone attributes to offer me lessons from the dream. The crone never appears in my dreams as the haggard witch-like woman. She appears in many forms but always with the wisdom of many years of love and loss and of life and death. As a crone, at this stage in my life, I am able to be—just be. I can let go of what is past that needs to stay in the past, but also embrace whatever I want or need from the past as well. I can accept that the years to come are much shorter than the years past. I can keep all the good that formed me and either leave behind or use to my benefit all that hurt me.

So, what does all that mean in the world of my dreams? I don't remember any of my childhood dreams. I wish I could—I believe it would help explain some of my complexities and even idiosyncrasies. However, even "as a woman of a certain age," I still have lots of life ahead of me, and my dreams are an integral part of where I am going. Only in my senior years did I realize that these dreams might have meaning beyond what I will call my "personal entertainment." Even when they were disturbing, I never gave them much thought. People dreamed, I dreamed—it was what it was. If nightmares occurred, they must have been because of a bad day. Certainly, there is nothing to learn from them—the delightful ones, the dreadful ones, the puzzling ones. They were just dreams—entertainment during my sleeping hours.

The community of my youth and young adulthood was not one to consider this work important. Actually, I would say my family and my culture thought just the opposite. The church, the Black church, was very much a part of my childhood and my early adult life. I believe it is unlikely that analyzing dreams to understand my inner self, my spiritual self, would have been considered valuable.

> *Summoned or Not, God is Present.*
> —C. G. Jung

## God and Dreams

And yet, the dream as a way for God to convey messages is biblical. There are twenty-one instances in the Bible in which God communicated through a dream. Most of the dreams are in the Old Testament, but six (four with a message to the same dreamer) are in the New Testament.

As a young child in Sunday school and vacation Bible school, I remember singing about climbing Jacob's ladder. Just as there are different interpretations of our dreams today, the movement of the angels up and down the ladder has been interpreted in several ways. The dream, however, is the way that God spoke to Jacob and through it to us today.

In the New Testament, dreams were instrumental in telling the story of the birth and early life of Jesus. Joseph, the husband of Mary and the earthly father of Jesus, has four visits from an angel in his dreams. These four instances of dreams by Joseph show us how God talked to Joseph, his instructions to Joseph, and his requirements for obedience to Joseph. For me, it is a lesson about our gift of the dream from God, and in the case of Joseph, it is a lesson on listening and obedience. For example:

> . . . *and her husband Joseph, being a just man and unwilling to put her to shame, resolved to divorce her quietly. But as he considered this, behold, an angel of the Lord appeared to him in a dream, saying, "Joseph, son of David, do not fear to take Mary your wife, for that which is conceived in her is of the Holy Spirit; she will bear a son, and you shall call his name Jesus, for he will save his people from their sins."* (Matt 2:19–25)

> *Now when they had departed, behold, an angel of the Lord appeared to Joseph in a dream and said, "Rise, take the child and his mother, and flee to Egypt, and remain there till I tell you, for Herod is about to search for the child, to destroy him." And he rose and took the child and his mother by night, and departed to Egypt, and remained there until the death of Herod.* (Matt 2:13–14)

> *But when Herod died, behold, an angel of the Lord appeared in a dream to Joseph in Egypt, saying, "Rise, take the child and his mother, and go to the land of Israel, for those who sought the child's life are dead." And he rose and took the child and his mother and went to the land of Israel.* (Matt 2:19–21)

> *But when he heard that Archelaus reigned over Judea in place of his father Herod, he was afraid to go there, and being warned in a dream, he withdrew to the district of Galilee. And he went and dwelt in a city called Nazareth, that what was spoken by the prophets might be fulfilled, "He shall be called a Nazarene."* (Matt 2:22–23)

Through these dreams, God spoke to Joseph, warned him of dangers, and guided his life and the life of his family.

As I mentioned earlier, I have dreamed all my life. I knew the story of dreams in the Bible and how God spoke to his people through them. I have always, even as a young child, had a deep and abiding faith. I, however, never connected God talking to his people in ancient times through dreams to God speaking to me. I did not think there were messages from God to me in my dreams. I did not think that I needed to or should look for messages about my life from the Divine. Just a few years ago, I completed the program for spiritual direction at the Haden Institute. For the first time, my eyes were opened to an opportunity to delve into what my dreams meant.

> *Dreams are impartial products of the unconscious psyche,*
> *outside the control of the will.*
> —C. G. Jung

## My Dreams

Learning about Carl Jung's work and dreamwork through the Haden Institute's spiritual direction intensives and dream conferences opened my eyes to a world unknown to me. Exposure to Jung drove me more deeply into my psyche than I had ever dared to go. Working on a dream has become a practice that is very important to my inner work and stability. This became clear to me when I reluctantly offered a dream while I was in spiritual direction training. This dream and working it became a pivotal part of my grief journey. Perhaps for the first time after my husband John suddenly died, I listened to both my own inner voice as well as messages from the Holy—from the God that I claimed as one who guided my life.

As a context, let me share that my husband died suddenly in July 2002. I did not seek counseling—looking back now, for many reasons, I really needed counseling, but that was not something I did. But in 2016, at the Haden Institute, when I shared this most important dream to my fellow journeyers, a new world opened to me. I was able also to look back and realize I had other dreams before this one that were trying to speak to me. A new world opened up to me.

Let me first share the dream and then share with you how it significantly impacted my life.

In my dream . . .

> John is standing in the doorway of the master bedroom in my condo. I am asleep, and he stands watching me. When I woke up, I was startled to see him there because he had died before I moved into the condo. He stands leaning on the door frame. He has just returned from Virginia, where he bought a car from a former corporate colleague. He tells me about his trip and the drive back to Florida. He wanted to buy the Lexus SUV from his friend, but it had been sold, so he bought the Mercedes SUV. He tells me how disappointed he is. He tells me the trip back was tiring, but he stopped in North Carolina to see his daughter. He said he is very tired. I ask him to come to bed with me, and he does. He holds me tightly in his arms and kisses me. I wake up. I physically felt the touch of his body against mine. I feel his physical presence—an actual physical presence—the human warmth of his body still lingering on mine. I began to cry when I realized this was a dream.

I awakened from the dream, startled and shaken. I was confused. In my waking moments, I wondered where John was—he was just here; he had just kissed me, hadn't he?

My colleagues in our spiritual direction cohort helped me see so many things about my life, including my love for John and his love for me, my grief, and the messages about his presence in my life. Those, perhaps, were the obvious things. The process led me to consider other dreams I had before this one. Dreams about losing something. After John's death and before this dream, I had multiple dreams about loss. As I worked this dream, I recognized the significance of two recurring dreams I had been having for months.

In the first dream . . .

> *I am lost in a building at the University of Richmond. I cannot find the classroom where my exam is being administered. It is important that I find the room. I am running all over the building, going from floor to floor—running in and out of classrooms. I cannot find my room. I am in a great panic.*

In the second dream . . .

> *I am in the first-class lounge at Kennedy Airport with John and one of his colleagues. We are waiting to depart for Europe on a business trip. We are having a casual conversation. They both have their luggage. I have no luggage. It is lost. Both are extremely calm, and I am not at all panicked about the loss of my luggage.*

Until I had the dream of John comforting me, I did not connect with the dreams that were speaking to me, that the dreams were connected and described how lost I really was. I also now recognize John as the crone figure in the second dream. In life, he had an extremely high IQ, but more importantly, he was wise. He was the crone speaking to me with the calming wisdom that things would work out. For me, dreamwork is not about an isolated dream. My dreams, my life, and my faith are all connected. God speaks to me through my dreams. Ancestors speak to me through my dreams. My unconscious psyche speaks to me through my dreams. My job is to listen.

## My Approach to Working Dreams

I am currently not a part of a dream group, but working my dreams is an essential practice for me, and Jeremy Taylor is my most important guide. Appendix 2 of Taylor's book *The Wisdom of Your Dreams* provided me a road map—but not one I had to stop in every "town" along my route.[1] Instead, the road map was one where I might skip some "towns" or even visit some more than once. I can use these techniques in any order. I can work the same dream using different methods. I

---

1. Taylor, *Wisdom of Your Dreams*, appendix 2, 308

might add, at this point, that working a dream several times using different approaches can truly be revealing.

I now offer the ten approaches from *The Wisdom of Your Dreams* without a detailed explanation. It is worth the read!

In *The Wisdom of Your Dreams*, Taylor offers the following approaches (he calls them hints; I call them approaches) to working a dream alone:

1. *Draw the dream*—Images are very powerful for me and often open up feelings that words cannot.

2. *Separate the emotional narrative*—As a TJ on the Myers-Briggs and equally a 1 and 8 on the Enneagram, identifying the emotional narrative is hard but very valuable.

3. *Do active imagination work with characters and figures in the dream other than the original dream ego*—In the Episcopal Church, our children learn through a program called *Godly Play*. We share Bible stories and ask them to wonder. Just saying "I wonder" about the characters in our dreams may open doors we did not imagine.

4. *Embody and act out the dream physically.* Depending on the dream, this can be fun!

5. *Find the image or situation in the dream that carries the greatest energy for you.* Finding the greatest energy in the dream for me is always an important step.

6. *Make a mask of an important character in the dream, wear it, and be that character.* Again, can be fun!

7. *Pray and meditate while focused on the dream.* As a person of faith, this is a step I always include.

8. *Look up images in a dream symbol dictionary.* Lots of resources to help in this area—many online.

9. *Rewrite the narrative, adding the phrase "part of me" to each image.* Many times, people in my dreams represent a part of me—my emotions, what I may be going through at the time of the dream. Pay attention to what others in the dream are telling you.

10. *Incubate further dreams to clarify and amplify the dreams you are working on.* Dreams are connected and not isolated events. It is important to keep a journal to find the connections.[2]

I have not used all these hints—I use the ones that are meaningful to my particular dream. It is important not to force oneself into a rigid pattern. Every dream is different, and the means of working it should also be personal to that dream.

Jung saw dreams as the attempt of the psyche to communicate important things to us. He believed that dreams help us to develop personality. He called this individuation. I believe that these dreams were just that for me. As living beings, at every age, we continue to grow and individualize. This is especially true after any kind of trauma. I know I had many dreams about John between the years of his death in 2002 and the nights I had the dreams I describe here. I do not remember any of them—I ignored them until the psyche would have no more. These dreams demanded that I pay attention.

There is a Lakota prayer that asks Wakan Tanka (the Divine) to teach us how to trust the heart, the mind, the intuition, and the inner knowing. Our dreams are a part of that inner knowing, and we must trust in the messages they offer.

## Deeper Conversation/Deeper Listening

1. What are the best ways to use dreams as a spiritual practice?
2. Have you noticed wisdom and eternal truth being a part of exploring your dreams?
3. Begin a dream journal by writing down dreams as they occur. Find a person that can support you through examining your dreams.

## Spiritual Practice

Two of my favorite things are nature and my camera. My walks, whether in a wooded area or just down my street, enable me to see nature, see creation, and meditate. I meditate, and I offer gratitude to the divine. With my camera, I capture a lasting glimpse of the sacred. As I notice creation, I often see the most insignificant things. One example is a series of photos

---

2. Taylor, *Wisdom of Your Dreams.*

of a pea pod in its natural environment. These photos have enabled hours of deep spirituality and centering for me.

Even as the outer pod looked dry and dead, the bright red peas inside were vibrant and full of life. My spiritual guide told me there is life even when there appears to be death. I spent much time looking at this pod in its natural environment but even more later because of my camera. While I practice meditating on nature in nature, my camera gives me the gift of a spiritual practice of meditating on nature again after my lived experience.

Take a camera along on your next walk. Select items that you are drawn to. Then, put together a collage of the photos. See how the items are a part of your dreams. Discern the meaning behind your selections. Contact a person who is familiar with dreams to assist you.

## Bibliography

Taylor, Jeremy. *The Wisdom of Your Dreams: Using Dreams to Tap into Your Unconscious and Transform Your Life*. New York: Penguin, 2009.

## Chapter 20
## Liturgy of the Hours
### A Need for Daily Practice

ROBERT BENSON, AUTHOR

*Robert Benson is the author of twenty books, including* Between the Dreaming and the Coming True, Living Prayer, Venite, The Echo Within, The Game, *and* Dancing on the Head of a Pen—*a book about the search for the Holy amid our ordinary lives. As a retreat leader and workshop teacher, Benson speaks on the life of prayer and contemplation, the disciplines and rituals of Christian spiritual practice, and the art and craft of writing. He is an adjunct faculty member for the Academy for Spiritual Formation and was named a Living Spiritual Teacher by Spirituality and Practice; Robert is a member of The Friends of Silence & the Poor, an ecumenical prayer community. Benson's roots are in Nashville, Tennessee, though he spends his time traveling, writing, and speaking these days. He does dance on the head of a fountain pen every day, no matter where he happens to be.*

WHILE THERE ARE MANY sources of inspiration and divine guidance, the most essential source of wisdom in my life has been the sayings and teachings of the *Daily Office of the Church*. An ancient practice uses daily prayers to mark the times of the day. For Anglicans, this generally comes in the form of the two main offices of Daily Morning Prayer and Daily Evening Prayer. They may be led by lay people and are said communally or individually.

I was raised in an evangelical part of the church, a part of the church that did not use liturgy and such prayer. My only real exposure to liturgical practice and the ways of such prayer and worship came from Christmas Eve services. One of my grandfathers was an organist in a Lutheran church, and I would go with him to the midnight mass. He would hand me the book while I sat next to him on the balcony and try to follow along.

For much of my early years, I did not know anything about these things called prayer and worship. I received much wisdom and insight from my parents and grandparents, teachers and ministers, and editors and publishing partners with whom I have worked over the years. The same is true of what I drew from the folk with whom I worshiped when I was young. Their way of extemporaneous prayer is one I learned from them, and it is still an essential part of my prayer to this day. But the Daily Office is the most consistent source of wisdom for the last four decades of my life. Indeed, I have been saying these prayers, studying them, and writing about them for years. Since I stumbled onto them, they have shaped my life and my work.

The Office is known by different names in different parts of the church—the Daily Office, the Liturgy of the Hours, and Common Prayer—but the essentials remain the same. The original "version" of the hours came from the Jewish people. It was first written down some four thousand years before Christ came among us. Read and recited each day for all those years, such a way of prayer would have been a part of the prayer that Jesus himself would have prayed. The form, shape, and rhythm of those prayers were the way of prayer practiced by the first Christians, who were, in fact, primarily Jewish people. Though the ways and practice of such daily prayer remained the same, the language reflected their new understanding of the revelation of God in the person of Jesus.

As the Christian faith grew, the practice of daily prayer was passed along to the ones who became the monks and nuns of the desert and then on to the Middle Ages, the days of the Reformation, and to our time. Rooted in this way of prayer, even as it has evolved over thousands of years, the prayers offer a wisdom that seems extraordinary and powerful. It is a rich tradition that grounds me in the devotion and the wisdom of the faithful of Yahweh. It does so in particular ways.

### First of All Is the Use of Scripture in the Daily Office

When one prays these prayers regularly, the Holy Writ becomes something that one does not just read but somehow mystically enters and informs one's prayer. It becomes something that becomes part of one's ongoing conversation with the One who made us.

Being guided daily into reading stories from the Old Testament, the hymns and prayers of the Psalms, the Gospels themselves, and the chronicles from the New Testament letters, all in an ongoing and consistent pattern, begins to center those things in one. I cannot explain precisely how that works; I only know it does. The words of Scripture become not just words of wisdom that one reads; they grant a wisdom that enters one's daily thought and language. Ultimately, they become a part of how one moves through the world, treats other people, and does the work to which one has been given.

Many of us have the experience of reading a book or a story at some time in our life, rereading it later, and discovering some truth or insight that we did not catch before. One of the most potent parts of saying the Office is that it requires one to go through the same pages repeatedly until we finally begin to stumble upon things we did not see or hear before. And to learn to hold those things dear. For example, on the seventeenth day of every month, I read this sentence in one of the prayer books I have used for many years: "Love your enemies." On that day each month, I am required to think about what the word *enemy* means to me, about how I am reacting to such folk in my head and my heart, about the anger I may be holding toward them, and about the person they are and what they might be feeling, and about how I might go about loving them. I do not have many personal enemies, but I do have political and philosophical ones. The Scripture itself, delivered to me by way of the Office, makes me very uncomfortable each and every month.

### Therein Lies Some Wisdom

A second thing that the Office offers to me is the expanding of the "my" in my prayer. It enables me to say words that are larger than just my own words of concern for my own circumstances. *Enable* is just a gentle word, for it *forces* me in the direction of prayer larger than my sweet self. I find myself less likely to pray for a good parking place and more likely to pray for those who are genuinely in need. Each day in the Office, I am called to pray for the Holy Catholic Church and for all who seek the truth. (Catholic being a word that means "universal," not simply a word describing one part of the crowd practicing the faith as best they know how.)

I am reminded to pray for all those whom *"we have loved and no longer see."* Not only for my family but also for those who have been and still are my friends along my journey. I am invited to say prayers for all bishops, priests, ministers, and leaders, a crowd who do not necessarily and immediately jump to mind each day, save for when I am unhappy with them. The Office reminds me to say prayers for my companions on my spiritual path, those to whom I have promised my faithfulness and prayers. The Office calls me to recognize that *"God said, let there be light"* again this day and later to note that the sky is dark and the day is done and to ask for protection *"from all perils and dangers of this night."* And to say, *"Keep watch, dear Lord, with all who work or watch or weep this night."*

These prayers keep calling me to move beyond myself to be part of a universal Church praying for others. We certainly can do that on our own; I have no question about that. But the wisdom of the Office is that it encourages me to say such prayer each and every day, whether I happen to think about doing so or not. I read the words in front of me and find myself praying my way into the larger world.

There is wisdom in there as well.

## And Then, There Is the Sheer Art of It

Over the years, through all the translations—from Hebrew to Latin to Greek to English to all the other languages in which it can be found—there has been a consistency and art to the careful translations of the words. I am not a scholar and am only fluent in only one language. But it is still a mystery to me, a welcome mystery to be sure, as to how the beauty of these prayers has held up over time and across the various parts of the church.

At a Catholic church near my home, I used to go there some days for Lauds, where the prayers were in Latin. I went to the Basilica of the Sacred Heart and to Notre Dame for Matins and Vespers in Paris. I could barely recognize a word in any of those places but knew precisely what was being said in them. Therefore, I could share in the prayer itself.

The art of the Office not only has to do with language, it has to do with shape, form, and structure. These things combine to move one to pray from one's own gratitude to praise to confession to intercession to reflection in a truly wonderful way. I am always struck by the patterns and phrasings I find in the Office, struck by how it moves me through those things and constantly calls me to be more aware of the things of the Spirit that I might overlook where I am left solely to my extemporaneous devices. There is wisdom in the history and language of the prayers, but there is also wisdom to be found in the structure of the prayers themselves.

After all these years of considering myself as a person of prayer and saying the Office, I am convinced that my life would never have been the same without it. The Office has turned out to be the most constant source of wisdom that I know.

*Amen. Amen. So be it.*

## Deeper Conversation/Deeper Listening

1. How should we respond to an unanswered prayer?
2. What is the one book or reading besides sacred text that has been essential to your prayer life?

# Chapter 21
# Spiritual Guidance in the Qur'an

IMAM JAMAL RAHMAN

*Imam Jamal Rahman is a popular speaker and author on Islam, Sufi spirituality, and interfaith relations. Along with his Interfaith Amigos, he has been featured in The New York Times, CBS News, BBC, and various NPR programs. Jamal is a co-founder, Muslim Sufi imam at Interfaith Community Sanctuary, and an adjunct faculty at Seattle University. He travels nationally and internationally, presenting at retreats and workshops. Jamal's passion lies in interfaith community building and activism*

## Introduction

*This Book of Blessings We have sent down to you so that they may meditate on its signs, and that people of insight might take them to heart.* (Q Sad 38:29)

*Listen closely to all that is said and follow the best of it.* (Q Zumar 39:18)

FOR MUSLIMS, A QUARTER of the world's population, the primary source of spiritual wisdom is the Holy Qur'an, which describes itself as a wellspring of guidance, discernment, remembrance, and mercy. The Qur'an is believed to have been revealed to the Prophet Mohammad over a span of twenty-three years, during which he received divine revelations, little by little, directly from the Angel Gabriel.

Like every other holy book, the Qur'an has two kinds of verses: particular and universal. Particular verses are in desperate need of historical and textual context; universal verses are timeless, placeless, and filled with wisdom. In this chapter, we will focus on universal verses. Over the centuries universal verses have resonated deeply in the souls of Islamic sages and inspired their writings. The thirteenth-century teacher Rumi exclaimed, "*I am a slave of the Qur'an; I am dust on the path of Muhammad.*"[1] The poet Muhammad Shamsuddin, who lived in fourteenth-century Persia, memorized the Qur'an in its entirety and is known as Hafiz, a title bestowed on someone who knows the holy book by heart. Rabia, the beloved female sage of eighth-century Iraq, spent countless nights reflecting on verses of the Qur'an.

In my spiritual training ever since childhood, my treasured teachers would give me a qur'anic verse accompanied by another qur'anic verse, a saying of the Prophet Muhammad, poetry, or a teaching story that illuminated the original verse. By meditating on the verses and stories, I was told that I might feel a shift within me and grow in higher consciousness.

In this chapter, I will be commenting on various verses of beauty and wisdom from the Holy Qur'an in order to understand some of its deeper meanings and its relevance to our time and our world today. We invite you, regardless of your faith or no faith, to join us on this journey of discovery.

I have chosen the following topics: becoming a seeker; the mystery of God; compassion; transforming the ego; polishing the heart; faith in God; trust in God; prayers of praise and gratitude; remembrance of God; righteous deeds; learning from nature; community; and the mystery of death.

## Becoming a Seeker

*Say, "Truly, my prayer, and all my acts of worship, and my living and my dying are for God alone, the Sustainer of all the worlds."*
(Q An'am 6:162)

*Something missing in my heart tonight*
*Has made my eyes so soft,*
*My voice so tender,*
*My need for God absolutely clear.* —Hafiz

---

1. Mackenzie, Falcon, and Rahman, *Finding Peace through Spiritual Practice*.

Sufis say we are all spiritual seekers, but sadly, often, it takes a crisis of "health" or "wealth" to awaken us. It may be the death of a loved one, a divorce, or a sudden downturn in financial or emotional security. In our desperation, we turn to the Source for help and consolation. We yearn to become more authentic and find greater meaning in life. For some of us, life changes forever.

In 1991, my mother fell ill, and, shockingly, in seven days, she died. After twenty grievous days, my father also passed away. My parents were deeply bonded as a couple. These two events shattered my world, but in the process, they also opened my heart to profound inner shifts. My life priorities rearranged themselves, and I felt a deeper connection to what Sufis call *"traffic and trade in the invisible realms."* I felt a greater clarity about my life and the need to bond with Spirit. To my amazement, I also discovered that, instead of losing my connection with my parents, I now actually feel an even deeper bond with them.

## Mystery of God

*We are closer to him than his jugular vein.* (Q Qaf 50:16)

*God sighs and complains, "Why does my servant wander to seek Me, forsaking Me." —Tagore*

In every tradition, there are stories of aspirants who journeyed to distant sacred places in search of God. In the end, they realized that the Beloved they so desperately sought also resided within the innermost chambers of their own heart.

At every moment we have access to Divinity. An eighth-century Sufi master was preaching to his students gathered outside his house, saying that we need to constantly knock on the door of God. Out of divine Mercy, God will open the door one day. The beloved sage Rabia, who was passing by, overheard the teaching. She remarked, *"Brother, when was the door ever closed?"* The teacher stood up, turned to her, and bowed.

## Compassion

*In the Name of God, Boundlessly Compassionate and Infinitely Merciful.* (Qur'an)

> *If kindness were a visible creation, nothing which Allah
> has created would be more beautiful than it.*
> —Hadith *of Prophet Mohammad*

In my early childhood, my parents taught me by word and example that the core teaching of Islam is the divine attribute of compassion, and to this day, compassion is the value that I most treasure and try to express in my own life. The compassionate nature of our Creator is invoked at the beginning of virtually every chapter of the Qur'an: "*In the name of God, Boundlessly Compassionate and Infinitely Merciful.*" This invocation, called the *Basmala*, inspired the Prophet Muhammad to conclude that all the teachings of the Qur'an can be distilled into a message of Divine Compassion. When a Bedouin asked him about the inner meaning of the *Basmala*, the Prophet replied, "*Have compassion for yourself and for others.*"

To expound on the astonishing power and beauty of practicing compassion in our lives, Sufi teachers use the metaphor of water in nature. They teach that water can be wonderfully soft and yielding, but over time it can also overcome the hardest granite. We also know that wherever water falls, life flourishes. Thus, the person who is gentle and merciful is not only possessed of authentic strength, but his or her compassion is life-affirming and life-bestowing.

## Transforming the Ego

> *The tyrannical self certainly impels me to evil,
> unless my Lord bestows Mercy upon me.*
> (Q Yusuf 12:53)

> *I call to witness the self-reproaching soul.* (Q Qiyamah 75:2)

> *O serene soul, return to your Sustainer,
> well pleased and well pleasing to God.*
> (Q Fajr 89:27–28)

The qur'anic verses above identify three stages of the ego. In the first stage, know that our ego can incline us toward wrongdoing. Therefore, maintain compassionate vigilance over the wiles of your ego. Through awareness and effort, little by little, strive to transform the ego from a commanding master into a personal assistant. Divinity will readily help us in our exertions. The Prophet Muhammad said, "*Walk towards God, and He comes running towards you.*"

In the second stage, we are asked to participate fully in the bazaar of life and mature from our experiences. If we make mistakes, our conscience will alert us. We can grow from our mistakes.

In the third stage, we make it a lifelong habit to align elements of our personality with our higher self as we continuously strive to become a better human being. This commitment and devotion to doing so bring us inner peace.

## Polishing the Heart

*The truth is that their hearts have become rusted on account of their evil deeds.*
(Q Mutaffifin 83:14)

*If you get irritated by every rub, how will the mirror of your heart ever be polished?* —Rumi

The Qur'an explains that every act of wrongdoing stains the heart. If untreated, this creates, metaphorically speaking, a veneer of rust on the heart. Thoughts and feelings become mangled and distorted. We experience separation from our true nature. Life feels burdensome.

The Prophet Muhammad suggested a remedy using the same metaphor of rust. For every rust, he explained, there is a polish. The polish for rust of the heart is "remembrance of God." Remember to use Divine solvents such as love or patience to cleanse the heart. Through spiritual practices, we are asked to remove our impurities and infuse our being with divine attributes.

The inner work of self-purification is difficult, inconvenient, and irritating. We are strongly encouraged to persist in the work of purification. The rewards are astonishing: a polished heart reflects the Face of Allah!

## Faith in God

*As for those who have attained to faith in Allah and hold fast to Him, He will cause them to enter into His Compassion and His abundant blessing and guide them to Himself in a straight way.* (Q Nisa' 4:175)

> *Allah has caused faith to be dear to you*
> *And has made it beautiful within your hearts.* (Q Hujurat 49:7)

Spiritual teachers ask us to attain to faith by moving from "borrowed certainty" to "inner knowing." The Qur'an suggests that it takes time, effort, and patience for faith to grow inside of us. Taking a metaphor from nature, Sufis say that only in stages does the crescent moon grow into fullness. It is important to listen to the words of elders and teachers as they instruct us about belief in God. But know that at this stage, we are reclining in the convenience of "borrowed certainty."

Resist the temptation to rest in blind faith. Move deeper, say the spiritual teachers. Build faith from within. Observe yourself as you move through the trials and tribulations of life. Ask critical and meaningful questions: "*Am I conscious of God or Higher Intelligence as I act on my decisions? Do I really have faith in divine attributes? Do I live them? Am I truthful, patient, compassionate, just and forgiving? Or do I compromise my divine principles for the sake of personal advantage?*"

As you go through this process of compassionate self-witnessing while you continue to be and do good, something beautiful blossoms in you. In your heart, you will feel the beautiful glow of Presence. A light from within guides you and consoles you in times of affliction.

The words of the poet Tagore capture the beauty and power of faith: "*Faith is the bird that feels the light and sings when the dawn is still dark.*"[2]

## Trust in God

> *And whoever puts all his trust in God, He will be*
> *enough for him.* (Q Talaq 65:3)

> *That man can have nothing but what he strives for.*
> (Q Najm 53:39)

One day the Prophet Muhammad noticed a Bedouin leaving his camel untethered. When the Prophet asked why the camel was untied, the Bedouin replied, "I have placed my trust in Allah." Replied the Prophet, "*Tie your camel to the post, then trust in Allah.*"

In our yearning for relief, peace, joy, or success, God is the best of providers. Have faith and trust in Spirit. But let us do our part by

---

2. Tagore, "Faith Is the Bird."

making every possible exertion of our body, mind, heart and soul before surrendering to God.

Some of our fervent and desired outcomes, unknown to us, are not in our highest interest. Out of mercy and grace, they are withheld from us. At other times, help is delayed for reasons not understood by the human mind. We are not privy to the larger story.

With sincerity, do your best; be conscious of Spirit and abide in faith. The holy book promises that in times of difficulties, "God provides for him from sources he never could imagine" (Q Talaq 65:2–3). Or, as Rumi imagined: *"In times of affliction, a stretcher will come from grace."*[3]

## Prayers of Praise and Gratitude

*Bow down in adoration and draw closer to Allah.*
(Q 'Alaq 96:19)

*One prostration of prayer to God frees you*
*from a thousand prostrations to your ego.*
—*Traditional Islamic Sufi saying*

Several times a day, Muslims bow and prostrate themselves, uttering words of praise and thanksgiving to God. In the final step, in a sitting position, the practitioner turns the head to the right and the left, offering greetings of peace to angels who, Muslims believe, rush into spaces where God is worshiped.

The Islamic body prayer, called *Salat*, is derived from the Prophet Muhammad's observation of angels in prayer. In a mystical experience described in the Qur'an as the Night Journey, the Prophet ascended seven levels of heaven. In that enchanting ascent, the Prophet saw angels bowing and prostrating to God while expressing praise and gratitude. From this, he concluded that true prayer, in imitation of angels, consists essentially of glorifying and thanking God and using the human body to express adoration.

Muslims believe that these series of prostrations, done with humility and sincerity in the course of the day, help us let go of our attachment to our ego and bring God into the center of our lives.

A classic story about Mulla Nasruddin illustrates the practicality, majesty, and beauty of body prayers. Imprisoned for life, Mulla is near despair, but he lightens up when he hears that his spiritual teacher has

---

3. Rumi, "Zero Circle."

received permission to visit him. Surely his teacher will slip in a concealed weapon or key to help him escape. But when the teacher arrives, all he brings is a prayer rug. Mulla is deeply disappointed and feels the need to escape, not to pray. But since he has time on his hands, he reluctantly does his body prayers, praising and thanking God by rote. He doesn't mean what he says. However, as he bows and prostrates to God over the days and weeks, he finally notices a special design on the prayer rug. It is the design of an escape route from the prison!

## Remembrance of God

*Truly, in the remembrance of God do hearts find rest.*
(Q Ra'd 13:28)

*Call to your Sustainer humbly, and in the*
*secrecy of your hearts.* (Q A'raf 7:55)

*Who has a better dye than God?*
(Q Baqara 2:138)

When we evoke the sacred name of Divinity as often as possible, we will experience in course of time a deep sense of being uplifted, nourished, and comforted. We begin to feel the blessing of Presence in our life. Sufi teachers offer an explanation. When we arrive here on Earth, we are separated from Source. This detachment pains our soul, and it yearns for union. No matter how many of our material wants are fulfilled, a mysterious ache persists.

This repetition of a mantra during meditation and in our waking hours conjures in the soul a memory of the joy it felt when it was united with God. We experience a connection with Mystery. This connection invites Presence that softens and diminishes the dissatisfaction caused by dramas and melodramas of the ego.

But will this sense of Presence abide in us as we repeat the sacred names again and again? Yes! Several traditions use the same metaphor to explain the amazing power of repeating a sacred mantra. Dip a piece of cloth in a vat of dye and the cloth assumes a beautiful color. However, the color fades over time. But if you dip the cloth repeatedly in the dye, there comes a time when the color abides. It becomes colorfast!

Similarly, by repeating the mantra continuously, the vibration of God consciousness, little by little, makes its home in our being. We become colored by the dye of God. Thus, when a Bedouin begged the Prophet Muhammad for a simple but powerful practice, he said, "Keep your tongue forever moistened with the name of Allah."

### Righteous Deeds

*Good deeds, the fruits of which endure forever are best in the sight of your Sustainer, and yield the best return.*
(Q Maryam 19:76)

*Truly, the most highly regarded of you in the sight of God is the one who does the most good.*
(Q Hujurat 49:13)

What takes us to heaven is not our religion or gender, but having faith in God and, especially, doing righteous deeds. I say "especially" because the words "righteous deeds" occur repeatedly in the Qur'an. Service to God's creation is the key to heaven.

To drive this point home, Sufi teachers explain that on the day of our passing into those celestial realms, our wealth and titles will be left behind at our palace. Our loving circle of family members and friends can accompany us only up to the grave site. What propels us further and beyond into those mysterious realms is the record of our good deeds.

### Signs of Nature

*Verily, in the creation of the heavens and the earth, there are messages indeed for people who use their reason.*
(Q 'Imran 3:190–91)

*There is only one holy book, the sacred manuscript of nature, the only scripture that can enlighten the reader.*
—Hazrat Inayat Khan

One of the best ways to grow in spiritual wisdom is to reflect on divine signs in nature. More than seven hundred verses of the Qur'an extol these natural signs. Many chapters are named after natural phenomena, and some chapters start with mysterious invocations, such as: "*By the fig and the olive*" or "*By the dawn.*" Nature teaches us everything we need to know about life.

For example, nature can help us learn about unconditional love. How can one explain the concept of unconditional love? In the fourteenth century, Hafiz exclaims that the Earth would die if the Sun stopped kissing her. But, even after all this time, the Sun never tells the Earth, "Hey, *you owe me!*" What happens with a love like that? It lights up the entire sky! Just like unconditional love!

Nature also helps us understand, honor, and celebrate our diversity. To expound unity in diversity, sages use the metaphor of trees, which appears often in the Qur'an. The branches of the tree sway differently in the wind, but they are all connected at the roots. In our essence, we are all one. To help us overcome our bias about religious superiority, we are asked to meditate on the following metaphor of nature: All rivers flow into the Ocean. I might be following one river. However, I should not mistake my river for the Ocean.

## Community

*Help one another in furthering virtue and God consciousness.* (Q Ma'ida 5:2)

*Ah! What a beautiful fellowship!* (Q Nisa' 4:69)

Spiritual teachers tell the story about two men, one blind and one lame, who were invited to the king's banquet. Both were overjoyed until reality set in. Then the blind man lamented, "*Alas, I can't see, and the road is treacherous. How will I ever find my way?*" The lame man bemoaned, "*What a tragedy! The way is long and my legs won't make it.*" But when their circle of close friends heard about the problem, one of them came up with a solution: The lame man could piggyback on the blind man and use his eyes to guide the strong legs of his blind companion. In this manner they were both able to attend the king's banquet. This is how it is in life: We all carry pain and insecurities that can blind or disable us in one way or another, but we can still get to the banquet. All we need is support and advice from what sages call our "Circle of Love" and a willingness to collaborate.

## Mystery of Death

*Every soul will taste death.* (Q 'Imran 3:185)

> *I learned that every mortal will taste death.*
> *But only some will taste life.* —Rumi

Death is not only inevitable but can happen to us at any moment. We lose sight of this reality as we get absorbed and preoccupied in our daily struggles of life.

Remembrance of this simple truth of the mystery of death helps us to live a life of fullness and fulfillment. It dawns on us that time is precious. This awareness helps us to arrange our priorities and make sound decisions in life. We avoid getting enmeshed in trivialities, the endless dramas and melodramas of our life that end up in tears and dissatisfaction.

The tendency to procrastinate is diminished. What is it that we want to say or do? Maybe we need to tell someone, "*I love you,*" or "*Please forgive me.*" The time is now, and the place is here. The Prophet Muhammad said, "*It is better to blush in this world than in the next.*"

What do we want to do that will give us meaning in life? Take risks now; do not make excuses. If you made an error, learn and grow from the experience. The words of Tagore resonate: "*I spend my days stringing and unstringing my instrument but the song I came here to sing remains unsung.*"[4]

The Prophet Muhammad said that when you arrived here on Earth, everyone was laughing and smiling, but you were crying. Live such a life that when you depart, everyone is weeping, but you are laughing and smiling.

## Deeper Conversation/Deeper Listening

1. Is there a correlation of what the Imam explores from the Qur'an with your personal beliefs?
2. How can the views expressed in this chapter be used to further interfaith understanding?

## Spiritual Practice

The concepts within the chapter are considered a spiritual practice. The Imam Jamal invites you to participate in one of the selections included in this chapter.

---

4. Tagore, "Gitanjali 13." https://poets.org/poem/gitanjali-13.

# Bibliography

Ali, Abdullah Yusuf. *The Holy Quran: Text, Translation and Commentary*. New Delhi: Kitab Bhavan, 2016.

Mackenzie, Don, Ted Falcon, and Jamal Rahman. *Finding Peace through Spiritual Practice: The Interfaith Amigos' Guide to Personal, Social, and Environmental Healing*. Turner, 2016.

Rumi. "Zero Circle." All Poetry. https://allpoetry.com/Zero-Circle.

Tagore, Rabindranath. "Gitanjali 13." Poets.org. https://poets.org/poem/gitanjali-13.

———. "Faith Is the Bird . . ." Goodreads. https://www.goodreads.com/quotes/101391-faith-is-the-bird-that-feels-the-light-and-sings.

# Chapter 22

# The Bursting of Bubbles

### Leslye Colvin

*Leslye Colvin is a contemplative activist, spiritual companion, and writer. Inspired by the Catholic social justice tradition, she is passionate about encouraging diversity of thought and has a wide range of experience in promoting the mission and expanding outreach, including faith-based nonprofit, government, corporate, and academia. She has been published by the* National Catholic Reporter *and interviewed by* America Magazine, Radio Veritas, U.S. Catholic, *and* Vatican Radio *on the construct of race. Leslye is a contractor with the Center for Action and Contemplation. She has previously served on the board of directors for NETWORK for Catholic Social Justice and also serves on the board of Future Church.*

SEEING YOUNG CHILDREN BLOWING bubbles immediately transports me to memories of the awe and wonder I experienced as a child at play. These elusive and delicate amoeba-like forms of soap and air capture our attention as they mysteriously float. Then, in an instant, the object of our fascination vanishes without warning by bursting.

When experiencing an epiphany, it may feel as though a bubble has burst. Something in our awareness or thinking shifts, allowing us to see or understand with a new sense of clarity. It is as if a perceived obstacle no longer exists or a light is turned on in a dark room. At once, we are free to move in a new and unimagined manner. Instead of seeing only black or white, grays, blues, reds, and yellows come into view in varying shades and tones, along with greens, oranges, and purples.

Our lives are influenced and shaped by our lived experiences within a specific context. From the moment of birth, we begin to receive information from the persons we encounter and the environment we were born into. Over time, all of this contributes to our perceptions and understandings. The practice of spiritual direction and other forms of intimate conversation create safe spaces in which bubbles can burst. As we explore our journey and recognize the abiding presence of the Divine, epiphanies occur. While the process may include discomfort, it helps me realize my response to the patterns and systems I dwell in and invites me to hold space for the tension generated.

The bursting of bubbles contributes to personal growth and the evolution of humanity, as it reveals the movement of Spirit. Even so, some are vested in preventing epiphanies and restricting the human capacity for intellectual curiosity and growth. They choose to distort and insulate the thin membrane of bubbles by preventing the natural floating and bursting. The objective of this fear-based control serves the agenda of those with some degree of power and those who orchestrate oppressive systems. The practice is neither new nor exclusive to our time and place. It can be in abusive and unhealthy personal relationships or larger structures that shape our society. If we are members of a dominating group, it is easy to accept the mainstream or dominant narrative as being the only accurate perception of reality. Our perceptions can be deepened and enhanced by relationships with people who have other experiences or are fortunate not to belong to the dominant group and, therefore, have different ways of seeing.

So many of us are bound by bubbles of untruths and delusions. My writing of this piece coincides with the second celebration of the national holiday in honor of Juneteenth, the day when a bubble of deceit burst and enslaved African Americans in Galveston, Texas, were told that chattel slavery had ended two years prior. What splendid effort had been expended to keep these people in bondage? The deception was an extension of White supremacy, a system based on the denial of human dignity for economic gain.

Juneteenth is a bursting of the bubbles of July 4, 1776. It acknowledges the tarnished and flawed independence our nation celebrates. It requires us to question the patriotic ideals espoused. The colonies were liberated from the oppression of British rule, but liberation was denied to my African ancestors on this land. Why would those who resisted oppression choose to apply it to others? What lies were created to justify this? What wounds can we now see that need to be addressed?

Generations later, there is an ongoing struggle to burst the fear-based lies of White supremacy, anti-Blackness, and racism. One of the greatest gifts I received from my parents and other elders was the encouragement to think creatively and critically. When my writing began to pierce the aforementioned systemic bubbles, my mother responded, "*Lord, please protect my child.*" Meanwhile, my aunt would say, "*Keep writing.*" As African-American women born in 1933 and 1929, respectively, they recognized the risk and value of truth-telling. Now that they are both gone, I still hear their words as affirmations for using my words to burst bubbles.

My creative and critical thinking skills also invite new ways of contemplating Scripture and experiencing the Divine. Born less than one hundred years after the end of chattel slavery in the United States, I am only five or six generations from this massive crime against humanity. As a Black Catholic, my understanding of Scripture and Tradition is influenced by my lived experience. I feel a strong connection to the enslavement of the Hebrew people and their exodus. When God instructs Moses to tell Pharaoh "*Let my people go*"—it is personal.

The labels we use to identify ourselves place us in a context. They are not to be used as weapons of division. My ability to burst bubbles has resulted in life-giving friendships with people from other cultures and faith traditions. In turn, my desire for inclusion invites me to be inclusive. It is a continuing process that compels me to move beyond the hard restrictions of dualism while freeing me to consider other perspectives and transcend perceived barriers.

My view of Jesus as an oppressed Palestinian Jewish man living in a territory occupied by Rome influences my understanding of my faith as I contemplate the incarnation. After being baptized and spending forty days praying and fasting, the Gospel of Luke tells us that he returned home to Galilee and then Nazareth. In both places, he visited synagogues. One of these moments is recorded in the Gospel of John.

Jesus stood up to read and was handed a scroll of the prophet Isaiah. According to Scripture: "*He unrolled the scroll and found the passage where it was written: 'The Spirit of the Lord is upon me, because he has anointed me to bring glad tidings to the poor. He has sent me to proclaim liberty to captives and recovery of sight to the blind, to let the oppressed go free, and to proclaim a year acceptable to the Lord'*" (John 4:16–19).

What a powerful message! Since it was written by Isaiah, these words have been proclaimed by countless others, including Jesus at the beginning of his public ministry. Have they been heard so often that they are now impotent, moving no further than our ears? Are Isaiah and Jesus calling for the bursting of bubbles?

What bubbles must be burst to bring glad tidings to the poor? Why are so many people economically poor in our wealthy society? Do I recognize my personal poverty? What bubbles prevent us from proclaiming liberty to captives? Why are our incarceration rates so high, especially for people who are Black and Brown? What fear holds me down? What bubbles stop the recovery of sight to the blind? What are we taught not to see? What is before me but unseen? What stops us from freeing the oppressed? Who benefits from the oppression of others? From what do I need to be liberated? How do we proclaim a year acceptable to the Lord when we idolize injustice? What altars must be dismantled? What idols must be demolished? What are my addictions?

Years ago, I began pondering the Gospel of John's account of Jesus weeping before returning Lazarus to life. His command to his deceased friend to "come forth" receives a great deal of attention. However, as I spent time with this narrative, a bubble burst, and my perspective expanded. How had I missed a message, a command, that was as clear and concise then as it is now?

> He cried with a loud voice, "Lazarus, come out!" The dead man came out, tied hand and foot with burial bands, and his face was wrapped in a cloth. So Jesus said to them, "Untie him and let him go." (John 11:43–44)

## Untie him and let him go?

After restoring Lazarus's life, Jesus is commanding the onlookers to get involved. "*Untie him and let him go.*" Why would they need to be told what seems to be apparent? A person is standing before them in need, and they have the capacity to respond accordingly. How do these words speak to us, or are they too impotent in the face of injustice? Who is standing before us bound? Whom do we choose not to see? What are we to do?

For many people, the murders of George Floyd and Ahmaud Arbery led to epiphanies about the role of White supremacy, anti-Blackness, and racism in our society. There was a collective gasp as bubbles burst, and people moved beyond the restriction of their bubbles. They began to process what they had been taught not to see. Many sought ways to learn and become more aware of the systems that structure our world. Some began to see how they were bound by the status quo. They began to recognize their privilege and how they benefited from an unjust and oppressive system.

Revelation generates awe and wonder like that of seeing a large bubble float away, carried by the wind. Epiphanies happen, and bubbles burst when we assume a posture of openness. They do not happen on demand. Begin by affirming your lived experience and allowing the questions stirring within to arise. While the answers may not be apparent, hold the unresolved questions. In time, you will recognize that there are more than two opposing perspectives on any issue. Enjoy the perspective of bursting bubbles!

## Deeper Conversation/Deeper Listening

1. What is your bursting bubble about yourself?
2. What is your bursting bubble about something outside of yourself that could change or enhance a community?

## Bibliography

New American Bible. Confraternity of Christian Doctrine, 1970. NAB Online. https://bible.usccb.org/bible.
Metzger, Bruce Manning. *The New American Bible, 1970.* Princeton, NJ: 1971.

www.ingramcontent.com/pod-product-compliance
Lightning Source LLC
Chambersburg PA
CBHW050344230426
43663CB00010B/1977